THE SENTIMENTAL LIFE OF INTERNATIONAL LAW

THE SENTIMENTAL LIFE OF INTERNATIONAL LAW

LITERATURE, LANGUAGE, AND LONGING IN WORLD POLITICS

GERRY SIMPSON

OXFORD
UNIVERSITY PRESS

Great Clarendon Street, Oxford, OX2 6DP,
United Kingdom

Oxford University Press is a department of the University of Oxford.
It furthers the University's objective of excellence in research, scholarship,
and education by publishing worldwide. Oxford is a registered trade mark of
Oxford University Press in the UK and in certain other countries

© Gerry Simpson 2021

The moral rights of the author have been asserted

First Edition published in 2021

Impression: 1

All rights reserved. No part of this publication may be reproduced, stored in
a retrieval system, or transmitted, in any form or by any means, without the
prior permission in writing of Oxford University Press, or as expressly permitted
by law, by licence or under terms agreed with the appropriate reprographics
rights organization. Enquiries concerning reproduction outside the scope of the
above should be sent to the Rights Department, Oxford University Press, at the
address above

You must not circulate this work in any other form
and you must impose this same condition on any acquirer

Public sector information reproduced under Open Government Licence v3.0
(http://www.nationalarchives.gov.uk/doc/open-government-licence/open-government-licence.htm)

Published in the United States of America by Oxford University Press
198 Madison Avenue, New York, NY 10016, United States of America

British Library Cataloguing in Publication Data

Data available

Library of Congress Control Number: 2021940844

ISBN 978–0–19–284979–3

DOI: 10.1093/oso/9780192849793.001.0001

Printed and bound in the UK by TJ Books Limited

Links to third party websites are provided by Oxford in good faith and
for information only. Oxford disclaims any responsibility for the materials
contained in any third party website referenced in this work.

for EF

Preface and Acknowledgements

> As these things were going through my mind I was watching the sand martins darting to and fro over the sea. Ceaselessly emitting their tiny cries they sped along their flight-paths faster than my eyes could follow them. At earlier times, in the summer evenings during my childhood when I had watched from the valley as swallows circled in the last light, still in great numbers in those days, I would imagine that the world was held together by the courses they flew through the air.
>
> W. G. Sebald, *The Rings of Saturn* (Vintage, 2002 [1995])

At the height (or in the depths) of the Great Terror in 1937, Joseph Stalin came across Boris Pasternak's name on an NKVD list of those to be liquidated. He crossed Pasternak's name off the list, appending the words: 'Do not touch this cloud-dweller'.[1] Pasternak, of course, was a cloud-dweller who wrote *Dr Zhivago*, the novel that, for some western readers in the post-war era, defined the Soviet enterprise.

This book, in a way, belongs in the clouds, far removed from the cut and thrust of international legal life. There is hardly a word on foreign investment law or collective security or the Paris Treaty on climate change. But in another sense—and looking at clouds, as we must, from both sides—this book is an argument against cloud-dwelling, against the idea that bodies of law exist in a space detached from the earthbound lives (sentimental, literary, material, friendly, pastoral) of international lawyers and their subjects, and that, instead, our world—with its sociopathically unequal distribution of life chances and its casual everyday cruelties, its enclaves of redemptive hope and human kindness—is held together by the courses of law and language as they fly through the air.

---

1. Sometimes, in the story, 'cloud-dweller' becomes 'holy fool'. Andrew McCulloch, 'First Frost by Boris Pasternak' (*Times Literary Supplement*, 2017) <https://www.the-tls.co.uk/articles/public/poem-week-first-frost/>. Irving Howe, 'Lara and Zhivago' (*New York Times*, 5 February 1978), section BR, p. 1.

Many people helped me hold the world of this book together by reading chapters, offering comments, urging me on. I want to single out, though, my two research assistants, Quito Tsui and Tanmay Misra, as well as my various readers (especially my sisters, Linda Reavley and Sheena Carmichael) and six of my international law friends—friends who happen to be international lawyers or honorary international lawyers but with whom I rarely talk about international law: Sundhya Pahuja, Raimond Gaita, Philippe Sands, Barry Hill, Matt Craven and Catriona Drew (who has had faith in me ever since I came second in the 1984 Jurisprudence course at the University of Aberdeen, confirming the old adage that no one ever remembers who came first).

All of this would have been impossible without the support, over the past few years, of my many colleagues and friends at the two law schools I have been most closely associated with, the London School of Economics Law Department and the University of Melbourne Law School.

Impossible without the kindness of Laura Corsini and Ged Lethbridge in 2014 and 2015.

Impossible without the lucky break I experienced when I first met Esther Freud one wintry evening at 'The Flask' in Hampstead Village.

And impossible without my golden daughters, Hannah (who helped me with chapter vii) and Rosa. Hannah Arendt's old apartment was very close to me as I sat writing parts of this book in Ruti Teitel's apartment in the East Village, the 'Rosa Luxemburg Stiftung' was thirty blocks north on Madison Avenue.

★ ★ ★

An earlier version of chapter ii ('the sentimental lives of international lawyers') was published as 'The Sentimental Life of International Law', 3(1) *London Review of International Law* (2015) 3–29, while chapter iv ('"bluebeard on trial": the experience of bathos') is drawn from 'Unprecedents', an essay in Immi Tallgren and Thomas Skouteris, *The New Histories of International Criminal Law: ReTrials* (Oxford University Press, 2019).

Chapter v ('an uncertain style: after method in international legal history') appears in shorter form as 'After Method' in *History, Politics, Law: Thinking Internationally* (eds. Megan Donaldson, Annabel Brett and Martti Koskenniemi, Cambridge University Press, 2021).

contents

list of abbreviations	xiii
i. a plea for new international laws	1
ii. the sentimental lives of international lawyers	30
iii. international law's comic disposition	55
iv. 'bluebeard on trial': the experience of bathos	88
v. an uncertain style: after method in international legal history	113
vi. a declaration on friendly relations	147
vii. gardening, instead, or, of pastoral international law	185
postlude: last thoughts on sentimentality	211
select bibliography	213
Index	225

What differs from the existent will strike the existent as witchcraft.

Theodor Adorno, *Negative Dialectics* (Continuum, 2007)

I'm sentimental, if you know what I mean . . .

Leonard Cohen, 'Democracy', *The Future* (1992)

list of abbreviations

ASIL	American Society of International Law
GATT	General Agreement on Tariffs and Trade
ICC	International Criminal Court
ICJ	International Court of Justice
ICTR	International Criminal Tribunal for Rwanda
ICTY	International Criminal Tribunal for the former Yugoslavia
IMT	International Military Tribunal
IMTFE	International Military Tribunal for the Far East
NAM	Non-Aligned Movement
TWAIL	Third World Approaches to International Law
UNDHR	Universal Declaration on Human Rights
UNGA	United Nations General Assembly
WTO	World Trade Organization

i

a plea for new international laws

---

i. language and crisis   1
ii. relevance and play (the 'last of the humanities')   4
iii. sentimental life   6
iv. international law   11
v. writing and style   15
vi. literature and law   21
vii. politics and sentiment   25

'In considering this strangely neglected topic', [the dissertation] began. This *what* neglected topic? This strangely *what* topic? This strangely neglected *what*?

Kingsley Amis, Lucky Jim (Victor Gollancz, 1954)

i. language and crisis

This is a book about our age-old longing for a decent international society. It is published, though, as public international law seems to be enduring, perhaps relishing, its latest crisis—an apparent deepening of the recession experienced since the end of a starry-eyed, post–Cold War interregnum. There is a fair bit of unease around: a disaffection with the foreign investment regime, a lot of muttering about the spate of withdrawals and would-be withdrawals from the International Criminal Court (ICC) and about judicial institutions incapable of making appointments, a nagging worry that the split between Europe and Britain or between the United States and the liberal democratic consensus prefigures something unpleasant, a belief that a highly personalised, capriciously authoritarian politics is displacing the long, slow boring of legal-diplomatic holes or a concern that international lawyers fresh from coming in from the cold are about to be again cast out into it.

As always, we need to be alert to the possibility that these are symptoms of a more fundamental problem. In 2017, I saw at the National Theatre in London a play called *Consent* about the fractious relationship between the private idioms of love, betrayal and regret, and the jurisprudential languages of guilt, responsibility and punishment.[1] The characters—including an earnest lawyer rarely seen without his collapsible bike—struggle to reconcile a language of rationality and cool wit with the turmoil of the human heart. Inevitably, the proximate matters—a divorce, an alleged sexual assault—end up in trial proceedings. But as the Programme Notes informed us: 'The courts are a poor place for a resolution'. In the end, the law runs out of road, and whenever the characters in the play speak law to passion, it sounds faintly prim or maladroit, sometimes even disabling.

In this book, I want to think about how we might be disabled by the governing idioms of international lawyering and, then, importantly, re-enabled, by speaking different sorts of international law or by speaking international law in different sorts of ways. To a certain extent, this initially might be approached or read as another glum assessment of a world gone wrong, but the glumness here is not directed at specific individuals (Bezos, Erdogan, Johnson, Musk, Modi, Afwerki), catastrophes in the making (fires, floods, extinction, viruses) or even the obviously structural causes of cruelty and maldistribution, but instead at the prison-houses, holding pens and detention centres of language itself. And along with diagnosis, I want to offer, too, if not hope then at least solace. Auden wrote that 'poetry makes nothing happen'.[2] The same could be said of this book. But each chapter does end with a promise of, or description of, some redemptive practice or thought, a message in a bottle. Sometimes this will be a pointer towards writing history that is not 'method' (chapter v, 'after method'), sometimes a modest prescription (chapter iv, 'the experience of bathos'), sometimes a rush of

---

1. Nina Raine, *Consent* (2017) performed at The National Theatre, London, 4–17 April 2017. See also Pierre Hazan, *Judging Wars* (Stanford University Press, 2010) 10 (on the introduction to the world of international law of 'terms, often of religious, or psychoanalytic inspiration . . . reconciliation, truth, punishment, pardon, repentance, catharsis').
2. W. H. Auden, '*In Memory of W. B. Yeats*': *Collected Poems* (Faber and Faber, 1940).

blood to the head (chapter vii, 'gardening, instead'), occasionally a plea for some ironic hopefulness (chapter iii, 'comic international law') and sometimes a romantic aside (chapter vi, 'a declaration on friendly relations'). At the very least, I like to think it might alleviate the odd discontent or lift the occasional mood.

The preoccupations of the book are organised around a series of questions. Are we at the point where enunciating our collective tragedy in the language of international law risks a degree of bathos or absurdity, when to keep speaking it might invite a certain cynicism not so much from its opponents but from within the field itself: cynicism as a condition of necessity?[3] Is international law—as a prescription for a good life—no longer compatible with living well, or has it become/has it always been a cluster of promises that obscure and inhibit the conditions for flourishing? Is international law subject to 'cruel optimism'?[4] Could it be that we are not thinking and writing about the world in quite the right way? Might it be the case that the imperatives of authority, relevance, solemnity, seriousness and conviction are part of our collective problem? In short, is international law an apt way to think about and change the world?

Describing the problem is at least one aspect of this study. Here I assume the dominance of a certain way of going about international law: a mode of thought, method, speech and a set of professional expectations and instincts that define the field every bit as much as the content of its rules. These are what Edward Said referred to as the 'pressures of conventions, predecessors, and rhetorical styles'.[5] Mostly these constitute or limit the parameters of the field by exiling some work to the margins or wilderness. International law is not alone in doing this, but since it tends to think of itself as a discursive exercise par excellence (a form of persuasion, technical agility, world-making word play), these conventions become unusually constitutive.[6] This book, then, is intended to be part of a broader project to open up the space in which international lawyers can live and work.

---

3. I develop this idea in a longer unpublished paper, 'How to be Cynical', delivered in Berlin in the late summer of 2019 at the German Society of International Law, Freie Universität. See an edited volume from this conference (not including that paper): B. Baade et al., *Cynical International Law? Abuse and Circumvention in Public International and European Law* (Springer, 2020).
4. Lauren Berlant, *Cruel Optimism* (Duke University Press, 2011).
5. Edward Said, *Orientalism* (Pantheon Books, 1978) 13. (He goes on to say that it is these conventions and styles that 'limit what Walter Benjamin once called "the overtaxing of the productive person in the name of ... the principle of 'creativity'"'.)
6. See Duncan Kennedy, 'Legal Education as Training for Hierarchy', in David Kairys (ed.), *The Politics of Law: A Progressive Critique* (Basic Books, 1998), 54–75.

But there is no getting away from the fact that work like this will be experienced as interesting or, perhaps, compelling only by those with an awareness that the distribution of material, moral and cultural power in the world is askew and that it is necessary to act and think in dramatically different ways in order to reverse this distribution. And even people who think like this will worry that writing a book about what it might mean to write a book about international law may not be the most direct way to challenge these existing wrongs (as I write this, commuters are dragging a man off the roof of a London Underground train for daring to protest about the coming climate disaster, Chilean students are being tear-gassed and shot in the eyes with rubber bullets as they gather to call for a more equal society, and an experiment in political self-determination is being slowly suffocated in the Rojava province of Northern Syria). Yet, international lawyers are a privileged caste in society. What we say and think matters (though it has been a tendency of public international lawyers to claim that this isn't so). As teachers of international law, in particular, we have in our care each year hundreds of students. For some of them, our course will be their only exposure to sustained reflection about global politics. There is a responsibility and power in this.

ii. relevance and play (the 'last of the humanities')

This is all especially pertinent in a period when the humanities are under threat (from technology, from cuts in funding, from perpetual auditing). In a melodramatic gesture, then, I want to think of international law as the 'last of the humanities': the final resting place in an over-professionalised curriculum for a relatively unfettered and playfully serious account of the world around us—an account that does not entirely give itself up to the demand for absolute utility. Isobel Armstrong has said that the best way to defend the humanities is to practise them.[7] This book, then, attempts a practice of the humanities that is more than the instrumentalised transmission of knowledge.

In 2004, I gave a public lecture in Melbourne on the Iraq War (arguing against it, declaring it illegal, providing illustrative examples, suggesting a peaceful solution, warning about the fragmentation of the Baathist

---

7. Marina Warner, 'Learning My Lesson', 37(6) *London Review of Books* (2015) 14.

state).⁸ After the speech, people gathered round me with various words of encouragement and praise while I ran through an itinerary of self-effacing gestures. A former prime minister approached me and said that he had found my lecture . . . 'relevant'. A little bit of me died in that moment. And yet, this book was born. 'Away with relevance and utility!', as Nietzsche might have said.⁹

A few years ago, the editors of a book for which I was writing a chapter came back to me with tremendously useful comments. In my chapter was a passage that I was especially proud of. Beside it, one of the editors had written, 'Beautifully written, but is it necessary?' The idea of necessity and usefulness, then, is one target of the book.¹⁰ My former LSE colleague, Stan Cohen, resisting the idea that history or text could simply be mined for lessons, once said of the trial of Klaus Barbie in Lyon that it was 'a postmodernist trial—a text from which no-one could learn very much'.¹¹ The culmination of this train of thought would be an Adorno-esque refusal of language itself, but, though it is all too possible to not-publish a book, it is not possible to publish a non-book: a book that refuses to publish. One must attempt to eff the ineffable.¹² So, this book belongs in the tradition (but it can't be anything as po-faced as 'a tradition') of the proverbial rather than the philosophical: a clandestine, barbarian international law of misreadings, perverse readings, marks, jokes, slips, accidents, (unintended) verbal resonances.¹³ Joe Smith, my teacher in Vancouver when I was first a postgraduate student,

---

8. A few weeks before that lecture I was taking part in a debate at the Institute of Contemporary Arts in Pall Mall, and when I said all of this, the right-wing commentator on the other side of the debate said: 'That's the trouble with people on the Left, they are all so pessimistic'.
9. The recent government-mandated research exercise in the UK has asked scholars to account for the 'impact' their research has had, as if scholarship was an asteroid colliding with the world of work and finance. Imagine my delight, then, when I read recently that a former director of the LSE, Sir Alexander Carl Saunders, is alleged to have 'proscribed all non-academic publication by anyone identifying himself as a member of the LSE'. Stefan Collini, *Absent Minds: Intellectuals in Britain* (Oxford University Press, 2007) 379 fn. 391, quoting Kathleen Burk, *Troublemaker: The Life and History of A. J. P. Taylor* (Yale University Press, 2000) at 206.
10. Sara Ahmed, *What's the Use? On the Uses of Use* (Duke University Press, 2019).
11. Stanley Cohen, 'State Crimes of Previous Regimes: Knowledge, Accountability, and the Policing of the Past', 20(1) *Law & Social Inquiry* (1995) 7–50.
12. This is a phrase of Samuel Beckett's.
13. See also Jacques Derrida, *The Post Card: From Socrates to Freud and Beyond* (University of Chicago Press, 1987). 'Proverbial' in the sense that I intend to speak without describe international law, and 'clandestine' in the sense that it involves an indirect approach on the subject. Meanwhile, I am happy to connote 'barbarian' in its many senses here. The barbarian has always been understood as savage, or foreign, of course, but also as pagan (not conforming to the Christian orthodoxy). David Hume described Oliver Cromwell as a barbarian, though not one 'insensible to literary merit': *Oxford Shorter English Dictionary* (Oxford University Press, 1993). And another Edinburgh Scot, James Lorimer, was happy to place the Ottoman Empire

argued relentlessly for this sense of legal theory as both psychoanalytic investigation and playful lily-hopping.[14] Later he wrote at length about the importance of doing political and theoretic work for its own sake:

> We can, through social action, accomplish limited set tasks such as preserving park land ... alleviating specific distress ... not because any of this will make a substantive difference to the world but because it is what we want to do at the time. This is action as play rather than action as pathology.[15]

In any event, I want to engage in a kind of belle-lettrist insurgency: an underground skirmish in the struggle to outflank the desire to be relevant, or an agonistic rejoinder to international law's rational-technocratic lifeworld or a book-length de-instrumentalisation of the field. Another way to put this is to say that you hold in your hands the most useless book in the history of international law.

Either way, it's a strangely neglected topic.

iii. sentimental life

But what is this book about? One way to answer this question is to say that it is about what it means for something to be 'about international law'. In particular, I ask what it might be to engage in a professional practice that has become, to adapt a title of Janet Malcolm's, not just impossible but difficult.[16] I do this by making the effort to discern, or better still to bring to the surface, international law's 'hidden literary prose': its bathetic underpinnings (chapter iv), its friendly relations (chapter vi), its neurotic foundations, its screened-off comic dispositions (chapter iii), its anti-method (chapter v), the life-worlds of its practitioners (chapter ii).[17]

in the category of a barbarian civilisation (neither savage nor quite civilised but occupying the borderland). Peter Fitzpatrick has talked about the way in which non-European peoples were 'called to be the same yet repelled as different, bound in an infinite transition which perpetually requires it to attain what is intrinsically denied to it'. See Peter Fitzpatrick, '"We Know What It Is When You Do Not Ask Us"': Nationalism as Racism', in Peter Fitzpatrick (ed.), *Nationalism, Racism, and the Rule of Law* (Dartmouth, 1995) 11.

14. J. C. Smith, *Course on The Western Idea of Law* (University of British Columbia, 1987–1988).
15. J. C. Smith, The *Psychoanalytic Roots of Patriarchy: The Neurotic Foundations of Social Order* (New York University Press, 1990) 386.
16. Janet Malcolm, *Psychoanalysis: The Impossible Profession* (Knopf, 1977) 1.
17. The phrase 'hidden literary prose' belongs to Jean-Paul Sartre in *Situations IX* (Gallimard, 1965). For a historical study arguing that pre-platonic language was mythic, narrative and proverbial, see Jan Swearingen, *Rhetoric and Irony* (Oxford University Press, 1991) 20–38.

But why a 'sentimental life of international law'? The phrase and title are an effort to encapsulate at least three ideas or suppositions. The first involves what might also have been termed a *literary* life of international law. Here I treat international law as a form of writing and thought capable of being understood as a literary endeavour, capable, perhaps, of being written in a self-consciously literary form. So, on one hand, the book applies some literary devices to certain aspects of international law (e.g. bathos and the history of war crimes law) or juxtaposes international legal forms (solemnity, professionalism) with comic irony. On the other hand, it takes what might be regarded as literary themes or objects (friendship, gardening) and brings them into relations with international law (sometimes this involves a reading of literary texts such as Alice Goodman's libretto for *Nixon in China*, George Steiner's *The Portage to San Christobel of A. H.* or Voltaire's *Candide*) in order to bring to the surface a certain possibility in international lawyering).[18]

Second, this is a literary *life* of international law. Like many others, I take the field to be composed of more than its text-based rules or ethico-political diktats. Instead, it is a life lived by people as international lawyers with a bundle of professional orientations (e.g. chapter ii), a technology for organising life on the ground and a micro-politics of political and personal interaction governed by standards and prospectuses (of friendship, chapter vi; of writing styles, chapter v).[19]

Third, this is a *sentimental* life, the title of an essay from which this book was originally derived. I chose this word partly because of its associations with Sterne's *Sentimental Journey* and the sentiments at the heart of a Scottish Enlightenment understanding of culture and society, partly because sentimentality, while itself a literary form, also encompasses a broader field than the literary (it includes professional sensibility, feelings, instincts and so on) but partly, too, because 'sentimental' has a double meaning (the lachrymose absence of proportion and the presence of a human, anti-technocratic sensibility) that haunts the life and practice of international lawyers (this is discussed in the next chapter).[20]

---

18. For work in this vein, see Peter Goodrich, Maks Del Mar, Joseph Slaughter, Desmond Manderson and Vasuki Nesiah.
19. In this context, see the work of Luis Eslava, David Kennedy and Sally Engle Merry.
20. See e.g. Naz Modirzadeh, 'Passion and the International Law of War Scholarship', 61(1) *Harvard International Law Journal* (2020) 1–64.

I have found it useful here to think through all of this drawing from a diverse group of writers (such as Diogenes, Sterne, Nietzsche, Rebecca West) who were willing to rethink and unthink playfully, rebelliously and scurrilously with a view to upending convention. So, for example, I return at the end of the book to the figure of Diogenes and the concepts of 'kynicism' that have grown up around him—not 'cynicism' as in the failure to live by a set of beliefs or an attitude of sneering dismissiveness, or a Faragist manipulation of voting preferences or the cynicism of 'inexpert rule'—but a *kynical* sensibility—derived partly from Diogenes himself, partly from the ironies of modernist thought—that puts international law into conversation with the dirty materialism of gardening and with the genre of comedy. The idea, then, will be to get to a place where we can combine cynicism with speculative hopefulness, where we might become kynics without cynicism, where we might uncover a sentimental international law of passionate, puckish, kind-hearted scepticism.

How might we discover—even create—this sentimental life of international law? I explore this possibility through a combination of indirection and bricolage. First, the book will enact the virtues of a slow, meandering, circuitous, approach to legal and literary material, one that privileges the tentative over the authoritative, *indirection* over coming to the point.[21] I have no doubt that this will be understood as a book about theory to be contrasted, say, with a book about the law of the sea or about treaty law. One of the 'ways of seeing' that international law insists on—indeed it is a law of international law—is that there are two separate domains of theory and practice/doctrine.[22] But the idea that international law can be disassembled in this way is both highly politicised and insidious. I cannot begin to count the number of times I have been told *sotto voce*, before a conference presentation, that I could 'deal with the more theoretical issues', or—this usually a compliment—that my presentation was not 'too theoretical'. Here, 'theory' is understood as deliberate abstruseness or over-complication or 'influenced by unreadable continental philosophers' or self-indulgent. This book does advance a 'theory' of international law, but it does so through stealth and

---

21. I take this to be the argument Derrida is making at the beginning of *The Post Card* when he talks about the bad reader, the reader who wants to finish her reading, wants her reading to confirm some sort of pre-reading, wants to move onto another reading and declare the original reading 'read': (n 13) 5.
22. Another law of international law is that most people claim to be committed to breaking down this barrier. I taught a course at LSE with Sundhya Pahuja and Christine Chinkin called 'The Theory and Practice of International Law', but the students immediately concluded that it was about 'theory' (everyone knew this from the title and teachers).

indirection, the international legal tonalities pursued through the book representing a kind of Dickinsonian international law: 'tell all the truth but tell it slant, success in circuit lies'.[23]

There is often a moment in psychoanalysis at the beginning of a session when the analysand will describe what she has been doing, who she has seen, where she has travelled: an itemisation of the conscious life designed to precede the disclosure of, or conceal, her deepest preoccupations. In an old cartoon, the analysand is busy describing this surface life while the analyst is depicted writing a shopping list on her notepad: 'eggs, milk, bread . . .'. Increasingly international lawyers, too, are rejecting these surface manifestations of international law—'courts, treaties, custom . . .'—in favour of an engagement with international legal diplomacy's dark heart, its recurring pathologies, its traumatic histories, its authoritarian vibes, its forbidden materials. What can't be done? And why not?

Public international law could still be redemptive, but this would be a flickering redemption: a modernist account of international law, then, but one that emphasises not the combination and recombination of primitive desire and formal experimentation but instead a commitment to hesitancy and delicacy in legal-political strategies.[24] This might require attending to the contours of what is unsaid, or, what *cannot* be said.[25] Or it might involve a reckoning with international law's acts of unsaying (or 'unprecedenting', as I call them in one of the chapters here), a covert approach on Žižek's 'known unknowns': the things we know but choose to 'unknow' by hiding them in plain sight.[26] It might be possible, then, to catalogue or register the losses incurred when international legal language displaces earlier moral epiphanies, when, for example, Siegfried Sassoon's 'frantic, butchered gestures of the dead' become 'serious violations of the laws of war'.[27]

---

23. This is from Emily Dickinson's poem, 'Tell All the Truth' (1868), in *The Poems of Emily Dickinson* (Harvard University Press, 1998), No. 1263.
24. For stirring work on interwar modernism, see e.g., and predominantly, Nathaniel Berman, '"But the Alternative Is Despair": European Nationalism and the Modernist Renewal of International Law', 106(8) *Harvard Law Review* (1993) 1792–1903 ; Rose Parfitt, 'Empire Des Nègres Blancs: The Hybridity of International Personality and the Abyssinia Crisis of 1935–36', 24(4) *Leiden Journal of International Law* (2011) 849–972.
25. Virginia Woolf has one of her characters say that he wants to write a book about silence, the things people don't say. See Virginia Woolf, *The Voyage Out* (Duckworth Books, 1915).
26. This is the gravamen of Maria Aristodemou's *Law, Psychoanalysis, Society: Taking the Unconscious Seriously* (Routledge, 2014).
27. Siegfried Sassoon, *Counter-Attack and Other Poems* (1918); *Rome Statute of the International Criminal Court*, Article 8 (1998).

In one of a small number of brilliantly accomplished psychoanalytic encounters with international law, Maria Aristodemou, paraphrasing Lacan, describes a world in which we kill God, but he refuses to die—refuses to be abolished—and becomes instead unconscious.[28] Here, (international) law is just one more of the placeholders for the dead/unconscious God (along with Father, Mother, Man, Markets, Freedom, Human Rights).[29] But now, the substitutes themselves are busy dying. In the case of international law, the act of dying is a distinguishing preoccupation of the field itself. It is often found advertising its own death, or failure to come to life (the 'vanishing point of a vanishing point of a vanishing point' or 'a discipline in paralysis').[30] Maybe it's time then to search again for international law's unconscious soul?

J. C. Smith argued thirty years ago that the foundations of the social order were largely neurotic. This is why that 'order' seems so irrational to so many people (15,000 nuclear weapons? Brexit? The 2 trillion dollar corporation?). The policies and practices underwriting that order attend to our neurotic needs or unconscious desires and cannot be understood—indeed are encountered as enigma or absurdity—in the absence of an attention to these needs and desires.[31]

It is not my intention, and it is beyond my capacity in any case, to put international law on the couch. But I do draw on at least two Freudian insights in this work. First, the idea that the unconscious presents itself or reveals itself through indirection, error, quip, pun, juxtaposition.[32] International law is a language, and that language has its conscious life (the effort to say something or many things in its texts and utterances) and its unconscious life, perhaps to be gestured at, indirectly, through the application of literary theory (bathos, chapter iv) or present in its comic life (chapter iii), or revealed in its private life (chapters i and vi) or found in image (film, painting) or literary text or material object (chapter vii).

---

28. Lacan, *Four Fundamental Concepts of Psychoanalysis* (1979) 59, quoted in Aristodemou (n 26) at 12.
29. Calling for an attention to the place as opposed to the thing in its place, see Gilles Deleuze, *Pure Immanence* (Zone Books, 2001) 71.
30. The original quote is from Thomas Holland, *Elements of Jurisprudence* (1924).
31. Smith (n 15).
32. See Marianne Constable, *Our Word Is Our Bond: How Legal Speech Acts* (Stanford University Press, 2014).

Along with indirection, and second, I will place in relation to each other materials that are not often thought of as having much of a relationship *with* each other. This *bricolage* (comedy and war crimes trials, gardens and international legal idealism, 'after method' and historical research) is intended to bring out the unexpected, perhaps unconscious, expressions of political desire at the base of legal-technocratic procedure: international law's intimate subterfuges, its exiled subjects. I tried to deploy, then, a technique derived from Freud's Basic Rule of Psychoanalysis:

> You will be tempted to say to yourself that this or that is irrelevant here, or is quite unimportant, or nonsensical so that there is no need to say it. You must never give into these criticisms ... indeed you must say it precisely because you feel an aversion in doing so.[33]

He then demands that the analysand freely describes to the analyst 'the changing view which you see outside'.[34] This of course can never be an entirely free activity. There is always, as Edward Said reminds us, 'a strategic location'.[35] Even free association—perhaps especially free association—is never entirely free.[36]

iv. international law

Having said something about what a 'sentimental' or 'literary' 'life' of international law might involve, let me return now, and with these thoughts in mind, to the second half of that phrase, namely, what counts as 'international law'? Just prior to giving a talk at Washington and Lee Law School in Virginia, and after delivering a set of slides—a photograph of a brooding Nabokov smoking a cigarette, an imperious Rebecca West wearing a

---

33. Sigmund Freud, 'On Beginning the Treatment (Further Recommendations on the Technique of Psycho-analysis I)', in J. Strachey (ed.), *The Standard Edition of the Complete Psychological Works of Sigmund Freud, Volume XII (1911–1913): The Case of Schreber, Papers on Technique and Other Works* (Hogarth Press and the Institute of Psychoanalysis, 1958) 121–144, 134–135.
34. But we do so in order to avoid becoming the sort of 'naïve' readers who merely look out of the window in the absence of a psychoanalyst. As Pamuk puts it: 'the naive reader ... [is like a person] ... who sincerely believes that he understands the country and the people he sees from the window as the car moves through the landscape ... he may begin to talk about the people and make pronouncements which evoke envy in the sentimental-reflective novelist'. Orhan Pamuk, *The Naive and the Sentimental Novelist* (Faber and Faber, 2010) 135.
35. Said (n 5) 29.
36. Donald Spence, *Narrative Truth and Historical Truth* (Norton, 1982) 81–82.

fetching fascinator, a garden in Bloomsbury full of irises—to the administrative assistant there, I was told that she had asked whether the wrong set of slides had been sent. These slides she said 'had no connection to international law'. What does it mean for something to have a connection to international law?

It has been a long time since Rosalyn Higgins told us that international law is more than rules.[37] But how much more than rules? What are the limits of this 'more-ness'? Hayden White said: 'every discipline is constituted by what it forbids its practitioners to do'.[38] What, then, does international law forbid its practitioners to do?

One answer to the question, 'what is international law about?' is found by asking what people who style themselves as international lawyers do and feel unable to do. But it is a risk describing back to international lawyers what they have been doing. When Rebecca West visited Florence in 1921, she was informed by her host that D. H. Lawrence had only just arrived in the city for the first time a few hours before but was probably already hammering out an essay 'vehemently and exhaustively describing the temperament of the people'.[39] West called this a silly thing to do. Let me now do that silly thing.

Just casting an eye over a programme for a conference on international law in Edinburgh in 2019, say, suggests a capacious field: here were papers on utopia, on cyberspace, on the Mandates system at Versailles, on indigenous law, on biometric data, on psychoanalysis in New Haven, on water.[40] But then, over the years, I have heard people speak on air-conditioning, on electricity supplies to the barrios, on monsters, on boredom, on the liberation of Nelson Mandela, on the Lacanian desire for fresh brains, about Jane Austen's influence on international law, about international law's influence on Jane Austen, on regret and repentance, on the picaresque novel, on luxury goods, on paper shredders . . . remember: these are all from conferences advertised as being about something called 'international law'. Clearly, international law *already has* a sentimental life.[41]

---

37. This is, of course, the first line of a book by my predecessor at LSE. See Rosalyn Higgins, *Problems and Process: International Law and How We Use It* (Clarendon Press, 1994).
38. Hayden White, *The Content of the Form: Narrative Discourse and Historical Representation* (Johns Hopkins University Press, 1987) 126.
39. See Geoff Dyer, *Working the Room* (Canongate Books, 2010).
40. Edinburgh–Glasgow Joint Meeting on International Law, 8–9 April 2020.
41. This is quite the contrast to the period when I began thinking about the subject and we were busy trying to figure out if humanitarian intervention was a good idea or not, or whether

But at the same time, scholars—young scholars especially—are experiencing a narrowing of range and opportunity. Now, to be heard and noticed amid the surrounding din of Stakhanovian over-production requires situating oneself in a field, armed with keywords to attract hits and cites and downloads: the numbing, career-enhancing data of contemporary academic life. And so—in the journals—we are confronted with a certain well-intentioned repetitiveness. A lot on crimes against humanity but not so much on capitalism and its links to avoidable and premature infant death, a bottomless pit of essays on anticipatory self-defence but very little on the way international law might help facilitate the homogenisation of London's or New York's urban landscapes. Viewed in this weakly ethnographic vein, then, international law is undergoing at the same time a narrowing and broadening of its multiple horizons.

Another sort of answer to the question, and an alternative to this anthropology of academic practice, might instead offer a conceptual view of international law. A vast array of 'international laws' has been advanced over the years: international law is rules, more than rules, authoritative decision-making by recognised epistemic communities, what international lawyers do, what states do and think, an expression of cosmopolitan values, the 'conscience of mankind', a gendered expression of transnational fantasy. At different times, I have found each of these answers attractive and illuminating (in some cases, I still do). As a preliminary matter, then, and having outlined the nature of the intervention being made here, it might be worth locating this project amid other projects of international legal thought and within a broader argument about the centrality of style and language.

We are familiar, I think, with the idea of international law as a field of progress or rationality slowly extending its regulatory reach, international law as a bag of tricks, or assemblage of norms designed to smooth interstate commerce and diplomacy. In this picture (upbeat, blasé), the world is

---

Article 38 of the ICJ Statute had 'exhausted' the sources of international law or how the right to self-determination might be extended to postcolonial circumstances. I added to a truly giant pile of articles and books on *that* subject, many of which, more or less, said the same thing. In my contribution, and bearing the gift of a totally impractical 'practical proposal', I called for an 'index of validity' to be applied to aspirant peoples. Indeed, I had one to hand. A version of this was published as 'The Diffusion of Sovereignty', by which time I had, alas, dropped the rather authoritarian index of validity in favour of a safer and blander appeal to constitutional tolerance, basically a plea that we all should get on better with each other. See Gerry Simpson, 'The Diffusion of Sovereignty: Self-Determinations in the Post-Colonial Age', in Robert McCorquodale (ed.), *Self-Determination in International Law* (Ashgate, 2000).

held together and (almost) fully governed by a network of rules and norms. The aim is to bring nearly everyone in (to the World Trade Organization, to the human rights system, to the ICC) in order to establish a truly global international legal order. The (underdeveloped, benighted) outsiders are aberrant. They lack—but this is remediable, and there is the endlessly and fatally deferred promise of remedy—democracy or capitalism or law or food. There are also recalcitrants, necessary, we might say, to humanity's self-realisation. A procession of figures has filled this role: pirates, outlaws, war criminals, terrorists, refugees, starving or bombed civilians, rebels and the world's proletarian and slum classes. In this version, humanity's potency is derived, partly, from its interventions—juridical, financial, humanitarian, military, cultural—in relation to these marginal figures. It is these interventions that help hold the world (of privilege) together.

Associated with this is an important body of writing arguing that international law is a tool to be deployed *against* poverty or maldistribution or empire or malevolence.[42] This idea, then, is grounded in a belief in the power of law *as it is now understood* to make amends somehow: for the state of the world or the excesses of capital or nationalism or war. The human rights movement, for example, is configured around this thought.

A third project regards these depictions of law as ahistorical or politically unattractive. International law, according to this view, is neither simply a neutral arbiter of political preferences (or management style) nor an immanently progressive tool for change. The idea here is to turn international law against itself, pointing to certain forms of international law as a way of thinking, or form of rhetoric or a diplomatic language, that forbids more emancipatory or dissident 'forms of life' and ways of going about things—or just closes off a bit of our humanity.[43] Those taking this third view will tend to offer an alternative vision of international law as a language or culture, or collection of people who call themselves 'international lawyers' and do things in particular ways employing distinctive speech patterns or tics, and operating within an identifiable matrix of cultural

---

42. See: Gerry Simpson, 'International Law in Diplomatic History', in James Crawford and Martti Koskenniemi (eds.), *Cambridge Companion to International Law* (Cambridge University Press, 2002) 25–46.
43. See also the work of Mark Antaki who says at one point and in a similar vein: 'The basic idea is that our forms of life—not necessarily visible to, or palpable for, us—are bound up with our language games—which we often play unwittingly. Allowing ourselves to become puzzled, even arrested, by how we speak, may allow us to better ask who we have become' (unpublished paper on file with author).

mores.⁴⁴ They will want to deploy this vision, then, against those very same progressive values that might be thought to have consolidated projects of empire and racial difference or obscured poverty or misshapened our languages or eaten up valuable political capital and so on.⁴⁵

v. writing and style

In the spirit of this final project, and returning to my initial thoughts about form and convention, I want to say a little more about what might it mean to engage in international law as a literary, rather than technical, task. Of course, this could mean a lot of different things. A simple awareness of the operations of language and an attentiveness to its grammatical and rhetorical moves might help us, perhaps, write better. In the spirit of the letter to a young contrarian, though, we might ask: How *should* we write? I have no answer to this question, but I will say that the two most pervasive voices in the field are respectively the voice of the disembodied, disarticulated discipline, and the ventriloquised voice of another writer (chapter ii). The temptation, in other words, is to sound like somebody else (the Anxiety of Influence) or to sound like nobody (the Anxiety of Professional Anonymity).⁴⁶

The narrative arc of my own writing career, in a way, has hewed close to these patterns. I had begun by speaking and writing in a mishmash of voices. My first essay took as its subject matter indigenous rights, and I wrote it in a style that fused mescaline-era Aldous Huxley with a strangulated imitation of Australian High Court legalese.⁴⁷ In some ways, it was a mess. In other ways, it was quite good. A couple of similar essays followed. Later I developed a mid-period style in which I learned to write like a mid-career academic (bereft of either youthful vim or ancient wisdom). There I was, introducing this, concluding that, making a sensible institutional proposal about another thing (in one article I suggested that the UN establish a new committee (a new committee!) to look into something or other). At times

---

44. For a fuller theorisation around this point, see Pierre Bourdieu, *Language and Symbolic Power* (Polity Press, 1991). See also Jacqueline Mowbray, *Linguistic Justice: International Law and Language Policy* (Oxford University Press, 2012) 4–8.
45. Respectively, Vasuki Nesiah, Margot Salomon, Madelaine Chiam, Wendy Brown.
46. The first phrase is, of course, Harold Bloom's. See *The Anxiety of Influence* (Oxford University Press, 1973).
47. Gerry Simpson, 'Mabo, International Law, Terra Nullius and the Stories of Settlement: An Unresolved Jurisprudence', 19(1) *Melbourne University Law Review* (1993) 195–210.

I sounded like a man who had lost the will to write, or live. When I read these mid-period essays now (which I don't), they seem witless. It wasn't until later that I began to write in the way that I wanted to write (aspiring to, but never quite achieving, what Andrea Bianchi calls 'levity and depth'), where writing began to feel like an emanation from some approximation of an authentic self.[48]

Of course, form is not simply a matter of finding a signature writing style or making a reasonable effort to write well. International law is itself a form, a prose that we find we have spoken all our lives. To speak of the world is to speak international law. Can we imagine, then, or will into existence, a sentimental, or at least, essayistic, maybe even *poetic*, international law?

The dangers are manifest. What if international lawyers simply don't make very good poets? We have our novelists (Philip Allott, Rob Howse, Joseph Weiler, Simon Chesterman).[49] There is now even some poetry in *The European Journal of International Law* (van den Meerssche, Crawford) and, while this is welcome and diverting, we still tend to treat international law and poetry as separate.[50] What if, instead, we take seriously the possibility that all philosophical (and juridical) thought begins with poetry, that our first thought is a metaphorical one that is then translated into a rational intervention: 'all thought begins with a poem' (Alain)?[51] The idea would be to revive this poetic origin. This would not require poetry (though Wittgenstein contemplated writing his *Tractatus* as a sequence of poems after all) but rather attentiveness to the stylistic choices one is making in one's writing life. Why do I write in this form? Could I write differently in order to get closer to this thought?

But why? One of the purposes of international law must be to get people to do or think things that ought to be done or thought. This book is animated by a sense that the diplomatic world is, if not quite Pirandello's 'very sad piece of buffoonery', at the very least somehow ungraspable in the

---

48. Andrea Bianchi, letter to author, 5 March 2018.
49. E.g. Philip Allott, *Invisible Power* (Xlibris, 2005); Robert Howse, *Mozart: A Novel* (Xlibris, 2004);Robert Howse, 'Semi-Detached' (unpublished on file with author); Joseph Weiler, *Der Fall Steinmann* (Piper, 2000).
50. Dimitri van den Meerssche, 'Calling Themis', 26(1) *European Journal of International Law* (2005) 310; James Crawford, 'Mr Kadi and Article 103' (EJIL:Talk!, 2013), at https://www.ejiltalk.org/mr-kadi-and-article-103-by-james-crawford-a-poem/. See also Philip Allott, 'Self-Determination: Absolute Right or Social Poetry?', in Christian Tomuschat (ed.), *Modern Law and Self-Determination* (Martinus Nijhoff, 1993) 177–210.
51. George Steiner, *The Poetry of Thought* (New Directions, 2011) 12.

ordinary language of professionalism; that our idioms for understanding and re-describing that world have shrunk at the very point where the world has increased in complexity.[52]

To make this more explicit, we might ask what it is that tends to get said in the language of international law?[53] What sorts of lives are lived by international lawyers (chapter ii)? What sort of writing is demanded of the international law professor or academic or advocate (chapter iv)? And what possibilities are foreclosed by this way of writing (chapter iii)?[54] This is the book's descriptive task. Something turns on what we want international law to *do*.[55] And my impression is that along with the dispute resolution and the cultures of formalism and the language-games of diplomacy, some of us at least are attracted to the idea that it might offer a shift in consciousness (perhaps reversing 400 years of empire, hegemony, indecency and lovelessness

---

52. I stand on the shoulders of others here (see Philip Allott, 'Language, Method, and the Nature of International Law', in 45 *British Yearbook of International Law* (Oxford University Press, 1971) 79–136. See, more recently, Richard McAdams, *The Expressive Powers of Law: Theories and Limits* (Princeton University Press, 2015).
53. Madelaine Chiam, *International Law in Public Debate* (Cambridge University Press, 2021); Dino Kritsiotis, 'The Power of International Law as Language', 34(2) *California Western Law Review* (1998) 9.
54. This is the thought that has inspired generations of modernists from James Joyce's *Finnegan's Wake* (Faber and Faber, 1939) to Samuel Beckett's *Malone Dies* (Les Éditions de Minuit, 1951) and onto Tom McCarthy's *Remainder* (Vintage, 2005). See also Franco Moretti, *Atlas of the European Novel, 1800–1900* (Verso, 1998); Virginia Woolf's *Orlando: A Biography* (Hogarth Press, 1928).
55. I am not the first person to have made such a demand. Peter Goodrich, in an account of the impoverished lives of international lawyers (nasty, brutish, solitary), seems to be calling for a new 'life of the law', a law ('a different and spectral law') that is not just words but a 'scholarly, humanist discourse' consummated or traced through 'literary sensibility'. See Peter Goodrich, 'On the Relational Aesthetics of International Law', 10(2) *Journal of the History of International Law* (2008) 321, 351, 324. I agree with the *telos* but Goodrich seems to describe an international law I don't fully recognise. Have international lawyers really 'vacated' the public sphere (Anne-Marie Slaughter, Christine Chinkin)? Have they really 'peddle[d]' a variant form of positive law' (ibid. 322) (Fleur Johns, Karen Knop, Vasuki Nesiah, Kerry Rittich)? Goodrich goes on to lament international law's 'scholarly apathy' and this is the picture of international law often offered from the outside: a field of study that has lost its mooring, or lacks intellectual courage. But I have to say I neither experience, nor encounter, 'apathy' when I read, say, the current generation of committed and brilliant young international lawyers, or when I teach the roughly 100 students each year at the London School of Economics, Australian National University or Melbourne University. When I pick up the pages of the *Leiden Journal of International Law* or the *London Review of International Law* or books published in the past decade or so—such as Fleur Johns, Richard Joyce and Sundhya Pahuja (eds.), *Events: The Force of International Law* (Routledge, 2010); Fleur Johns, *Non-Legality in International Law: Unruly Law* (Cambridge University Press, 2013); Cait Storr, *International Status in the Shadow of Empire* (Cambridge University Press, 2021); Madelaine Chiam, *International Law in Public Debate* (Cambridge University Press, 2021)—I see assuredness of tone, a sense of purpose, a sensitivity to political effect, and a striving for new forms of expression.

in international diplomatic life). So, to offer an example from the Scottish Enlightenment, when Hume describes 'sympathy' as that 'which makes me concerned for the present sorrows of a stranger', we must feel that a language that responds to those sorrows through law could be useful.[56] When it comes to the misery of the other, 'the present sorrows of a stranger' are, these days, rendered invisible in official circles where there is either a language of coldness (the insistence by the Australian Department of Immigration that Department documents describe asylum seekers as 'illegals') or a legal vernacular of abstraction ('refugee claimants'). The drownings of strangers barely elicit a flicker of recognition now in most liberal-left circles.

When it comes to shifts in language and consciousness. Philip Allott is thinker-in-chief: 'We make the human world, including human institutions, through the power of the human mind. What we have made by thinking, we can make new by new thinking'.[57]

This book is partly motivated by this thought but derives its inspiration, too, from a general preoccupation with the continuities and discontinuities of literary and juridical accounts of life, and it explores a hunch I have (though it is really the hunch of the 20th century) that most of what is interesting in life occurs off-screen, that surprisingly little is facially explicable and that the informal (to render things sociologically)[58] or the unconscious (to think psychotherapeutically)[59] or the emotional (in its neurological, or philosophical or affective dimensions)[60] or the micro-political (to make a contrast with formal legal arrangements)[61] are largely obscure to us without quite a bit of effort and that, as a consequence, our patterns of engagement can become stultifying and familiar and, yet, also obscure and muddy.[62]

---

56. David Hume, *A Treatise on Human Nature* (Thomas and Joseph Allman, 1817) 70.
57. Philip Allott, *Eunomia: New Order for a New World* (Oxford University Press, 2001) xxvii.
58. Moshe Hirsch and Andrew Lang (eds.), *Research Handbook on the Sociology of International Law* (Edward Elgar, 2018).
59. Aristodemou (n 26).
60. See studies suggesting that cognitive reflection is partly emotional, so that in processes of ethical deliberation, emotions have a serious role to play. This is supported by studies in political psychology and neuroscience. See Renée Jeffery, 'The Promise and Problems of the Neuroscientific Study of Individual and Collective Emotions', 6(3) *International Theory* (2014) 584–589.
61. See Antaki (n 43).
62. This is related to the need for attentiveness. A point taken up by both Simone Weil, who said that morality was a matter of attention not will (Iris Murdoch, 'Against Dryness', XVI *Encounter* (1961) 16–20, at 20), and Hannah Arendt, who bemoaned Eichmann's thoughtlessness. On micro-politics, see Michael Shapiro, 'The Micropolitics of Justice: Language, Sense and Space', 8(3) *Law, Culture and the Humanities* (2011) 1–19.

Even more specifically, I would argue that our sense of what a piece of international legal scholarship or teaching has achieved is bound up with a sense of its literary style or, in a stronger version, that it *is* its literary style. Virginia Woolf was once asked what her books were about; she responded by saying that they weren't about anything, they *were* the thing. Her style was, in a way, her content.[63] International law, similarly, is not about something else. It *is* the something. In a more serious vein, we might refuse the invitation to see international law as merely a language by which we engage in or re-describe legal-diplomatic work. Instead, what we do with words *is* the diplomatic work.[64]

We respond to style as a matter of aesthetic judgement of course, but also as a matter of experience and sentiment. Words in the right order make us feel differently about the world.[65] I suppose that it is this commitment to content and style that makes unsatisfactory descriptions of our own work or the work of people we admire. I turn in terror to the pages of some textbooks when they pay a perfunctory visit to that tiny, beleaguered principality called 'International Legal Theory'. Here a whole generation's worth of human endeavour and literary style is cut down—often accompanied by 'a tin ear for irony'[66]—to a few superannuated phrases about 'indeterminacy' or 'power' or, worst of all, 'cynicism'.[67] Indeed, when it comes to 'deconstructionism' or 'feminism', textbook writers often quote the views of *other* textbook writers instead of the original texts. Remember that this is not just wrong or bathetic; worse than that, it misrepresents a whole way of being and talking. It enacts, in other words, the very opposite of what it purports to encapsulate.

---

63. See Ed Morgan, *The Aesthetics of International Law* (University of Toronto Press, 2007) at 3: arguing that *Lolita*, like argument about international law, is more about 'modes of expression than content'.
64. Hayden White, of course, has made one of the largest contributions to breaking down this distinction between form and content in his work on the style of history.
65. See the idea of what Raymond Williams called 'structures of feeling' in *Marxism and Literature* (Oxford University Press, 1977).
66. Rai Gaita's phrase, in 'Literature, Genocide and the Philosophy of International Law' (unpublished work on file with the author, 2013).
67. Example One: 'critical legal studies argues that law is politics'; Example Two: 'deconstructionist theories see law as a smokescreen for behaviour that would have occurred in any event'. I don't mean to suggest that literary critics and reviewers don't riff brilliantly off particular texts. Barthes' *S/Z*, his book on Flaubert, is longer than the Flaubert short story that is its proximate subject.

The broader thought, here, then, is that somehow cognition and affect are enmeshed in ways that are under-explored. Bernard Williams tells the story of a philosopher who said to a colleague with whom he was writing a book: 'Let's first get the content right. Later, you can add the style'.[68] It would be crazy and inane to ask someone to summarise a short poem *in lieu* of reading out. But I want to suggest that all writing is a bit like poetry in this regard.[69] This is what makes translating poetry (something Philip Larkin thought was pointless, but then he also said that he would like to go to China only if he could return on the same day)[70] so difficult or only possible if one thinks of it as a whole new poetic enterprise. This is why I say, non-facetiously, that it would be better for textbook writers to leave a blank space under the heading 'Critical Theory'.

During the 1983 British General Election, a former LSE law student called Cherie Booth was the candidate for Margate in Kent. Her father, a well-known British soap star, knew Tony Benn—then the most powerful left-wing politician in the Labour Party—and had Benn come down to Margate from London to give a rousing speech to the party faithful. Cherie Booth sent her husband, Tony Blair, to pick Benn up from his flat in Holland Park. Blair thought Benn's speech was inspiring: 'I sat enraptured, absolutely captivated. If only I could speak like that'.[71] The strange thing about the whole episode is that Blair didn't agree with anything that Benn had said. He didn't understand Benn's way of speaking to be somehow derived from a tradition and style of radicalism that was its own content. Style, for Blair, was something that could be added later.

So, if we can accept for these purposes that style matters a great deal and not just as decoration, and that our demarcations around style and content may not be useful, then we can begin to approach the sentimental as a particular way of writing or being, and international law as a mode of communication and discipline perpetually in need of new resources, even if these new resources seem eccentric or magical.[72]

---

68. Bernard Williams, *Truth and Truthfulness: An Essay in Genealogy* (Princeton University Press, 2002).
69. In Iris Murdoch's phrase: 'Poetry is the creation of linguistic quasi-things; prose is for explanation': (n 62) 19.
70. See Tom Courtenay, *Pretending to Be Me* (Hachette Audio, 2005), a one-man play about Larkin.
71. Tony Blair, *A Journey* (Arrow, 2010) 36.
72. T. Adorno, *Negative Dialectics* (Continuum, 2007) 33.

vi. literature and law

There is already, of course, a formal practice of reading law against literature itself.[73] The general literature in law and literature is by now enormous, and I can barely scratch the surface of it here.[74] But when we read literary texts against law, what are we doing? In some cases, this might be part of an effort simply to illuminate the legal texts or to effect a kind of transference whereby the law is revealed as fantastic, opaque and enigmatic, while literature becomes textually transparent and relatively univocal.[75] This, I take to be at least one of the arguments performed in Ed Morgan's exercise in what we might call comparative law and literature, *The Aesthetics of International Law*, his book-length plea for a new self-conscious international law.[76]

Law and literature have been placed in relation to each other in at least three different modes.[77] The survey of favourite books for fresh portraits of legal process (*Bleak House*) or concepts of usury (*The Merchant of Venice*) or in the name of lawyerly self-improvement is a well-travelled field of scholarship (law in literature).[78] Melville's (and Britten's) *Billy Budd* (because it is about a trial) and Kafka's *The Trial* (also about a trial) and *In a Penal Colony* have kept law and literature scholars busy for decades. More subtly, there are texts such as Richard Weisberg's *The Failure of the Word* (taking in Kafka, Dostoevsky, Camus) that seek to discover new things about law in a more

---

73. An earlyish classic is Robin West, *Narrative, Authority and Law* (University of Michigan Press, 1993). Or from the literature side, Joseph Slaughter's ground-breaking *Human Rights, Inc: The World Novel, Narrative Form and International Law* (Fordham University Press, 2007).
74. The earliest 'humanist' (to use Julie Peters' typology in 'Law, Literature and the Vanishing Real', 120(2) *PMLA* (2005) 442–453) interventions are by James Boyd White in *The Legal Imagination* (Wolters Kluwer, 1973) and later in *Heracles' Bow: Essays on the Rhetoric and Poetics of the Law* (University of Wisconsin Press, 1985) and *Acts of Hope: Creating Authority in Literature, Law and Politics* (University of Chicago Press, 1994). See also Richard Weisberg, *Poethics, and Other Strategies of Law and Literature* (Columbia University Press, 1992). For an overview, see Gary Minda's *Postmodern Legal Movements* (1995) (situating law and literature among contemporaneous developments in legal theory).
75. This would at least reverse the more common reductive tendencies of interdisciplinarity in this field. See Peters (n 74).
76. Morgan (n 63) 169. Morgan's book wants to compare the modes of expression found in international legal texts with somewhat analogous writing in literature (at 4). Of course, Morgan's book is much richer than this account suggests, but the chapters do engage in a comparison between legal and literary forms, e.g. Ibsenian realism and Brechtian symbolism are read into the performance of detachment and involvement that we see in war crimes trials (16–21).
77. See Ian Ward, *Law and Literature: Possibilities and Perspectives* (Cambridge University Press, 1995).
78. Richard Posner, *Law and Literature* (Harvard University Press, 1988). To say nothing of a *law of literature* (encompassing copyright, intellectual property, libel and obscenity).

general literature of responsibility, guilt, or shame and to provoke a more authentically human engagement with legal material and language, or what he called, in a phrase that didn't quite catch on, 'poethics', or Robin West's work on re-establishing the boundedness of lives lived outside liberal law or Nicola Lacey's study of character in criminal trials.[79]

In other instances, law has been treated as a literary enterprise: law as literature.[80] And, academics have long been fond of the judges who quote literary texts in academic opinions: literature in law. For some reason, the judge who references Bob Dylan seems especially popular here (Dylan-quoting establishing the judge as both hip and irredeemably out-of-touch at the same time).[81] And there has been a mountain of scholarship concerned to think into law and literature through hermeneutics.[82] 'Wrong Again' may be one of the best law review titles; it arrived in the midst of a battle between Ronald Dworkin and Stanley Fish over the autonomy of texts and in the wake of Dworkin's effort to think of adjudication as a literary as well as constitutional enterprise: law as interpretation.[83]

International lawyers have been a little slower on the uptake, but when they have shown an interest in literature, Shakespeare has been a tremendous favourite, almost an honorary international humanitarian lawyer.[84] There

---

79. Nicola Lacey, *Women, Crime and Character* (Clarendon Press, 2008); Richard Weisberg, *The Failure of the Word* (Yale University Press, 1984).
80. For an examination of confession via Camus and Dostoevsky, see Peter Brooks, *Troubling Confessions: Speaking Guilt in Law and Literature* (University of Chicago Press, 2001). See also Kieran Dolin, *Fiction and the Law: Legal Discourse in Victorian and Modernist Literature* (Cambridge University Press, 1999); Guyora Binder and Robert Weisberg, *Literary Criticisms of Law* (Princeton University Press, 2000).
81. Maureen Cain, 'Necessarily Out of Touch', 23 *Sociological Review* (1975) 226. Not to mention that Dylan quotes tend to be conveniently plastic: 'There's no success like failure and failure's no success at all' (indeed, but also, *what?*), or, more often, 'to live outside the law you must be honest' (hugely popular among criminologists).
82. Andrea Bianchi, *International Law Theories: An Inquiry into Different Ways of Thinking* (Oxford University Press, 2016) 289–291.
83. Stanley Fish, 'Working on the Chain Gang: Interpretation in the Law and in Literary Criticism', 9(1) *Critical Inquiry* (1982) 201–216; Stanley Fish, 'Still Wrong after All These Years', 6(3) *Law and Philosophy* (1987) 401–418; Ronald Dworkin, 'My Reply to Stanley Fish (and Walter Benn Michaels): Please Don't Talk about Objectivity Anymore', in W. J. T. Mitchell (ed.), *The Politics of Interpretation* (Chicago University Press, 1983). On interpretation in international law, see Ingo Venzke, *How Interpretation Makes International Law: On Semantic Change and Normative Twists* (Oxford University Press, 2014). See also, in a productive and contemporaneous countermove: Robert Cover, 'Foreword: Narrative and Nomos', 97(4) *Harvard Law Review* (1983) 4–68.
84. See, in general, Kenji Yoshino, *A Thousand Times More Fair: What Shakespeare's Plays Teach Us about Justice* (Harper Collins, 2011). David Seymour, 'Letter from Shylock', 8(2) *Law and Critique* (1997) 215–222, Ian Ward, *Shakespeare and the Legal Imagination* (Butterworths, 1999),

have also been, of course, literary treatments of international lawyering in, say, Muriel Spark's novel about the Eichmann Trial (*The Mandelbaum Gate*) or Robert Harris' lightly fictive account of the indictment of a British president for crimes against humanity (*The Ghost*). Meanwhile, Frank Moorhouse's trilogy on the League of Nations traces with élan the biography of an Australian diplomat at the League of Nations, while Shirley Hazzard's own literary life is, in some respects, a mini-history of the different ways of writing international law, switching back and forth between formulaic insider indictments of United Nations 'failure' and the recasting of bureaucratic manoeuvring UN in short-story form.[85] In work by Christopher Warren, a rather unfamiliar figure, John Milton, is positioned as an international legal avatar. Warren and Chenxi Tang have sought to approach the history of international law (or the law of nations) as a history of literature.[86] From the other side, there have been efforts to treat international law as a language: to think about authorial will and intention, rhetorical device, grammar, meaning and so on.[87] And of course there is a whole field of international law *and* language studying the ways in which international law secures or fails to secure what Jacqueline Mowbray calls 'linguistic justice'.[88]

Alongside, or not quite alongside, all of this has been more experimental writing that has sought to disturb or redistribute relations between law and literature, and in particular, to de-essentialise each element of the relationship.[89] In her keynote to the 2019 Conference on International Law and Literature at the Edge, part of a bigger project to reimagine international

---

and in international law specifically, Theodor Meron, *Bloody Constraint: War and Chivalry in Shakespeare* (Oxford University Press, 2000); John Sutherland, *Henry V, War Criminal?* (Oxford University Press, 2000). Quentin Skinner's more recent, *Forensic Shakespeare* (Oxford University Press, 2014) comes to the playwright from a different direction, arguing that Shakespeare was influenced by contemporaneous trends in judicial rhetoric.

85. Frank Moorhouse, *Grand Days* (Random House Australia, 2011); Shirley Hazzard, *People in Glass Houses* (Picador, 1967); Shirley Hazzard, *Defeat of an Ideal: A Study of the Self-Destruction of the United Nations* (Little, Brown, 1973).
86. Christopher Warren, *Literature and the Law of Nations, 1580–1680* (Oxford University Press, 2015); Chenxi Tang, *Imagining World Order: Literature and International Law in Early Modern Europe, 1500–1800* (Cornell University Press, 2018).
87. James Boyd White is a leading figure in this regard.
88. These include books on international human rights law and the protection of languages (the authorities are numerous) and work like Mowbray's which attempt to get at the way in which language capital is allocated and (mal)distributed within the field of international law. See Mowbray (n 44).
89. 'Literature and International Law at the Edge' project (Christopher Gevers, Joseph Slaughter, Vasuki Nesiah, Gerry Simpson): conferences in New York City (Gallatin School), December 2018; London (LSE), July 2019; Nairobi, June 2021).

law and literature, Aristodemou called for a disruptive relationship—perhaps even bad relations—between law and literature. This bigger project, in a way, performs this 'bad' relation by placing an international law of the Global South into conversation with its literature and by contrasting these with more conventional depictions of international law and literature (and 'international law and literature'). So, received accounts of Robinson Crusoe are displaced by readings that rewrite Defoe as the story of Man Friday's dispossession or as a tale of mercantile expansion; stories of self-determination and corporate expansion are understood through the picaresque East African novel rather than through one more invocation of Conrad.[90] All of this work is conscious of the price we might pay for enjoying law and literature. In particular, it worries about approaches that have seen literature as a utilitarian (Posner) or humanising (Weisberg) aspect of the lawyer's work.[91] I have not engaged in a law and literature of international law in this book, but clearly there are traces of this interdiscipline scattered throughout from the reading of literary texts as prompts for misrecognitions and misreadings of international law to a humanist spirit (but absent the hubris of seeing in literature a 'path to justice readily available in these stories'—Weisberg) of longing and renewal derived from literary sensibility to a more disruptive account of law's and literature's, and 'law and literature's', potential to realign our prevailing languages and patterns of thought and behaviour (something powerfully present in literary reconstructions of the relations between law and gender) to a willingness to acknowledge the vulnerability of law to 'the justice of humour' (Peter Goodrich).[92]

To read literature with law risks engaging in a civilising mission or celebrating a culture that 'discharges us from the obligation to think'.[93] Instead, what is demanded from the more recent law and literature encounter is what Joey Slaughter called a 'contrapuntal' style.[94] Sometimes

---

90. Stewart Motha, 'Fiction as Archive of Sovereignty', *International Law and Literature at the Edge Conference* (LSE, 2019). See also Vasuki Nesiah, 'Freedom at Sea', 7(2) *London Review of International Law* (2019) 149–179.
91. Weisberg (n 74).
92. Peter Goodrich, 'Lex Laetans: Three Theses on the Unbearable Lightness of Legal Critique', 17(3) *Law and Literature* (2005) 293–319; Nicola Lacey (n 79); Carolyn Heilbrun and Judith Resnik, 'Convergences: Law, Literature and Feminism', 99 *Yale Law Journal* (1990) 1912–1956; Richard Weisberg, 'What Remains "Real" about the Law and Literature Movement?', 66(1) *Journal of Legal Education* (2016) 38.
93. Aristodemou (n 26), quoting Freud.
94. The phrase is Slaughter's. See Warren (n 86). See also Joseph Slaughter, 'Pathetic Fallacies: Personification and the Unruly Subjects of International Law', 7(1) *London Review of International Law* (2019) 3–54.

this might involve keeping the two disciplines apart or at length (for some reason, I'm reminded here of the UN Bookshop in Geneva refusing to stock Solzhenitsyn) or emphasising the discordant nature of the encounter, a modernist international law and literature that seeps into the pages of this book along with a more typically humanist effort to reimagine international law as a literary field. In her powerful late novel, *The Great Fire*, Shirley Hazzard grafts the love affair between a war crimes investigator and a nurse onto a story of hopeful post-war reconstruction.[95] This masterpiece enacts the idea of law as literary enterprise, literature as a form of law and the performance and disturbance of both simultaneously.

vii. politics and sentiment

The aesthetic obsessions of this book do not disqualify it as a contribution to the politics of international law. It is, of course, a plea for a politics of international law, or better, an international law of politics. But what might this mean? Not so long ago, the politics of international law was that it was not recognised—indeed it refused to be recognised—*as* politics. Now, the idea of 'international law as politics' has become the kind of commonplace that even the most doctrinal international lawyers are happy to repeat to whoever will listen. To concede that international law has a politics is, often, just a prelude to a tactical withdrawal into the cosy space of legalism. In one especially banal, theoretically innocent version, it is agreed that of course international law is political because it is made by states and, after all, states are political, but that there remain spaces of apolitical judgement amid this system (tribunals, academic lawyers describing the law, the International Court of Justice (ICJ), a foreign investment arbitration tribunal) where a law free of politics is interpreted, enforced, adjudicated, described.

Much has been written about this: on hermeneutics, on indeterminacy, on the deep structural politics of international legalism. And now it has become an act of dissent to retrieve the lawfulness of law *from* politics, or at least, from the facile enunciations of law's politics. By avoiding the collapse of law into politics, law takes responsibility for the world around us. Instead of international lawyers arguing that politics constitutes law (and thereby letting law off the hook), law constitutes politics and puts itself back on the

---

95. Shirley Hazzard, *The Great Fire* (Virago, 2003).

hook. I make an intervention along these lines—if a rather indirect one—by thinking of international law's aesthetic surface as a politics of law where projects win and lose, where people and their voices are subject to an institutionalised no-platforming, and where certain styles of thought, syntax, dress or gender are as likely to determine reception as any particular 'content', where a micro-political world of gesture, code, clubbability or cool is as much 'international law' as the Treaty on Celestial Bodies or the Articles on State Responsibility.

But this book's own *internal* politics are complicated in some respects. On one hand it might be read, at times, as a plea for civility, perhaps even quiescence (the exchange of letters between Khrushchev and Castro in the chapter on friendship; the celebration of a gentle pastoralism in the chapter on gardening). This would not be an outrageous reading. Like many people, when I watched the funeral of George H. W. Bush in December 2018, I was struck by the regular pleas for civility and decency in politics. But this 'high-mindedness' is also something I want to argue against in diplomacy, law and politics: a high-mindedness that has so often been the cover for varieties of imperial violence.[96] I hope this book, then, helps us retrieve a place for a certain sort of civility in legal diplomacy (but stripped of the obvious hypocrisies and cheapening effects of the Bush funeral coverage) combined with an attentiveness to sentiment and a radical politics that civility might neuter or defang (absent the sheer playground capriciousness and emotional instability of contemporary Anglo-American politics).[97]

As a political gesture, this book will not convince anyone who thinks international law is 'working effectively' or that it successfully describes and represents the world or that it is a coherent project of enlightenment rationality or that there is such a thing as 'the international community'. So, along with its negotiations around civility (how to be sentimental without being apolitical, chapter ii; how to write history without method, chapter v; diplomacy during nuclear crisis, chapter vi), the substantive politics of the book can be understood as, to use Fredric Jameson's term, anti-anti-utopian, or

---

96. This is a phrase of Nancy Fraser's.
97. In some ways, this plays into a broader politics where the space between rampant neoliberalism and ethno-nationalist populism either becomes vanishingly small or unbridgeably vast, depending how one looks at it. It is small in the sense that it gets harder and harder to operate in that space without adopting a soft liberal defence of the status quo (the Brexit debate in the UK was conducted around these two poles) yet wide in the sense that the possibility of a common ground between the two seems to be disappearing.

as a kind of chastened utopian longing; it is this hope that I take up in the final chapter where I point to the possibility of utopia after the death of utopianism and in chapter vi where I offer up a declaration on friendly relations among nations.[98]

The distinguishing feature of so much left-liberal politics today (perhaps its greatest failing) is that its foundational economic commitments are largely compatible with hyper-capitalism.[99] Successive 'progressive' regimes in the United States, Australia and the United Kingdom (Clinton–Obama, Keating–Hawke, Blair–Brown) have more or less left untouched the fundamentals of this system or, worse, have facilitated and promoted the power and influence of the toweringly wealthy as well as the growth of a distressed precariat. There have been advances (especially in the cultural field, e.g. gay marriage, anti-discrimination law), some soft but significant public investment (late-Blair), the odd intervention in the field of immiseration (Obama's healthcare initiative, Brown's expenditure on the National Health Service), but overall the picture has been one of a sustained assault on public space and life, spasmodic war-making (Iraq, Libya) and a bio- and techno-politics which long ago surpassed, in form at least, Orwell's or Atwood's worst fantasies.

I make a normative argument, then, by pointing to the need for a sentimental life of international law to re-energise our (legal) politics in the face of all this. Many of us feel cut off from a genuine reckoning with global warming, the lived experience of starvation in Syria, anarchy in Mexico or oligarchy in the United States. Meanwhile, international legal instruments remain abstractions careening between technocracy and gush, between lazy cliché and lawyerly standoffishness. Does anyone really believe in 'the scourge of war' (the UN Charter) or the 'mosaic of humanity' threatened by war crimes (the Rome Statute)? Does anyone think 'serious violations of the laws of war' captures the essence of bodily and mental harm caused by explosive devices or torture?[100] To think our way into a common humanity

---

98. Fredric Jameson, *Archaeologies of the Future: The Desire Called Utopia and Other Science Fictions* (Verso, 2005).
99. Samuel Beckett apparently said that 'perhaps' was his favourite word.
100. How might we understand the literary economy of international law? In order to approach this question we might contrast, say, Elie Wiesel's *Night* with the work of Primo Levi. A lot of survivor memoir fails as literature and fails as an account of the special wrongs of the Holocaust. But if some Holocaust memoir is 'banal and sentimental', would that matter if we could capture the underlying truth of the account? Of course, sentimentalism could obscure the underlying truth of the account or at least its compellability as witness testimony, but

or a possible future takes imagination, a reckoning with the things we did not see coming or do not see in front of us.[101]

In 2019, the London School of Economics hosted a photographic exhibition on the Syrian Civil War. In one image, a father is driving his sons back from the front line where they have been caught up in a blood-soaked military campaign. The boys are in the back seat of a pick-up truck. It is only when we look more closely at the photo that we see that where their legs should be the boys, instead, have two stumps each. One boy's face is contorted in an epic pain. It is the pain of pain but also, one imagines, the pain of violation (his legs removed through the action of other men) and the pain of future loss (running, walking, driving, playing football). It is a pain that mocks our legalistic resort to the fictions of 'proportionality', 'discrimination', the casual references to 'civilian losses'. Suddenly, all of these seem less like descriptive techniques or normative projects and more like mechanisms of repression through language.

So the literary account of international law enacted in these pages is already a politics of international law: a plea for a combination of ironic laughter and earnest commitment as a response to the problem of private doubt and public cruelty or wrongdoing.[102] This is not an escape into shoulder-shrugging but a realisation that legal politics is an intensely private reckoning with the self (and its neurotic, libidinal urges) as well as a series of solidarity gestures with others, that in these groundless, post-metaphysical times, we simply have to keep on, making things grow, failing to describe—but re-describing again and again—unassuageable sadness or grotesque cruelty, caring for friendships, laughing at the pomposity of liberal rationalities and the cruelties of illiberal tyrannies, offering sympathy and hospitality to strangers.[103]

You, dear reader, may be asking by now: what are the chapters about? The second chapter, 'the sentimental lives of international lawyers', originally formed part of a lecture to mark the launch of the *London Review*

---

the idea of stripping away literary artifice to get at cognitive truth is surely a flawed account of how reading (or truth) works: 'If we need the terribleness of what it is to commit and to suffer genocide to be vividly and soberly before our minds, they ask—usually rhetorically—is it not art rather than philosophy that will do it?' See Gaita (n 66).

101. Ibid.
102. Peter Sloterdijk, *Critique of Cynical Reason* (Verso, 1988).
103. See Richard Rorty's efforts to bring together the worlds of private irony and public action through a commitment to description through literature and, sometimes, philosophy. Richard Rorty, *Contingency, Irony and Solidarity* (Cambridge University Press, 1989).

of International Law.[104] In it, I set out a manifesto for thinking and speaking carefully about international law in a position somewhere between tears, (cheaply sentimental), laughter (blasphemous) and expertise (cold). This position I describe as 'close to tears', a hard-boiled sentimentality about the world and international law's place in it. In this second chapter, I offer up some thoughts on humanitarianism and where it might be going wrong. This is a more specific indictment of two projects I have been engaged with: international criminal justice and international human rights law. The problem here I take to be a form of sentimental excess, an over-attention to some realms of sadness and pain as a form of displacement activity. It seems to me that these two projects also have bequeathed us languages that have lost moral traction and literary power.

Can international law be funny? In chapter iii, I consider this question, and ask, in particular, what kind of funny it might be. Here I contrast two kinds of comedy: ironic and blasphemous. Chapter iv, "bluebeard on trial': the experience of bathos', continues in this vein by specifying bathos as an effect produced by the application of international criminal law to the disasters of war. The end of this chapter then adopts what I take to be the book's anti-anti utopian aspect. This manifests itself as a search for spaces or enclaves in which resistance to the orthodox modes of being, feeling and speaking might be discovered or played out. In this instance, the chapter argues for acts of memorialisation or reckoning that escape the old routines.

Chapter v, 'an uncertain style', then wrestles with ways of seeing as a response to international law's recent turn to history: not a history of international law but rather a history of histories of international law, a compendium of arguments around the turn to history in international law.[105] The hunch here is that we might see history more imagistically and suggestively, perhaps by deploying an anti-method. The final pair of substantive chapters, then, makes more explicit pleas for different kinds of international law based on a politics of lawful friendship in one case, and on the idea of gardening as a practice of redemptive international legal pastoralism in the other.

---

104. Gerry Simpson, 'The Sentimental Life of International Law', 3(1) *London Review of International Law* (2015) 3.
105. On history of histories, see Simpson in Kevin Jon Heller and Gerry Simpson, *The Hidden Histories of War Crimes Trials* (Oxford University Press, 2013) 1–9.

ii
the sentimental lives of international lawyers

i. the absence of life	32
ii. the (auto)biographical moment	36
iii. notations on the sentimental lives of international lawyers	41
sentimental excess	43
moral simplicity	46
sentimental solipsism: advertisements for myself	47
depoliticising sentimentality	49

There is properly, no history only biography

Ralph Waldo Emerson, *Essays* (1841)

Every writer needs an address

Isaac Bashevis Singer, *New York Times* (6 July 1987)

On 11 June 1956, the then recently appointed Professor of Poetry at Oxford, W. H. Auden, delivered his inaugural lecture entitled 'Making, Knowing and Judging'. Reading a poem, he claimed, raised two sets of questions. The first was technical. How does a poem work as a formal matter or as a 'verbal contraption'? What was the rhyming pattern? What were the sorts of techniques used to convey meaning? But late Auden was more interested in the second set of questions: 'What kind of guy inhabits the poem? What does he conceal from the reader? What does he conceal from himself?'[1]

---

1. W. H. Auden, *Making, Knowing, and Judging* (Oxford University Press, 1956) 23. Seven years later, Dwight Culler, the editor of *Poetry and Criticism of Matthew Arnold*, was to write: 'To be a Professor of Poetry is tantamount to declaring that one is not a poet' (See Paul Muldoon,

II. THE SENTIMENTAL LIVES OF INTERNATIONAL LAWYERS

If, to adapt a well-known international legal aphorism, international law is what international lawyers are, what, then, is an international lawyer? In this chapter, I want to stage an answer to this question in three acts. In the first, I will consider the absence of 'life' in the writing of international law and especially the way in which most international lawyers position themselves as a 'person from nowhere': a man with a suitcase, a woman in a rush, a group of people wearing wigs and chatting to each other in a courtroom but most of all, a person with little or no inner life to speak of (or worth speaking of in the context of professional engagement). In the second act, I will document and re-describe a recent move towards biography or micro-history or 'life' in the field of international law. What is it that has provoked this burst of interest in the interior lives of international lawyers?[2] And why now? Third, I will suggest that there is a sentimental life available to international lawyers through which they might weave a path between teariness (with the attendant risks of cheap sentimentality) and a too-cool dispassion (that is in danger of lapsing into an alienated technocracy). In this final and lengthier section of the chapter, I will describe four sentimental vices found in international legal work and read these vices alongside the sentimentality of the late 18th-century 'sentimental' English novel. At the end, I will try to reclaim, via *Tristram Shandy*, some space for tears or tearfulness in international law.

At the beginning of Book 16 of Christopher Logue's modern account of Homer, with Troy under siege and the battle evenly poised, Patroclus 'comes crying to the Greek'.[3] Achilles teases him: 'Why tears Patroclus? Someone is dead, Patroclus? Your father? Mine?' Patroclus is affronted: 'You know Odysseus is wounded? Orontes too—his thigh: King Agamemnon even. Yet, still you ask: Why tears?'[4]

Why tears?

The End of the Poem: Oxford Lectures (Farrar and Giroux, 2007) 323). 'The guy' (suggesting that Auden might have been adopting the patois of beat generation 1950s) here seems all wrong—particularly because Auden is concerned with the large questions of this 'guy's conception of his literary task (though the lecture does not follow through on this).

2. Here we might want to draw a distinction between the lives of international lawyers (thought of as somehow existing apart from 'international law') and their contribution to the discipline (e.g. Hersch Lauterpacht's friends and family as opposed to the arguments he constructed at the Nuremberg Trials in 1945). This could be reframed as a difference between the directly personal and the indirectly biographical.
3. Christopher Logue, *War Music: An Account of Books 16–19 of Homer's Iliad* (Faber and Faber, 1988); See also, for a powerful audio recording by Logue himself, Christopher Logue et al., *Audiologue*, A seven-CD set of recordings 1958–1998, Unknown Public (2001).
4. In fact, there is a lot of crying in *The Iliad*. Homer was able to use countless adjectives to describe tearfulness. In the end, Achilles, too, cries tears over Patroclus (even the horses cry over

i. the absence of life

Flaubert once suggested that the greatest goal in art is to provoke neither laughter nor tears. Later, Brecht called for and wrote anti-empathetic theatre: a theatre that refused to engage the theatregoer's emotions. And modernist high art was in general a repudiation of romantic sentiment and naturalistic description of the sort that continues to dominate the market in popular fiction. For the most austere modernists: plot, character, emotion and content were all suspect. Or, as Jose Ortega y Gasset said, in a similar vein to Flaubert, 'tears and laughter are, aesthetically, frauds'.[5]

Might international legal practice, then, be understood as a form of austere modernism, a commitment to raise neither laughter nor tears? Beckett insisted that theatre be reduced to its barest of bare life or 'hacked to the bone'.[6] So, in Beckett, we watch two characters doing and saying nothing much (*The Irish Times* said of *Godot* that 'nothing happened, twice') just as we watch a trial continue on interminably through its interlocutory phases (think of the *Tadic* Trial with each of its phases happening twice, once in the trial chamber, once on appeal). From a certain perspective, saying something definitive seems suspect in both cases: bourgeois theatre in one instance, show trial in the other.[7] Instead a certain slowing down is required.

Late one Friday evening, in what will certainly now be my last ever interview with the *News of the World*, I was asked, by a journalist, some questions concerning the trial of President Milošević. After a worrying start—this very nice young man made a passing reference to 'Hitler's trial at Nuremberg'—the interview settled into a wide-ranging discussion of contemporary war crimes law. On the Sunday, I rushed to the paper shop, hid the *News of the World* inside *The Observer*, and sat down at 'Café on the Hill' to read that I had described Milošević, on page 5, as 'one of the most evil men on the planet'. Milošević, of course, was a 'monster' to the tabloid press. But as lawyers, we are bound to reject the idea that accused war criminals

---

the death of their master). See generally, Hélène Monsacré, *The Tears of Achilles* (Center for Hellenic Studies, 2018).

5. What was required instead was a 'high noon of the intellect'. See Jose Ortega y Gasset, *The Dehumanisation of Art and Other Essays on Art, Culture, and Literature* (Doubleday, 1925).
6. Terry Eagleton's phrase. See Terry Eagleton, 'Determinacy Kills', 30(12) *London Review of Books* (2008) 1–7. Though Beckett also said that *Godot* was really, like this book, all about laughter and tears.
7. Gerry Simpson, *Law, War and Crime* (Polity, 2007).

are 'monsters'. Indeed, Kevin Jon Heller once made a plea for 'boringness' in international criminal law.⁸ So instead Milošević is, for us—and as I tried to tell the *News of the World*—a man accused of having 'participated in a joint criminal enterprise to violate Article 5 of the Statute' and so on. The point, then, is to make things less interesting not more interesting; the point is dispassion not passion.⁹

As an important aspect of this dispassion, we have tended to take relatively little interest in the interior life of international lawyers themselves. I want to begin by offering, then, a brief description of some surface manifestations of the sentimental lives of international lawyers themselves (as a prelude to probing a little deeper).

Lawyers have not traditionally been much interested in feelings as an aspect of professional engagement. In our orthodox, Enlightenment image of the self, there is a separation of the mind and the body, and the mind is further divided into a calculating instrument of reason and a chamber of passion (Kant is a key figure here).¹⁰ The emotions (there is a substantial literature on the relationship between emotions and feelings) are then thought of either as bodily (William James) and chemical (Antonio Damasio) responses to external signals or are confined to a non-cognitive aspect of brain-work.¹¹ In either case, the tendency—unmistakably gendered and famously described by feminist scholars like Robin West—has been to regard the emotions as inferior or subordinate.¹² To be calm, reasoning, sober and position-less is the liberal ideal.¹³

---

8. Kevin Heller, 'Boredom', Presentation at conference on 'The Passions of International Law', Melbourne University (13–15 September 2012; on file with author).
9. See Hilary Charlesworth, Keynote Address, 'Passions of International Law', Melbourne University (13–15 September 2012).
10. John Rawls asks us to drop our affective life as we step into the 'original position'. The moral person is the reasoning individual deprived of particular interests and stripped of emotional identity. Little wonder, then, that Rawls has sometimes been criticised for assuming that we are all broadly risk-averse (risk, presumably, being a combination of cognitive appraisal and feelings of daring or fear). On the other hand Rawls, often taken to be the archetypal liberal-proceduralist, ends *A Theory of Justice* on this plaintive note: 'Purity of heart, if one could attain it, would be to see clearly and to act with grace and self-command from this point of view'. John Rawls, *A Theory of Justice* (Oxford University Press, 1972) 587. Similarly, as Mark Antaki has pointed out to me in private correspondence, Kant relies on feeling to move or motivate us in relation to the moral law.
11. For a discussion of socio-biological, and neurological findings on the role of emotion in cognition, see Antonio Damasio, *Looking for Spinoza* (Harcourt, 2003). See also William James, *What is an Emotion?* (Editions Le Mono, 1884).
12. Robin West, 'Jurisprudence and Gender', 55(1) *University of Chicago Law Review* (1988) 1–72.
13. For a much-anticipated jurisprudence of the emotions, see Emily Kidd White, *Emotions in Judicial Reasoning* (Oxford University Press, forthcoming, 2022).

International lawyers have tended to adopt or inhabit this *persona* in their public lives. But in this respect, they do not sound any different from lawyers in general or from a certain sort of professional in many fields of endeavour. What, then, are international lawyers *really* like? To ask this question is to ask whether there is anything that sets them apart from the rest of humanity. There is no shortage of associations. To self-describe as an international lawyer (at a party, say) is to call up an image of a person who travels a lot doing law, someone perhaps involved in the mercantile world, a trans-nationalist. This person carries a briefcase and a small piece of carry-on luggage, and she moves from town to town (accumulating air miles to be redeemed for upgrades on family holidays). In a more public-spirited variant, there will be some sort of relationship to the institutions of international law: the state, the UN, the World Trade Organization (perhaps). For my generation, working for the UN was probably the emblematic move for an international lawyer.[14] The UN represented the heart of the public administration of the world (Ronald Reagan's declaration that 'government

14. In the European summer of 2014, I was asked to speak at the United Nations. In the minds of my family and friends, this conjured up a mental image of me addressing the General Assembly. It got to the point where I began to think I really was going to be addressing the General Assembly. Perhaps, I would make a plea for world peace and personal happiness. So, I began writing my thoughts on world peace (more bicycles, a ban on advertising, smaller cars, periodic vegetarianism) and personal happiness (sauntering, day-dreaming, periodic vegetarianism). Soon, I had written many, many pages. If I *did* address the General Assembly I would end up like Fidel Castro. I looked up a speech of his once and it was dated, ominously but impressively, 23 *and* 24 December. On the day of my address to the General Assembly, I took a cab down 2nd Avenue and got the driver to drop me off eight blocks from the UN (just outside the Liechtensteinian Mission to the UN, where I was to have a meeting that afternoon). As soon as I got out of the cab, rain began to fall in insistent droplets on my new suit. I arrived at the UN drenched. But this was not really the UN. The lecture was to take place at the UN Plaza where the UN has two dilapidated buildings (UN 1 and UN 2). It is hard to say which is the least distinguished. I wandered through security—the security men were perfunctory and bored. The lecture took place in a tiny, slightly shabby, space where the Library of Lectures on International Law are recorded. When I finished my forty-eight-minute *tour d'horizon* on the history of international law in the diplomatic system, two interns—who had been kind enough to attend/had been commandeered into attending—clapped. This is what a smattering of applause sounds like, I thought. This is what working at the UN as an intern looks like. As I left UN 1 (or 2), the rain had stopped and now there was a little cloud of steam coming from my suit. Later, I watched the lecture. I was not, it turns out, a master of the autocue. Whereas others had looked totally at ease—as if addressing me across a dining table—I was to be seen staring unblinkingly at the camera's secret screen as if transfixed by its still beauty. What had made Ronald Reagan look so articulate all those years ago, made me look like a robot manservant from Woody Allen's *Sleeper*. No matter, I went to dinner that night in Brooklyn on a high—I had after all addressed the UN. I was a certain sort of international lawyer. Or I had become, I think, the international lawyer everyone imagined I had become or, at least, an anti-climactic version of the same figure. On long footnotes and intertextuality, see Brian Fawcett, *Cambodia* (Talonbooks, 1986).

was no longer the solution to our problem, it is the problem'[15] had not yet quite become the governing ethos of western political economies).[16]

Meanwhile, the inclination has been (with some exceptions) to express ourselves in a highly particular, contingent form. Generally speaking, the ideal is a deracinated, depersonalised, formally circumscribed, view-from-nowhere prose style.[17] It really is remarkable, given the variousness of our lives, how stylistically similar the majority of law review essays are.[18] To put it at its most basic, international lawyers tend to write alone and as individuals, adhering to what Robin West described as the 'separation thesis': the idea that physical and psychological separation is what marks the lawful human being, that 'I' is 'I', at the very least that the writer is 'I' (as it has been throughout this book, through any 'sole-authored' book).[19] Carol Gilligan's *In a Different Voice* makes it clear that this is a highly masculinised account of living and writing.[20] If women rather than men really do 'raise, nurture and cook for children', then it seems remarkable that this does not figure in the world of academic international law as an organising principle.[21] It is possible to read and work and live in international law without once thinking about, or arguing about, this proposition.[22]

---

15. Ronald Reagan, Speech, 'Inaugural Address' (1981 Presidential Inauguration, Washington DC, 20 January 1981).
16. See Donald Sassoon, *The Anxious World: The History of Global Capitalism* (Allen Lane, 2019).
17. See Pierre Schlag, *The Enchantment of Reason* (Duke University Press, 1998) 126.
18. See James Boyd White, *Justice as Translation* (University of Chicago Press, 1990) 9–10. Carl Landauer characterises one of Tom Franck's books as 'provid[ing] an elegant and at times emotional argument against the political questions doctrine. But it is not made clear what is emotional about Franck's argument or whether that was a good or bad thing. Carl Landauer, 'Book Review', 87 *American Journal of International Law* (1993) 465–467, at 465.
19. Though the use of the word 'I' is both an expression of this separation and at the same time a recognition of the writer's individuality.
20. Carol Gilligan, *In a Different Voice* (Harvard University Press, 1982).
21. 'Obviously, men can care, and love, and support, and affirm life. Just as obviously, however, most men don't'. Robin West, 'Jurisprudence and Gender', 55(1) *Georgetown Public Law and Legal Theory Research* (1988) 1–72, at 7.
22. The emphasis should be very much on the 'it is possible' aspect of this. There has been a substantial and invigorating literature around what used to be called 'Feminist Approaches to International Law'. This is not the place to rehearse the debates among different schools of thought on these issues and, in particular, whether the assumptions in Gilligan and West are 'essentialist' or whether different social and political practices are in some ways biologically mandated or grounded, or whether pregnancy and child-rearing should be treated in this way at all (see the recent debates over abortion in the United States). For a useful discussion see Dianne Otto, 'Feminist Approaches to International Law', in A. Orford, M. Clark and F. Hoffman (eds.), *The Oxford Handbook of International Legal Theory* (Oxford University Press, 2016) 105–118. For a famous before-the-fact rejection of these earlier cultural claims, see Shulamith Firestone, *The Dialectic of Sex* (William Morrow, 1970). For a more recent series of

And I have been surprised over the years how little emotion there is in the review pages of the international law journals.[23] Here a relatively genteel form of expression is the norm despite the enormity of what is at stake.[24] Indeed, one might expect the review essay to be a place where an angry exchange or two might flare up. I'm thinking of the bitter disputes found in the Letters page of the *New York Review of Books* or in the (usually politer) *London Review of Books*, where Terry Eagleton and Gayatri Spivak's supporters can slug it out over a few vituperative weeks.[25] There are some famous exceptions of course. The reader can certainly feel the irritation in Philip Alston's surprisingly candid demolition of Ian Brownlie's *Documents on International Law* ('In general it is difficult to comprehend how such a distinguished author and such a discerning publisher could have inflicted such an outdated collection on the academic market') or the intensity of feeling behind Nathaniel Berman's review of Hurst Hannum's book on sovereignty in the *American Journal of International Law* or in current controversies over the history of international law.[26] But these are the exceptions, and if we are to learn something about the inner lives of international lawyers it may be that we, instead, need to attend to what is written *about* them as individuals.

ii. the (auto)biographical moment

International law has not, traditionally, been especially hospitable to (auto) biography. The idea has always been to professionalise, to become scientific, to achieve objectivity, to offer something other than politics (either

---

qualifiers, see Janet Halley, *Split Decisions* (Princeton University Press, 2006). For chapter and verse, see Judith Butler, *Gender Trouble* (Routledge, 1990).

23. See Fred Rodell, 'Goodbye to Law Reviews', 23 *Virginia Law Review* (1936) 38–45.
24. See discussion in: Andrea Bianchi, *International Law Theories: An Inquiry into Different Ways of Thinking* (Oxford University Press, 2016) 36–38.
25. Terry Eagleton, 'In the Gaudy Supermarket', 21(10) *The London Review of Books* (1999) 3–6; 'Letters', 21(13) *London Review of Books* (1999).
26. Philip Alston, 'Book Review of Brownlie, Ian (ed.), *Basic Documents in International Law*', 13(5) *European Journal of International Law* (2002) 1285–1286; Nathaniel Berman, 'Review of Hurst Hannum, *Autonomy, Sovereignty and Self-Determination: The Accommodation of Conflicting Rights*', 85(4) *American Journal of International Law* (1991) 730–733. See Lauren Benton, 'Beyond Anachronism: Histories of International Law and Global Politics, 21(1) *Journal of the History of International Law* (2019) 7–40. See also Natasha Wheatley, 'Law and the Time of Angels: International Law's Method Wars and the Affective Life of Disciplines' (on file with author).

in its ideological guise or as a cypher for personal preference). Lived lives had been slowly evacuated from the life of international law. As tyro international lawyers, we learn about Grotius' escapades hidden in a trunk or Vitoria's religious commitments but, mostly, after that, it is a story of detached scholarly endeavour and the provision of depersonalised expert advice. There had been very little, then, that resembles the long-running debates about the relationship between the life and the art in, say, poetry (Ezra Pound, Elizabeth Smart, Virginia Woolf), or in music (Richard Strauss, Wagner, Shostakovich).

Now, we find ourselves in the midst of a biographical moment. Where has this come from? Undoubtedly, international lawyers have been influenced by historians who advocate a contexualised approach to the past in which men and women are depicted not simply as bearers of ideas and practisers of practice but as psychologically rich individuals embedded in political and cultural struggle.[27] If this is the historiographic impulse—a demand that one treats with the past honestly and with care—there has also been a political demand that international lawyers begin to think of themselves as individuals with moral agency and responsibility and not simply as enactors of a politics and agency found elsewhere: deciders not managers.[28] Of course, it may be that we are simply responding to a larger cultural requirement that scientific disciplines be made interesting. The general public will not read a book about the rules of treaty-making, but they might read a book about the treaty-makers (living, breathing souls who were born, ate, drank, made love and died).

There are several discernible strands to this development. The first is a biographical practice which attempts to connect a professionalised life story to the promotion and defence of international legal worlds (institutions, rules, norms). Think of the *European Journal of International Law* series on continental international lawyers, or the interest in the men of 1873, or the men (again) of the Manhattan School, or the life of Lauterpacht or the story of the American businessmen who made the Kellogg–Briand Pact.[29] The

---

27. This trend is taken up in chapter v. See Quentin Skinner, *Foundations of Modern Political Thought* (Cambridge University Press, 1978); John Noonan, *Persons and the Masks of the Law* (Farrar, Straus and Giroux, 1976).
28. For a general discussion, see Hannah Arendt, *The Human Condition* (University of Chicago Press, 1958) Chapter vi.
29. E.g. Elihu Lauterpacht, *The Life of Hersch Lauterpacht* (Cambridge University Press, 2013); Oona Hathaway and Scott Shapiro, *The Internationalists* (Allen Lane, 2018).

second is a form of memoirist history that combines the genre of family history with a story of the lives of great international lawyers and tells their stories *as* lives while at the same time trying to project those lives onto a canvas of international legal and political struggle.[30] A third inclination has been more autobiographical. This involves international lawyers describing their experience of doing international law as a way of bringing out the tragedy or comedy of this practice, or as a way of illustrating or bringing to life a contrast between a legal education and a lawyerly practice, or the public and private dimensions of a practice.[31] This is international law in its sentimental mode with its references to 'the tragic voice of post-war public law liberalism', or 'the sadness for what international law has lost'.[32]

In one recentish essay on life-writing and international law, Andrew Lang and Susan Marks discuss the question of autobiographical writing:

> Of course, there is a strong autobiographical aspect to everyone's writing. We are all always, in some sense, writing about ourselves, and it may well be that we are most eloquent on the subject insofar as we keep silent about it. But that kind of eloquence is presumably best left for the psychoanalyst's couch; what we will be concerned with here is the self-conscious thematizing of a connection between published works and life events.[33]

It's true that we are, all, always in some sense writing about ourselves.[34] But I think here we have a very nicely exposed distinction between two types of life-writing. In one, the self is presented as 'self-conscious', making the connections between life and work in a presentable way. In the other, there is a subject where silence might be more appropriate, a silence best kept on the

---

30. Philippe Sands, *East West Street* (Vintage Books, 2017).
31. In international law, David Kennedy, *The Rights of Spring* (Princeton, 2009) (originally 'Spring Break', 63 *Texas Law Review* (1985) 1377) and 'Autumn Weekends: An Essay on Law and Everyday Life', in Austin Sarat and Thomas Kearns (eds.), *Law in Everyday Life* (University of Michigan Press, 1995) 191–236; more generally, see Patricia Williams, *The Alchemy of Race and Rights* (Harvard University Press, 1991).
32. David Kennedy, 'A New Stream of International Legal Scholarship', 7 *Wisconsin International Law Journal* (1988) 1–50, at 2; Deborah Z. Cass, 'Navigating the New Stream', 65 *Nordic Journal of International Law* (1996) 341–383, at 383.
33. Though I want to bring out an important distinction hinted at in this piece, the essay does sensitively catalogue and describe the many forms of life-writing engaged in by international lawyers and show the salutary effects (anti-universalising, humanising) of this kind of writing. Andrew Lang and Susan Marks, 'People with Projects: Writing the Lives of International Lawyers', 27(2) *Temple International and Comparative Law Journal* (2013) 440–444.
34. Not everyone is happy with this shift. See Eagleton (n 6): 'The English fondness for biography ... goes hand in hand with their philistinism'.

couch.³⁵ In her work, Maria Aristodemou has done more than most people to explore the intimate (or 'extimate') life of international lawyers by bringing to the surface that which is already on the surface but somehow hidden from view or the see-able object that we refuse to see, hidden in plain sight.³⁶ As she puts it, following Freud: 'it is in our mistakes, jokes, our slips of the tongue or of the pen that the truth of our desire may be gauged'.³⁷ Law's unconscious 'talks and writes'; what we have to do now 'is to read and listen to it'.³⁸ But where should we look? This writing and speaking 'about ourselves' is likely to occur in unexpected or marginal places. To take some very obvious examples, we have all encountered the post-colonial scholar rigidly committed to a series of liberal-procedural norms in her professional existence, or, more commonly, the liberal thinker who is furiously illiberal in his micro-politics (failing to accord speech rights to relatively powerless junior faculty, aristocratic in his manners).³⁹ When I discuss later the sentimentalism present in the work and speech of humanitarians, I am engaged in an excavation of that which is unspoken, or already spoken but unheard.

We do know *something* about the sentimental lives of international lawyers from the lengthy first footnote in a law review essay or the acknowledgements at the beginning of a book. Indeed, one could write a whole law review article on the acknowledgements in monographs and the way in which a hinterland of emotional life is either obscured or (partially, reluctantly) disclosed. Quite often it turns out that there are children (neglected, agitated), a spouse or partner (long suffering, saintly, occasional grammatical advice). There are friends and colleagues (usually an improbably large retinue of cool people), and there are places the author has presented her ideas (for some reason this list always reminds me of the tennis tour: Shanghai, Montreal, London, Melbourne, Paris), often as 'keynotes' (meaning: 'I am giving the most important presentation at the conference'). There are humble brags to be bragged. And there are institutions to be thanked. The point seems to be to announce that the project was funded rather than to

---

35. Later the authors talk of work that 'teeters on the edge of solipsism'. Maybe this book is an attempt to push international law over the edge (impossible, of course, because a 'solipsistic' account of international law would be unpublishable). Compare, say, Claire Tomalin to Geoff Dyer here.
36. Maria Aristodemou, *Law, Psychoanalysis, Society: Taking the Unconscious Seriously* (Routledge, 2014) 2–3.
37. Ibid. 5.
38. Ibid. 6
39. Peter Goodrich, 'Laws of Friendship', 15(1) *Law and Literature* (2003) 25–26.

thank the anonymous and distant funders. And it remains the case that some authors insist on noting that 'all errors are mine'. Since we had originally little doubt about this, it is, I think, a way of implying that 'some of them are not mine'.[40] Such inversions are the very stuff of the sentimental life.

Maybe there will be a short paragraph or two on the motives for writing the book in question: 'I was inspired by an encounter I had at the United Nations' or 'Years ago, I was speaking to X on the red-eye from JFK'. These acknowledgements are working hard to establish the author as almost human (but always fully professional). Meanwhile, when it comes to love, the tendency has been to mask things with a jarring detachment. We want to acknowledge the most important people in our lives, and yet we cannot quite bring ourselves to make an unqualified declaration: hence, the frugal gestures of affection. These acknowledgements seem to want to present the author as absolutely solid (not incapable of love but perhaps incapable of outright public expressions of it), a dependable family man (we have no equivalent phrase for women—a dependable family woman is just a woman, after all), a person able to juggle the demands of work and family (sometimes by working like a maniac through the childhood of his children and then apologising for it in print afterwards).[41] The relationship of children to famous or industrious fathers (and mothers) is way beyond the scope of this book, but one thinks of John Updike going to his study at 6.00 am and emerging, for a round of golf, at 2.00 pm having written 2,000 words of *Couples* and contributed nothing to the domestic economy of the household: the price to be paid for genius. The typewriter in the bedroom is, after all, the enemy of childhood.[42] In any event, what we have is the 'mumble of humility masking the purr of self-satisfaction'.[43] We should probably put a stop to it.

To pause for a moment: there are some things that could be said about all of this. The first is that people read the acknowledgements; they are interested in the lives behind international law. What sort of person skips the acknowledgements and moves to the 'actual' text? Someone very clear-sighted,

---

40. In this book, not all errors are mine.
41. For extensive work on gender and the law school, see Richard Collier, *Men, Law and Gender* (Routledge, 2009).
42. 'The pram in the hallway is the enemy of promise': Cyril Connolly, *Enemies of Promise* (Routledge, 1938).
43. Alan Hollinghurst, 'When in Rome', *New York Review of Books*, 14 June 2007, at https://www.nybooks.com/articles/2007/06/14/when-in-rome/.

ambitious and a bit chilly perhaps? Most of the people I know do read and absorb the acknowledgements, talk about them, are intrigued by them. They seem to define, in some important way, the person writing the book. The author—emotionally dead in other respects—becomes a living presence in these few pages. These acknowledgements do so much work. They position a person in a certain way—they give her a sentimental life—and that seems important in how we might read that person's work, whether her thoughts on inequality might be compromised by or reread in the light of the hierarchical arrangement of her household, how we might reconstruct a vision of what that person is trying to say in her book.

Well, we can all think of other examples. This is just a sketch, and I will conclude this section simply by noting that the sentiments, in general, are experiencing a revival in moral theory and in scholarship more generally (there has been, for some time now, for example, a Centre for the Study of the Emotions, established with Australian Research Council funding).[44] Meanwhile, there is a large body of scholarship testing the relationship between feelings and judgements: some collapsing the two, others offering hybridised accounts of cognition and feeling.[45]

It is an exciting time to be sentimental.

iii. notations on the sentimental lives of international lawyers

I want, now, though, to come to an important distinction at the heart of this chapter. Some years ago, Jonathan Franzen gave a keynote address at the Melbourne Writers' Festival.[46] Franzen held up Philip Roth's *Sabbath's Theater* as an example of courageous literary work: a lesson to be learned by all the 'sentimental' American novelists and a reproach to what he calls 'the sentimentality of some young American writers who seem to believe that literature is about being nice'.[47] (Certainly, there is nothing 'nice' about

---

44. Martha Nussbaum is a key figure in the political theory of the emotions. See Martha Nussbaum, *Upheavals of Thought: The Intelligence of Emotions* (Cambridge University Press, 2001) and *Hiding from Humanity: Disgust, Shame and the Law* (Princeton University Press, 2004).
45. See Renée Jeffery, *Reason and Emotion in International Ethics* (Cambridge University Press, 2014b).
46. Melbourne Writers Festival, 'On Autobiographical Fiction' (2010).
47. Jonathan Franzen, *Farther Away* (Farrar, Straus and Giroux, 2012) 125.

Mickey Sabbath.)[48] In a printed essay based on this speech, Franzen goes on to list a bunch of things he doesn't like about the modern novel: 'weak narrative ... misogyny ... sterile game playing' and 'sentimentality'.[49]

It's a telling catalogue of defects. No one wants to come over as a sterile, game-playing misogynist. But 'sentimental' is a less harmful epithet, surely?[50] During the question-and-answer period, someone in the audience asked Franzen what was wrong with sentimentality; after all, this questioner asked, wasn't David Foster Wallace in favour of sentimentality? Franzen backtracked a bit at this point, and the ensuing exchange suggested for me the existence of at least two forms of sentimentality. I want to explore these models of sentimentality and what they might have to say about the work we do.

This relationship between two forms of the sentimental was at its most visible in the middle of the 18th century when we had Smith's *Theory of the Moral Sentiments* sitting alongside and working against a spate of sentimental novels culminating in the work of yet another Scotsman, Sir Walter Scott.[51] The Scots, of course, have a dual reputation for being both closed-for-business emotionally and excessively sentimental.[52] But there is something suggestive for international lawyering in this relationship. To put it bluntly, on one side, we need a language of sentiment to motivate us and render our lives meaningful, but on the other side lie the twin temptations of mawkishness and insincerity. Coming to the point, I think this danger can be partly avoided by adopting a sentimentality that repeatedly combines and recombines involvement and distance and applies

---

48. Philip Roth, *Sabbath's Theater* (Houghton Mifflin Harcourt, 1995).
49. Franzen (n 47) 125.
50. J. M. Coetzee has something similar occur in *Elizabeth Costello* (Knopf, 1999). Costello is invited to give a conference presentation on evil. She suspects this is because of the notoriety of some remarks she had made at a college in the US, comparing abattoirs and the production of meat to the concentration camps. She finds herself defended by people with whom she has no sympathy: 'anti-Semites, animal-right sentimentalists' (157).
51. Walter Scott, *Waverley* (1814); *The Heart of Midlothian* (1818); Adam Smith, *Theory of the Moral Sentiments* (1759).
52. In Edinburgh, an Enlightenment project was underway where the 'passions' (as Hume called them) or 'moral sentiments' (Adam Smith) entered the modern philosophical and political lexicon. This project understood the sentiments as an important engine of social, moral, political and financial life. Without them, the market collapsed into itself (Smith) and moral life was impossible (Hume). Arthur Herman, *The Scottish Enlightenment: The Scots' Invention of the Modern World* (Fourth Estate, 2003); James Buchan, *Capital of the Mind: How Edinburgh Changed the World* (Birlinn, 2012).

sensitivity to suffering allied to a suspicion of over-advertised sensitivity to suffering.⁵³

So let me now turn to 'sentimentality' coded here as moral, literary and juridical failure. I will touch on four dangers associated with sentimental failure: *sentimental excess, simplicity, solipsism* and *de-politicisation*.

sentimental excess

I think what Franzen is referring to and what most of us mean when we use the word 'sentimental' is an excess of emotion or a lack of alignment or proportion between event and expression.⁵⁴ I. A. Richards, the great literary theorist of the interwar period, devotes a chapter of *Practical Criticism: A Study of Literary Judgement* to 'Sentimentality and Inhibition'. For him, sentimentality is akin to a disease of the mind. This tendency to emote too readily or willingly is associated, he claims, with brass bands, nightingales and influenza.⁵⁵ Even Richards himself is prone to it: 'I reluctantly recall the last time I had influenza, a very stupid novel filled my eyes with tears again and again until I could not see the pages'.⁵⁶ The main characters in the sentimental novels of the 18th century are, unlike Richards, frequently moved to tears.⁵⁷ John Berger, in a discussion of Kim Phuc, the girl running from the napalm attack in the famous Vietnam War photograph, has written about the way in which these atrocity images have the effect of only moving

---

53. Someone once said 'involvement is death' and a certain sort of immersion in a particular scene might indeed bring in its wake artistic or critical death. Think of the artist who becomes a spokesman for his generation or an academic who becomes a legal adviser to government. See also Laurence Sterne, *A Sentimental Journey through France and Italy by Mr Yorick* (Penguin, 2005 [1768]).
54. Stephen Ahern calls this the 'aesthetic of emotion': Stephen Ahern, *Affected Sensibilities: Romantic Excess and the Genealogy of the Novel 1680–1810* (AMS Press, 2007). See I. A. Richards, *Practical Criticism: A Study of Literary Judgement* (Routledge & Kegan, 1929). For Richards, it is partly a lack of proportion (too much gushing, 'too great for the occasion' (258), partly a lack of refinement (the expression of sentiment lacking refinement), partly an inappositeness (sentimentality about war (bloody and gruesome) or about schooldays (nasty and brutish)) and partly an expression of emotion for its own sake (see contemporary Hollywood).
55. Ibid. 257.
56. But the aversion to sentimentality can be politically reactionary, too. Think of John Howard's antipathy to the 'maudlin' view of Australian history that calls attention to the dispossession and murder of Aborigines in Australia.
57. This is something akin to intoxication or fear: a state of being or mind that fatally compromises the capacity to see or present things as they are. I am grateful to Rai Gaita for this. See, again, his 'Literature, Genocide and the Philosophy of International Law' (unpublished paper, on file with author, 2013).

us to tears but never to action (otherwise, as he puts it, they would not be displayed by newspapers).⁵⁸ Others, meanwhile, have pointed out the ways in which such atrocity stories serve to prompt future retaliatory atrocity or are 'remembered as humanitarian'.⁵⁹ As one Belgian colonist put it during King Leopold's fantastically violent assault on the people of the Congo:

> I made war against them . . . my goal was ultimately humanitarian . . . I killed a hundred people, but that allowed five hundred to live.⁶⁰

We can see these excesses, too—related here to a sense of unearned emotion—in the syrupy evocations of distress or voluptuous descriptions of massacre that are stand-bys on the lecturing circuit and sometimes in written scholarship. This excess of sentimentality is present too in preambular international law. So, we have 'outrages to the conscience of mankind' or the Rome Statute's rather unlikely 'delicate mosaic of peoples'. The literary flourish is rarely an aesthetic or political success.⁶¹

But we can see why we took the sort of sentimental turn deplored by Heller and others.⁶² Because, in the world of international law, we have the spectre of the very opposite problems of dryness or technocracy: a ritualisation of evil, the conversion of the unprecedented into precedent, the apoetics of legal language, the reductiveness of lawful thought and the thinness of emotional life contained in judicial pronouncements or scholarly work. So, international law has worked against *this* problem of impersonal dryness by moving in the direction of the sentimental, or tearful.⁶³

---

58. Adam Hothschild, *King Leopold's Ghost* (Mariner Books, 1998) 296. John Berger, *About Looking* (Vintage International, 2009). See also, in a similar vein, Susan Sontag, *On Photography* (Penguin, 1979).
59. Bruce Robbins, 'Bad Atrocity Writing', 32 N + 1 (2018) 12.
60. Hothschild (n 58) 166.
61. The 'untold sorrows' of the UN Charter is better (even if drafted by a supporter of apartheid).
62. I haven't spent a great deal of time working through the distinctions between feelings, sentiments, passions and emotions. 'Feelings' tends to suggest an immediately experienced physical sensation but we have feelings about politics or social life that imply a combination of emotion and reason. Think about the way we are taught at school not to say 'I feel' when we are understood as meaning 'I think'. 'Emotions' are defined in the *Shorter Oxford English Dictionary* as 'disturbances of mind' (*OED*, 339). The word 'passion' is suggestive in different ways: some common derivations include the idea of physical agitation (perhaps, sexual), overwhelming emotion and the allusion to suffering, especially martyrdom, especially on the cross (The Passion of Christ). One of the literary examples of passion given in the *OED* is Virginia Woolf: 'His passion was for the law' (*OED*, 2117).
63. On this encounter, see Didier Fassin, *Humanitarian Reason: A Moral History of the Present Times* (University of California Press, 2011).

Perpetrators are brought to life in all their villainy, no longer able to shelter behind the state. Indeed, it was this very sheltering that the peacemakers at Versailles believed 'shocked the civilised conscience of mankind' and, in turn, led to a century-long effort to make international law responsive to the tears of victims. One of the standard complaints made about war crimes trials is that victims of mass atrocity are under-represented, in both senses. The result has been a series of compensation schemes or outreach projects or civil party involvement.[64] These are designed to give international law an emotional life, to soften the objections that lawyers are somehow soulless and to enhance international law's expressive or didactic or symbolic or sentimental life.[65]

But the problem with this attention to victims is that they are often given, as Richards has argued about the impoverished and destitute in the sentimental novels of the 18th century, a severely attenuated emotional life. They are *only* victims (not, say, class warriors or perpetrator-victims—look how much trouble Hannah Arendt encountered when she tried to develop this idea). Here, if you like, the problem is not the case of too much feeling but too little or too narrow a range of feeling.[66] Or, and to put this another way, the problem for the activist from the centre is too much feeling, the problem in representations of the victim at the periphery is too little. Sentimental feelings are the luxury of those in a position of safety. In the same way that a sentimental novel will treat the destitute as a blank screen on which to project the feelings of compassion experienced by an aristocratic class, so too in international law, the victims of mass crime often seem to have a curiously featureless internal life compared to the self-reflective agonies of the humanitarian. This is mirrored in the field's conceptual languages: crimes against humanity are precisely those crimes that disturb humanity's self-conception. So who is the real victim here? Humanity? Or the person who happens to be tortured? Perhaps it can be said that 'humanity' has been enriched, privileged, constituted at the expense of thinking of individual humans as individually harmed.[67]

---

64. 'Fifteen years of Outreach at the ICTY' (2016), at https://www.icty.org/x/file/Outreach/15-years-of-outreach/outreach-15_en_light.pdf.
65. Mirjan R. Damaska, 'What Is the Point of International Criminal Justice?', 83(1) *Chicago Kent Law Review* (2008) 329–365.
66. Mark Drumbl is good on this. See Mark Drumbl, *Reimagining Child Soldiers in International Law and Policy* (Oxford University Press, 2012).
67. Dostoevsky is reputed to have said that he loved humanity but hated human beings.

moral simplicity

Another way in which international law has worked against the problem of dryness and boredom and embraced sentimentalism is by moving in the direction of character, plot and moral tale. 'Human beings not abstract entities', to quote the International Military Tribunal at Nuremberg and to reverse the trajectory of modernist literature, is the motivating principle.[68] The new international law is plot-driven and 'character-full' with an 18th-century piety at its core. As Richard Goldstone put it: how can there be any international law without international trials?[69] Ahistorical as this is, when we hear it, we know we have moved from the abstractions of structure to flesh and blood monstrosity.[70]

Here, though, the sentimental risks becoming a form of moral simplicity (melodrama might be its aesthetic form) with a tendency to divide the world rigidly into perpetrators and victims, or tyrants and a vulnerable and abject populace. The whole idea of an international law (responsibility to protect, human rights interventions) of humanitarianism is also susceptible to this.[71]

To offer just one example of international law's melodramatic aspect, the way in which war is now thought of as either criminal or humanitarian seems configured around a narrative of moral simplicity.[72] This begins with Lloyd George and Clemenceau during the Great War and is carried through the modern project of international criminal law, whereby individuals with some sort of criminal intent—and through force of will or malevolent

---

68. 'International Military Tribunal (Nuremberg): Judgment and Sentences', 41(1) *American Journal of International Law* (1947) 221.
69. Richard Goldstone lecture, 'A Rule of Law for the International Community: Is It Achievable?' (Speech LSE, 2001).
70. Thus, we have Ribbentrop 'struggling in the air for twenty minutes' as he is hanged in Nuremberg. See Rebecca West, *A Train of Powder* (Virago, 1984) 77. Philip Allott once said, in one of my favourite international law quotes: 'the punishment for sin is death not responsibility for sin'. Philip Allott, 'State Responsibility and the Unmaking of International Law' 29(1) *Harvard International Law Journal* (1988) 1–26, at 12.
71. That is why rhetorical moves reversing the gaze of humanitarianism are so provocative. I'm thinking here of the Iranian government's condemnation of police brutality in the UK during the summer riots in 2011 or calls for the UN to intervene in the United States to end gun violence (far more lethal in the long view than the Syrian civil war).
72. Elaborated in my Gerry Simpson, 'Linear Law: A History of International Criminal Law', in Christine Schwöbel (ed.), *Critical Approaches to International Criminal Law* (Routledge, 2014) 159–179.

charisma—capture powerful states and transform them.[73] This leaves these leaders open to prosecution for the 'crime' of aggression.

In Klaartje Quirijin's film about the International Criminal Court (ICC), there is a scene in which the Prosecutor and others gather round a table and begin to talk about future trial strategy.[74] At one point, the Prosecutor stares at a map of Africa and says 'get rid of Kony, and the Lord's Resistance Army is destroyed'. An arrest warrant is issued. Thus: no man, no problem. This desire to transcend politics through a juridical universalism and a narrow individualism is not the exclusive domain of the ICC. It is increasingly present as part of the 'lock her up' and impeachment dramas that disfigure US politics today.

At the same time, the idea of the humanitarian war (introduced at around the same time) insists on sharp moral distinctions between interveners and those subject to intervention. This is what Perry Anderson, discussing the historical novel, called 'costume drama', and it typically features a narrative of progress and a melodramatic clash between good and evil played out in over-stylised term. And so this operatic international law of force is appealing more and more to the same sensibility that has book group participants complain about the lack of sympathetic characters in an experimental novel (as in: 'I just couldn't relate to the female protagonist' or 'I didn't like the husband').[75] Now, we have humanitarians we can relate to.[76]

sentimental solipsism: advertisements for myself

There are also more sinister implications of sentimentality, in particular the danger of a sentimental solipsism. The sentimental novel of the 18th century

---

73. I discuss some problems with this in 'Stop Calling It Aggression', 61(1) *Current Legal Problems* (2008) 191–228.
74. Klaartje Quirijins, *Peace versus Justice* (ITVS Films, 2012).
75. This was a post-romantic response to the anxiety about displays of emotions (the concern that these might be sentimental or unearned). So, we end up with 'Prufrock' not daring to disturb the universe and then the absolute dryness (almost to the point of self-parody) of, say, the *Four Quartets* with its 'cold friction of expiring sense without enchantment'.
76. I am being unfair to opera here. John Adams' *Nixon in China* or *Death of Klinghoffer* or Steve Reich's *Three Tales* or Britten's *Peter Grimes* offer examples—anti-operatic operas where moral ambiguity is the dominant theme. See e.g. John Adams, *Nixon in China* (libretto, Alice Goodman; 1987). In Chou's final aria, 'I am old and I cannot sleep', he reflects on his life's work: 'How much of what we did was good? Everything seemed to move beyond our remedy'. This gently Elizabethan final sentence offers a pretty decent characterisation of the work of, say, human rights lawyers or international criminal law practitioners. On the Adams opera, see chapter vi on friendship.

typically featured a fellow of fine feeling and sensibility experiencing exquisite distress, and documenting it, or having it documented, in florid prose. The effect is self-congratulatory rather than sympathetic, but the trick seemed to have worked well at the time. These novels were commercially successful and established an emotional economy of aristocratic benevolence. The encounter with trauma or with tragedy was always about the observer, the 'man of feeling' (to quote the title of one of these novels) rather than the victim or the situation (far less the social or economic structures that might have produced the situation and in which the sentimental protagonist might be implicated). A contemporary version of this is parodied in writers like Ann Patchett or Malcolm Bradbury.

But the parody is over two centuries old. In *A Sentimental Journey*, Laurence Sterne's protagonist, Yorick, travels in order to experience grief and sympathy and to advertise his own self-improvement. The idea of foreign experience itself is satirised in ways that might resonate with some international lawyers, their *curricula vitae* full of cosmopolitan identifiers.[77] Yorick is also the epitome of the look-at-me philanthropist or humanitarian.[78] He goes from place to place almost doing good deeds, or not doing good deeds and wondering how this reflects on him, or doing good deeds in exchange for some sort of sensual reward, or doing good deeds and enjoying the increased feeling of self-worth.

Perhaps in a sense, international law is one large project of sentimental solipsism advertising its virtues, obscuring its vices.[79] Considering what it does to reinforce the existing coinages of privilege and distributions of power, this is a remarkable trick. And this has been a success as far as the public mind is concerned. I once attended, in Melbourne, a series of lunchtime social gatherings with businessmen and the very occasional businesswoman. When it came to the formalities, and I was introduced as an international lawyer, I could see the typical arc of the thought processes: 'impressive . . . decent . . . marginal'. What follows might be a discussion of the taxation

---

77. At one point in *Tristram Shandy*, too, Tristram deplores travel writers who 'can't go quietly through a town and let it alone'. Laurence Sterne, *The Life and Opinions of Tristram Shandy* (Penguin, 1981).
78. Sterne, *A Sentimental Journey* (n 53).
79. David Kennedy writes on this, see esp. 'Law and the Political Economy of the World', 26(1) *Leiden Journal of International Law* (2013) 7–48. I take up the theme of virtue in my Cambridge Companion essay: Gerry Simpson, 'International Law in Diplomatic History', in James Crawford and Martti Koskenniemi (eds.), *Cambridge Companion to International Law* (Cambridge University Press, 2002) 25–46.

system or the trade in derivatives or the price of oil. At some point, there will be a brief discussion about 'Syria' or 'the boat people' (now more commonly wrapped into 'people smugglers'). There will be no sense that international law has anything at all to do with the first series of topics or that it is in any way responsible for creating the conditions for the second. My efforts to say something about this have been met with a blank and slightly pitying lack of comprehension. Searing radical critique as social *faux pas*.[80]

International lawyers, particularly humanitarians, will have to be very careful if they are to avoid being remembered as the aristocratic men of sensibility from the 18th century are remembered.[81] Indeed, this apparent combination of aristocratic sensibility, high morals and effeteness is captured in popular culture when, in the film *Bridget Jones' Diary*, we discover that the insipid, drippy but nice, character played by Colin Firth is a 'human rights lawyer'.[82]

depoliticising sentimentality

But the sentimental novel of the 18th century was not just a description of suffering (either the suffering of the victim or man of feeling) but also a normative statement about the virtuousness of feeling and responding to that suffering as well as a promotion of 'charitable impulses'.[83] The combination of didactic moralising and the display of intense feeling signals—perhaps even constitutes—a particular class sensibility.

Stephen Ahern rehearses the three forms of the sentimental novel (the gothic, the amatory and the ethical).[84] As he puts it, the language of love was 'first used to designate the relations between two individuals, but soon the

---

80. The critique of human rights tends to make absolutely no sense in some settings, so easily misinterpreted as a heartless lack of care.
81. I once told a Hague tribunal lawyer that I couldn't supervise his PhD at LSE. He then offered to send me a manuscript he'd written on the anonymity of witnesses or Rule 69 proceedings or something like that. I wrote back saying sorry I was finishing a book and I couldn't read that either. I then received a very angry reply to *that* accusing me of a lack of interest (guilty) and collegiality (partially guilty). It ended by saying something along the lines of: I happen to be prosecuting a major war criminal; the least you could do is read my work.
82. This image reappears in Nina Raine's *Consent* (Faber and Faber, 2017), with the slightly wet lawyer and his fold-up bicycle.
83. Dinah Birch (ed.), *The Oxford Companion to English Literature* (Oxford University Press, 2009) 903.
84. Ahern (n 54). These included *The Vicar of Wakefield* by Oliver Goldsmith (1766) and Samuel Richardson's epistolary novels *Pamela: or, Virtue Rewarded* (1740) and *Clarissa: or the History of a Young Lady* (1748) as well as *The Man of Feeling* by Henry Mackenzie (1771).

significance is widened to include the affairs of humanity in general'.[85] This amatory, operatic language existing in the midst of astonishing deprivation and inequality might remind us of, say, international human rights law with its high-flowing rhetoric about the rights of man but its indifference to the banking crisis.[86]

What we end up with in some forms of sentimentalism is the idealisation of classless humanity.[87] As Janet Todd puts it, 'Misery is alleviated by sensibility and sympathy, not by political action'.[88] Even more tellingly, Ahern suggests that that the alienation of the self from the world and the deterioration in material conditions require more tales of moral improvement: sentimentalism breeds in conditions of squalor.[89] This produces the combination of endless torment and sentimental encounter.[90]

As I have argued elsewhere, in human rights law and international criminal law, these tendencies are on full display.[91] The Genocide Convention literalises this tendency with its protection of national, ethnic, racial and religious groups and its occlusion of class struggle, but the decontextualisation of the sentimental encounter is a significant feature of some of our work.[92] Indeed, we might say the more contextualised the work human rights lawyers do, the lower their status (e.g. those who work in trade unions).

We can see this depoliticised sentimentality in the way people speak about the 'individual' in international law. There was a spate of essays and work not that long ago which took a very sentimental view of the individual. This was a character who had been neglected or elided in some way

---

85. Frank Baasner, 'The Changing Meaning of "Sensibilité", 1654 till 1704', 15 *Studies in 18th Century Culture* (1986) 77–96, 86.
86. But see Philip Alston, 'Report of the Special Rapporteur on Extreme Poverty and Human Rights on His Visit to the United Kingdom of Great Britain and Northern Ireland' (2019).
87. A book that avoids this is Ian Clark, *The Vulnerable in International Society* (Oxford University Press, 2013).
88. Janet Todd, *Sensibility: An Introduction* (Methuen, 1986). Ahern also invokes the Bakhtinian idea of carnival as a way of playing out but at the same time containing and domesticating rebellious urge and dissent. See Mikhail Bakhtin, *The Dialogic Imagination* (University of Texas Press, 1981) 259–422.
89. Ahern (n 54) 21. See also Wendy Motooka, *The Age of Reasons* (Routledge, 1998).
90. The rise of sentimentalism in the 1760s was a product of an optimistic response to Hobbes but also Hobbesianism from the perspective of the victim though, as Ahern points out, it's not as if this sentimentalism did not have its achievements: the Reform Bill, the anti-slavery movement and so on. It also produced a field of satire and irony.
91. A recent exception: Alston (n 86). See also Samuel Moyn, *Not Enough* (Harvard University Press, 2018).
92. See Hilary Charlesworth, 'Discipline of Crisis' 65(3) *Modern Law Review* (2002) 377–392 (Kosovo as a 'real life Jessup Moot problem').

by the statism of international law or the international order. It seemed important to retrieve or reposition the individual as a bearer of rights or duties at the international level. And yet, in this work, there didn't seem to be much awareness of the role of, say, individualism in producing a certain form of late capitalism to be set against the collective politics or endeavours of particular classes, or the relationship between anti-statism in international law and a corrosive hostility to the whole public realm in the dominant economic politics of the era. This too resembles, say, Henry Mackenzie's *The Man of Feeling*, where the indigent and impoverished are to be cared for, mourned and wept over as individuals but feared and despised as classes of people. Indeed, as Peter Gabel, showed us several decades ago, the consequence (maybe even the point) of sentimentality (for him 'rights talk') is precisely to neuter the expression of political resistance and the experience of impoverishment or injury.[93]

★ ★ ★

Let me come to some sort of conclusion by saying that what we seem to have is a concern about dryness (partly counteracted—but maybe also compounded—by the new international law of humanity and human beings) and an anxiety about melodrama (a nagging concern that all this focus on victims and individuals and narrative arc is sentimental and depoliticising).

I have been left in my work trying to overcome this dual problem: the spectre of technocracy (law, rationality) and the lure of sentimental indulgence (tears, melodrama). In teaching a class on, say, the law of war crimes, I like to embrace emotional austerity, but it can seem odd to teach war crimes law without mentioning any actual crimes. And, so my account of joint criminal enterprise in *Tadic* or command responsibility in *Oric* must come off as a bit soulless, perhaps even a re-enactment of the whole International Military Tribunal allergy to discussing the Holocaust itself by focusing instead on the technical aspects of the war or organisational criminality: anything but the actuality of the offence.

---

93. See Peter Gabel, 'The Phenomenology of Rights-Consciousness and the Pact of the Withdrawn Selves', 62 *Texas Law Review* (1984) 1563–1598. See also, in a Canadian context, Michael Mandel, *The Charter of Rights and the Legalization of Politics in Canada* (Thompson Educational Publishing, 1994). Also: Peter Gabel and Duncan Kennedy, 'Roll Over Beethoven', 36(1) *Stanford Law Review* (1984) 1–55.

On the other hand, as I have said, 'humanising' the field seems dubious too. I worry terribly about overcompensating for dryness by dwelling on the unspeakable.[94] Descriptions of massacres very, very often seem cheaply sentimental, not-fully-earned. So every course I teach in this area is a rehearsal of my own angst about these things. But then I worried that war crimes law shouldn't really be about my angst.[95]

What is to be done? I have tried to show in this chapter that international law possesses a sentimental life (but that this is not a commonly discussed aspect of our work) and that this sentimental life carries with it certain dangers (I discussed four of these: excess, simplicity, solipsism and depoliticisation). Adopting a specific genre of sentimental international law—with its desire to achieve affect and sentimentalise the encounter with otherness—risks trumping the experience of sympathy, the potency of political action and considerations of taste. The debate around the 18th-century novel might be a way of clarifying what is at stake in avoiding these dangers. By avoiding them, it might be possible to imagine a non-fraudulent, and less solipsistically affective, life for international law.[96]

To put this differently: I suppose a sort of hard-boiled, unillusioned sentimental life is what we might be after, sentiment without sentimentality. A sentimental life that takes the emotional pulse of the work we do but allies it to an economy of irony that is at the same time detached but involved. If that sounds both too abstract and too much like hard work, I try to give it content at different points in the following pages. It is an idea I take up in the final chapter on gardening and international law when I begin to offer a fuller account of this tough sentimentality. But it is present, too, in the

---

94. At one point, Mark Lilla discussing Margarethe von Trotta's film, *Hannah Arendt* (2012), states: 'it cannot be emphasised enough that the Holocaust is not an acceptable occasion for sentimental journeys'. See Mark Lilla, 'Arendt and Eichmann: The New Truth', 60(18) *New York Review of Books* (2013) 35–38.
95. In Coetzee's *Elizabeth Costello* (n 50), Costello, an Australian writer of some renown and possibly a Coetzee avatar, worries away about this form of sentimentality as prurience or voyeurism. She reads a book by a 'Paul West' (he might be a stand-in for the Martin Amis of *Koba the Dread*) about the horrors of the Stauffenberg Trial and wonders whether there should be limits on what is said and described in writing about torture and depravity. This becomes the basis for her keynote address at a conference in Amsterdam. West, inevitably, is in the audience. I have no idea what Coetzee's own views on this might be (he, too, describes or brings into the world, the very horrors Costello recoils from) but Costello's are a compelling defence of the limitable. There is an idea of an obscene or 'off-scene'; things that should not be described, stories that poison the soul. Coetzee (n 50) 156–182.
96. I am not so interested here in whether emotions are the slaves of reason or whether cognitive judgements must be also emotional judgements. See, for an overview, Renée Jeffery, 'Reason, Emotion, and the Problem of World Poverty: Moral Sentiment Theory and International Ethics', 3(1) *International Theory* (2011) 143–178.

chapters on comic irony (where the idea is to marry international legalism's seriousness of purpose to an awareness of absurdity), on bathos (where I call for memorialisation of atrocity without authority and 'closure') and in the chapter on friendship (where a freewheeling diplomacy of epistolary friendship is set against the hortatory and solemn expressions of amity often found in international treaties). I will end here with one literary example.

Laurence Sterne's life and work can be understood through the relationship between hard-boiled and soft sentiment. It is suggested, for example, that he switched tack from satire to sentiment in accordance with public taste (in particular, a growing taste for sentimentality). In *Tristram Shandy* there is a description of the death of one of the main characters Yorick (later to be found travelling through France on his sentimental journey).[97] The deathbed scene is conveyed in the style of the sentimental novel, but one can feel the loss of faith in romantic sentiment behind the words that Eugenias, Yorick's friend, speaks. 'He was within a few hours of giving his enemies the slip for ever "I hope not"', answered Eugenias, with tears trickling down his cheeks, and with the tenderest tone ever man spoke'.[98]

The scene continues in this vein, but the sentimentality is offset by two epilogues: one, a broad comic gesture backwards (Yorick is 'laid upon his grave with no more than these three words of inscription serving as elegy and epitaph: Alas, poor Yorick');[99] the other, a very postmodern black page (suggesting Yorick's eternal rest). In the end, we are permitted to feel for Yorick and Eugenias while at the same time 'feeling' the dangers of over-feeling.

Later in the book, I describe how Rebecca West works this seam of ironic sentiment when she writes about the Nuremberg Trial, and like West's, the best writing—the best theorising—resists the injunction to come to the point, to render the world transparent, to clarify the thesis, to achieve relevance, to simplify, to make explicit.[100] These are the standard vices of the sentimentality of excess and simplicity, of operatic international law. This chapter has been a plea for something else: a different register combined with a wariness of that different register, a poetic international law of the 'tingle',[101] an irony of the mind. This might involve an attentiveness to the

---

97. Sterne, *Tristram Shandy* (n 77).
98. Sterne, *A Sentimental Journey* (n 53) 60.
99. Ibid.
100. On the problem of explicitness, see Kate Soper, *Troubled Pleasures: Writings on Politics, Gender, and Hedonism* (Verso, 1990).
101. Nabokov's word: 'That little shiver behind is quite certainly the highest form of emotion that humanity has attained when evolving pure art and pure science. Let us worship the spine and

unseen and unheard, or the seemingly insubstantial or a commitment to an international law of style and love and smallness and an attentiveness to the everyday and informalities of power. A willingness to do what poets do: namely, to notice the micro-political humiliations that might entirely undercut the grand humanitarian scheme:

> [The] capacity to wonder at trifles—no matter the imminent peril—these asides of the spirit, these footnotes in the volume of life are the highest forms of consciousness, and it is in this childishly speculative state of mind, so different from commonsense and its logic, that we know the world to be good.[102]

When it comes to the sentiments, I suspect the prosecution mutters 'woolly, self-indulgence, incontinent', the defence cries 'sincerity, openness, creativity'. Perhaps, Martin Wight at the LSE was right all along that our feelings about international affairs (and your receptiveness to this paper) will depend partly on temperamental rather than conceptual or intellectual considerations.[103] Here I have offered some markers and warnings and some promises. This is not a science of the sentiments: it's art all the way down.

Maybe all I have done is to argue for an international law that keeps an eye on its own emotional life and one that adopts a form of life that resists tears but stays close to them.[104] In the end, I make a plea for the sentimental life of international law and against an international law of sentimentality: an international law of tears but not teariness and of irony but not frivolity.[105]

So, in the end, when Patroclus is dead and on the morning when Achilles is about to die, Achilles tells Odysseus that Patroclus was 'the only living thing that called love out of me. At night I used to dream of how when he came home to Greece, he'd tell them of my death ... and show my son ... my long green meadows stretching through the light'.[106] Achilles falls asleep beside his dead (who are really those about to die) and 'Odysseus goes off, as close to tears as he will ever be'.[107]

---

its tingle': Vladimir Nabokov, 'Bleak House', in Fredson Bowers (ed.), *Lectures on Literature* (Weidenfeld & Nicolson, 1982).

102. Vladimir Nabokov, 'The Art of Literature and Commonsense', in Fredson Bowers (ed.), *Lectures on Literature* (Weidenfeld & Nicolson, 1980).

103. Martin Wight, 'An Anatomy of International Thought', 13(3) *Review of International Studies* (1987) 221–227.

104. On the cultivation of empathy, see James Brassett and Dan Bulley, 'Ethics in World Politics: Cosmopolitanism and Beyond?', 44(1) *International Politics* (2007) 1–18.

105. This might also be part of what Flaubert and then Rorty calls the 'Sentimental Education'. The idea is to concentrate on this and forget the search for universal moral truths: Richard Rorty, *'Human Rights, Rationality, and Sentimentality', Truth and Progress: Philosophical Papers* (Cambridge University Press, 1998) 176.

106. Logue (n 3) 78.

107. Ibid.

iii

international law's comic disposition

i. simply laughing	55
ii. solemnity	61
iii. ironic laughter	63
iv. ironic lawyers	72
v. contrapuntal laughter: blasphemy and rebellion	78

> There is nothing in his writings from which it could be inferred that he knew of the existence of such things as wit and humour ... here are passages ... which it seems to us could have been written by no man who had ever laughed.
>
> John Stuart Mill, Auguste *Comte and Positivism* (Trubner, 1865)

> I was especially struck by his complete lack of humour.
>
> Avner W. Less, *Eichmann Interrogated* (Bodley Head, 1983)

i. simply laughing

When General Dyer, who ordered the Amritsar Massacre of 1919, was asked why he had shot so many innocent women, men and children, he replied, 'If I had asked them to disperse, they would have simply laughed'.[1] But then, as George Orwell had remarked in *Shooting an Elephant*, 'every white man's life

---

[1] See Hunter Inquiry into Amritsar Massacre (1946); Kim A. Wagner, *Amritsar 1919: An Empire of Fear and the Making of a Massacre* (Yale University Press, 2019); Nigel Collett, *The Butcher of Amritsar* (Continuum, 2005).

in the East was one long struggle not be laughed at'.² Laughter can be fatal after all. There is footage of Nicolae Ceaușescu waving from the presidential balcony in Bucharest for the last time, a supreme leader suddenly realising his dictatorship is over as he hears jeering and laughter below in the crowd. A few days later, on Christmas Day 1989, he is hauled before a star chamber, tried, and then executed along with his wife Elena (who had shouted at the crowd: 'Silence!'). To paraphrase Nietzsche, this was laughter as an epitaph on the death of a tyrant.³

Dyer's lack of proportion recalls the discussion of sentimentality in chapter ii and foreshadows my thoughts on bathos in the next chapter. In this chapter, though, I extend outwards from the specific topic of bathos as a literary device for understanding international law's linguistic and structural limitations and disappointments to a more general encounter with laughter as a response to, perhaps even an effect of, international legal solemnity. Again, the intention is to approach international law from the fringes and to put into conversation ideas that are not commonly thought about together. More particularly, General Dyer's comment and Orwell's gloss on it made me wonder if international law, too, had not spent its whole life trying not to be laughed at. Tom Franck once remarked that some legal arguments are right, some are wrong and some just don't pass the laughter test. They lack credibility *as* legal arguments. But what if international law itself somehow failed the laughter test? And, what if the whole history of international law has been a reaction to the threat of offstage or onstage ridicule? Isn't this what phrases like 'taking international law seriously' are responses to? Isn't this partly what the move to a science of international law was designed to counteract and what the interminable, undergraduate debates about whether international law is 'really law' are all about?⁴

In light of all of this, we might ask whether or not laughter is a promising way to begin exposing international lawyering's opacities, its pretences and its self-satisfactions? I want to begin by recalling something I said in chapter ii. The argument pursued throughout this volume is, in a way, drawn from a sense that international law can be a project of sublimation and from a

---

2. Ferdinand Mount, 'They Would Have Laughed', *London Review of Books* (2019) 9–12.
3. 'A joke is an epigram on the death of a feeling' (Nietzsche).
4. International lawyers are by now well versed in a variety of, sometimes mildly contradictory, answers to this latter question (it's a different species of law, law isn't 'law', national law is often unenforced or unenforceable, enforcement is the wrong subject) but a certain fatigue settles over a room when such questions are on the table.

conviction that its managerial structures, its pristinely acontextual rules, its professional habits, dress codes and its *lingua franca* can be artifice, mask or evasion.

This argument can be contrasted with the assumptions that circulate in two other international legal subcultures. In the first, the rules-based order (beloved of leading diplomats and a number of practising lawyers) is to be defended from its competitors (neo-conservatives, authoritarians, intransigents, illiberals) and its enemies (terrorists, tyrants, pirates). The second is a more sceptical, reformist account of international law that takes the best elements of this system (human rights, development, legal environmentalism) and tries to extend these progressive-liberal values across the globe.[5]

But another project turns international law against itself or places in question those very progressive values that instead might be thought to have consolidated empire or obscured poverty and so on.[6] This chapter—indeed, the whole book—is situated in this tradition. Uncovering the absurd or comic or ironic at the heart of this progressive enterprise is one way in which the dark, neurotic underpinnings of the system might be exposed. Certainly, the events at Amritsar and Bucharest suggest that maybe there are times when we should be laughing.[7] It is not unusual to think of laughter or comedy as a corrective to antisocial behaviour or bureaucratic routine (Bergson) or political crime (Brecht) or authority itself (Bakhtin).[8] But could the project of international law, too, be fruitfully exposed to laughter or, at least, understood through the frame of comedy?

Because this seems so counter-intuitive, and remembering Hayden White's dictum about disciplines being defined by that which they deem

---

5. For a persuasive treatment, see Ruti Teitel, *Humanity's Law* (Oxford University Press, 2011).
6. The works are legion, of course. Deborah Cass provides a sympathetic introduction: 'Navigating the New Stream', 65(3–4) *Nordic Journal of International Law* (1996) 341–383. More latterly, we have Thomas Skouteris on progress, Rose Parfitt on late-empire, Cait Storr on territory, Maddy Chiam on language.
7. Richard Evans, arguing against 'postmodernism', stated that there were limits to the ways in which one could emplot the Holocaust. See R. Evans, *In Defence of History* (Granta, 1997) 124. This was an argument against Hayden White made in Saul Friedlander's *Probing the Limits of Representation* (Harvard University Press, 1992): 'Auschwitz was indeed inherently a tragedy and cannot be seen either as comedy or farce' (124). But see, *Hitler and Pink Rabbit? The Dictator? Inglourious Basterds?*
8. Henri Bergson, *Laughter* (Macmillan, 1911); Mikhail Bakhtin, *Rabelais and his World* (Indiana University Press, 1965). I am recalling here Brecht's famous and rather hopeful comment (found by Arendt): 'The greatest political criminals must be exposed and exposed especially to laughter' (Interview with Hannah Arendt, *The New York Review of Books*, 26 October 1978).

impermissible, I would like to explore the way in which irony and laughter emerge out of the practice and history of international law, not as a deliberately comedic retort to the international legal solemnities (section ii) but as a reflexive response to the felt absurdity of international legal life (section iii), as a structural condition of its history (also section iii), as a way of being and behaving in the face of this disjuncture (section iv) and as an expression of unconscious desire or disgust (section v).

The first form of laughter, discussed in sections ii–iv, is an ironic comedy of scepticism and doubt (*via* Paul Fussell, Jonathan Lear and Søren Kierkegaard), and the second, in section v, is a blasphemous or grotesque comedy of rebellion (*via* Diogenes and Sloterdijk), and I read these as political responses to, and ways of thinking through, the self-consciously deep, but sometimes *faux*, seriousness of international law as well as its excessive sentimentality.[9]

Ironic laughter arises organically from the gap between our hopes and the abridgement of these hopes or in the abyss between illusion and experience. These gaps will be immediately recognisable to the student of international law brought up on a steady diet of unrealised expectations and normative overreach. Irony might indeed be international law's natural, often privately expressed tone. With this in mind, I want to think about two encounters between irony and international law. The first draws on Paul Fussell's account of irony in his book *The Great War and Modern Memory* in order to reflect on the parallels between Fussell's dead languages of Edwardian English (and the way in which irony arose to counteract and undercut these) and sometimes turgid solemnities of international legalism (section iii).[10] In passing, I note too the historical juxtaposition of Fussell's sardonic Great War idioms and the wholly unironic shift taken by international law in response to that war. The second section will ask, through a reading of Jonathan Lear, how the ironic international lawyer might experience her practice or how she might try to chart a passage for laughter—indeed, live an ironic life—amid the dangers of sentimentality (against which ironic laughter or the comedy of forgiveness seems a possible defence) and tastelessness (with which blasphemous laughter must always figure). At the very worst, we might simply end up with an anti-hubristic style, at best all of this could mark a tentative step towards a better or more supple language with which law might answer to murderous violence and preventable misery (section iv).

---

9. On the idea of the grotesque, see Bakhtin (n 8).
10. Paul Fussell, *The Great War and Modern Memory* (Clarendon Press, 1975).

I end the chapter by turning, albeit sketchily, to grotesque laughter: the rebellious, instinctive, subaltern, laughter of a world in which some deaths are more sacred than others—a laughter born of fear, anxiety, hysteria, aggression, disbelief.[11] This is the laughter we experience when we have narrowly avoided danger, or encountered a rationality-cancelling absurdity. This is a blasphemous comedy of rebellion, associated with the Greek anti-philosopher Diogenes and the contemporary German writer Peter Sloterdijk, whose roots are found in the playful rejection of dominant social and intellectual mores.[12]

★ ★ ★

Let me begin a little digressively by conceding that it is risky to be talking about laughter in any self-conscious way. It would be especially foolish to try to be funny. Camus once defined 'the absurd' as the sight of a man talking on the phone behind a glass partition. Anyone looking through the window of my rented apartment on East 10th and Broadway in the fall of 2018 would have recognised the absurdity of a man in a stone-faced struggle with his computer trying to write an essay on laughter. It is a grim subject: Freud's treatise on joking is one of the least amusing books I have ever read.[13] John Carey, the English literary critic, in an introduction to *The Joke and Its Relationship to the Unconscious*, describes a German joke as 'one of the few jokes collected by Freud that still seems funny to today's reader'. But that joke isn't funny either. And the implication that readers of the past were chuckling gaily over any of the other, sometimes baffling, jokes strikes me as unlikely.[14] This problem, of course, has been well documented over the years. Collections of humour are strictly for the comically challenged. Henri Bergson's rapidly multiplying taxonomies of comedy made me feel

---

11. There are no doubt other forms of laughter. One can imagine the satanic laughter of an untouchable offshore class who no longer care enough to care, whose power or wealth has taken them outside the system; a hyper-rich for whom the idea of a global law of constraint and humanitarianism must seem comic (or who might embrace it, cynically, through charitable work).
12. I had initially wanted to call it 'hysterical laughter', but in order to do so I would have had to reclaim the word 'hysterical' from the Victorian medical profession and from Freudian psychoanalysis. See Sigmund Freud and Joseph Breuer, *Studies on Hysteria* (Penguin, 2004).
13. Sigmund Freud, *The Joke and Its Relationship to the Unconscious* (Penguin, 1905). For Freud, the joke was rather like the unconscious: full of substitutions, condensations, slips, mistaken identities, inexpressible aggressions.
14. Though I had the same reaction to Karl Kraus' *Last Days of Mankind* (Ungar, 1974), which people claim as a great comic masterpiece of the Viennese early 20th century.

as if I would never laugh again. And I have not been immune to this effect myself. After a talk I gave in Geneva on 'international law and humour', a student took the time to inform me that she had hoped my presentation would be 'funnier'.

I sympathise.

Some further reservations, at this point, might be in order. Comedy as an instinctive expression of an unconscious will or an ironic response to absurdity and bathos could be helpful, but we should not overstate the case. A comic international law might prove to be fangless or authoritarian or unfunny. When Peter Cook opened his club 'The Establishment' in Soho, he said he had consciously imitated 'those wonderful Berlin cabarets which had done so much to stop the rise of Hitler and prevent the outbreak of the Second World War'.[15] And, as Jonathan Coe points out, satire can become a reflex that prevents thought. To aim barbs at everyone is to aim them at no one. Is the gentle ironic rebuke always the order of the day? And we now live in an era in which there is too much of a certain sort of laughter, too much of, what Sloterdijk calls 'a cheekiness that has changed sides'.[16] The British, for example, have political comedians who use humour to defuse criticism and distract from policy disaster. Boris Johnson's language, especially, is an often eloquent, sometimes witty, Etonian smokescreen of comic asides and wordy exaggerations straight out of *Hippolytus*:

> This is the thing which devastates well-ordered cities ... that's it, this art of oversubtle words! It's not the words ringing delight in the ear, that one should speak, but those that have the power to save their hearer's honourable name.[17]

We might want to reject, too, the rather stern Bergsonian idea of the comedy of correction, a comedy transmitting the harsh laughter of a God who knows us in our entirety and before whom we are ridiculous and transparent.[18]

---

15. Jonathan Coe, 'Boris Johnson and Laughter', 35(14) *London Review of Books* (2013) 258–299 (see too the reference at 299 to a comedy that ends up rendering everyone 'silly'—the term is Martha Nussbaum's).
16. Peter Sloterdijk, *A Critique of Cynical Reason* (Verso, 1988) 110.
17. Euripides, *Hippolytus* (Penguin, 1996).
18. I can't help thinking of Adolf Eichmann in *his* glass cage and in *his* opaqueness, a transparency that failed to reveal much at all except a lack of depth or further, descending, layers of transparency.

I want to take general inspiration instead from what the literary critic James Wood has called 'the comedy of forgiveness'.[19] This is an ironic comedy—a laughing *with*—a recognition of our shared predicament (a subject I take up again in chapter vi) not a cruelty about our buffoonery or silliness or ponderousness but instead a means by which we might interrupt linear or closed accounts of particular problems or circumstances in history.[20] To take up Freud again, the joke or the comic release undercuts or subverts the technical-rational requirements of professionalisation or status or argument.[21] It opens up a space for thinking and experiencing against the grain by introducing into a world of expertise a sequence of 'unconscious meanings and unwanted associations'.[22] The comedy of forgiveness manages our incompetence and lack of complete knowledge and concedes our collective failure to meet our aspirations. It is a form of Gogolian laughter through tears, something that might reveal the pathos of our dreams and aspirations (in order, maybe, that we dream a bit differently).

ii. solemnity

In this book, I have been exploring an intuition about the legal order I have worked with, and in, for the past thirty years, namely that there is something not quite right about it.[23] International law, of course, has been chastised on a number of counts: as imperial, gendered, selective, politically innocent, disingenuous and so on. But I wondered too if there wasn't a different problem, one that had something to do with the atmosphere surrounding the performance of international law—at war crimes trials, in lectures, in public speeches, at conferences—and in particular its indignant moral purity, its gestures of internationalist superiority, its Olympian detachments from political life and its sombre invocations of justice. I want to bracket all of this, for the time being, as 'solemnity'. This term, I hope, conveys some

---

19. See James Wood, *The Irresponsible Self: On Laughter and the Novel* (Cape, 2004) 6.
20. See T. Eagleton, *Humour* (Yale University Press, 2019).
21. See Freud (n 13).
22. This is what Jonathan Coe calls 'the incongruity theory of comedy'. See 'Grimace Called Laughter', 6059 *Times Literary Supplement* (17 May 2019) 17.
23. Some of the ideas here were first presented in 'Satires of Circumstance', my Inaugural Professorial Lecture at Melbourne Law School. The title was stolen from Thomas Hardy's 1914 collection of poems 'about' the Great War published in 1914 but written between 1870 and 1913.

of the self-regarding seriousness, emotional detachment and gravity that are characteristic of the project. Practitioners and scholars in the field take themselves and the field very seriously indeed (it would be strange if we did not). What indeed could be more grave a matter than the prosecution of those responsible for grave crimes or the allocation of economic advantage in an investment dispute or the protection through treaty-making of biodiversity? Irony seems to be positively excluded by the requirements of solemnity, legality and remembrance (a judge at the World Court once said to me, over supper, that a comedy about the Holocaust was scandalous).[24] But I want to argue instead, and following Peter Goodrich, that 'the dependence of law upon solemnization ... entails also the thesis that all law is vulnerable to humour'.[25]

The appeal of solemnity, even in adverse circumstances, is described in George Steiner's novel *The Portage to San Cristobal of A. H.*, where a group of Israeli agents is sent into the South American jungle to capture Adolf Hitler.[26] The book probes the distance between two worlds: civilised, bourgeois Berlin where lawyers argue about what should happen to Hitler when he is 'brought to justice' and the unstable, existential jungle where the agents, now with 'A. H.' in their precarious custody, are dying of disease while at the same time pondering Hitler's destiny.

Within both worlds, a solemn, muffled technocracy and a passionate retributivism are in tension. In Berlin, a young, headstrong lawyer, Rolf Haufmann, is frustrated with the usual legal forms. He proposes:

> a more striking procedure ... the accused stands outside the norms of law either common or specifically promulgated. Beyond any aim of judicial retribution. It is not so much a high and solemn bench we need as a school open to the world.[27]

His mentor, an older lawyer, responds by saying: 'history has too long been extra-legal' (this, a pithy restatement of the 20th-century's dominant international legal ethos).[28]

---

24. This was around the time that *Life is Beautiful* had won an Oscar for Roberto Benigni.
25. Peter Goodrich, '*Lex Laetens*: Three Theses on the Unbearable Lightness of Legal Critique', 17(3) *Law and Literature* (2005) 311–316.
26. George Steiner, *The Portage to San Cristobal of A. H.* (Faber and Faber, 1981).
27. Ibid. 92–93.
28. Ibid. 93.

Meanwhile, in the malarial swamp, the agents are bickering over procedure too. In the end they choose to try A. H. in the jungle. Passion seems to have prevailed. But has it? The agents concede they are forced to:

> state reasons for a procedure which ordinary good sense and world opinion would doubtless condemn as irregular ... [but which they] ... had resolved to enunciate with condign solemnity.[29]

These solemn rites, they believe, are as vitally necessary in the swamp as they are in the international legal order with its rule of law (violent, bloody and so on, as China Mieville called it in an updated Hobbesian flourish) operating amid an anarchic world of black finance, people smuggling, abject poverty, hyper-affluence.

iii. ironic laughter

> Every war is ironic because every war is worse than expected.
>
> Paul Fussell, *The Great War and Modern Memory* (Clarendon Press, 1975) 7.

But the gulf between this 'condign solemnity' and the messy realities of lived lives must inevitably produce openings for laughter. When international law purports to administer that which cannot be administered, the results are a certain lack of proportion, an ironic gap. Obviously, responding to international legal projects or institutions or writing with smugness would be in bad taste. Ironic laughter might hardly seem an appropriate or polite way to go about thinking about, say, genocide trials.

Nonetheless, I do want to posit, against this solemnity, international law's messy unconscious and its ironic subtexts, or, from the other extreme, its materiality (its universes of raging hatred, catatonic boredom and bloody death). The combination of official solemnity and unofficial chaos, of the desire for a fixedness of legal language and the ambiguity of the word, provokes in response an ironic language, throws up ironic historical juxtapositions and requires us at times to inhabit the position of the ironic lawyer (section iv). This is especially the case because of the professional

---

29. Ibid. 118. This resembles the ad hoc and provisional mechanisms established by the UN Security Council in The Hague: the International Criminal Tribunal for the former Yugoslavia (ICTY) and the International Criminal Tribunal for Rwanda (ICTR).

requirements and status anxiety of a field like international law. The elaborate rituals found amid legal forms—the International Court of Justice (ICJ), the United Nations Sixth Committee—signal a deep desire to be taken very seriously. Yet the system continues to be grounded in a primitive set of social and diplomatic relations where the play of caprice and violence remains the dominant motif.

Irony can be understood as a verbal technique (e.g. a relentlessly superior jokiness), an operation of fate (e.g. a reversal of fortune), a theatrical or literary device in which awareness of circumstance is unequally distributed (the knowing audience, the innocent character; a situation in which the participants lack information about something the observer (who may be a co-participant) knows already and which sheds a comic or subversive light on the behaviour or ideals of the participants), or a transmission and exchange between the conscious and unconscious mind.[30]

As international lawyers we are perhaps most familiar with the idea of irony as an effect of the gap between our linguistic, intellectual or political resources and the world of pain we inhabit. In *Radical Evil*, Carlos Nino, expanding on this gap, wrote:

> Our vocabulary for moral blame soon runs out when we want to condemn the murder of six million persons or the torture of children. To say that these acts are wrong sounds like a kind of irony.[31]

But if it sounds like a kind of irony to say that mass murder is wrong, then think how much more ironic (perhaps comically so) it might be to say that genocide 'breaches a norm of *ius cogens*' or that the use of nuclear weapons against an undefended city might 'not comply with the principle of discrimination in international humanitarian law'. To talk in these antiquated or prosaic languages about industrial slaughter is to hold to standards of civilised discourse in a way that is either heroism or folly.

Nino's comments are related also then to the familiar thought that law runs out when exposed to a certain extremity of wrongdoing. Karl Jaspers believed there was something wrong about using law to confront the unspeakable horrors of the Shoah: 'something other than law was at stake here and to address it in legal terms was a mistake', he argued. Hannah Arendt,

---

30. See William Empson, *Some Versions of Pastoral* (Chatto and Windus, 1935). See also my 'Satires of Circumstance: Some Notes on Irony and War Crimes Trials', in Carsten Stahn (ed.), *Future Perspectives on War Crimes Trials* (Asser Institute Press, 2009).
31. Carlos Nino, *Radical Evil on Trial* (Yale University Press, 1996), 141.

too, famously pronounced that hanging Eichmann was necessary but totally inadequate. In *St. Genet*, meanwhile, Sartre contrasts two forms of evil: a 'banal evil' present in unexceptional individuals who lack heroism or imagination but possess a certain facility for administering systems of cruelty and violence, and an 'extreme evil' he associated with charisma, daring and cunning (Iago is an obvious literary example here).[32]

In fact, both forms of evil cause problems for international law. In the case of extreme lawless violence, there is a problem—in the end an ironic gap—between the wrongdoing itself and a legal regime incapable of responding in juridical terms to such extreme violence (it is to this special problem of political violence and mass atrocity that I will turn first, using Fussell as my interlocutor).[33] Banal, systematic and administrative violence discloses a different set of weaknesses for international law, though, namely its tolerance of systemic starvation and human immiseration and the way it renders mass killings lawful (I discuss the possession and use of nuclear weapons under this heading later in the chapter). In both cases, there is an ironic disjuncture between the acts themselves and the legal language used to comprehend these acts.

One of the most resonant investigations of ironic disjuncture is found in Paul Fussell's *The Great War and Modern Memory*.[34] Fussell explored the ways in which an ironic tradition emerges in the trenches of France to displace a panoply of Edwardian virtues and attitudes ('tradition' and 'duty' being two obvious examples).[35] It does so because of the comically gaping chasm between the patriotic insistence on the imminent triumph or vindication of civilisation and what he calls the outright 'abridgement of hope' found in the trenches but spreading out from them. The experience of trench warfare is translated, too, into a more generalised ironic mood in the culture at large

---

32. On Jaspers, see Lawrence Douglas, *The Memory of Judgement* (Yale University Press, 2001) 174. See the discussion in Hannah Arendt, *Thinking without a Banister* (Schocken, 2018) 276–278.
33. See discussion in chapter iv.
34. Fussell (n 10).
35. The Great War's image in the popular imagination remains that of 'tragic senselessness and mass death': Isobel Hull, *A Scrap of Paper* (Cornell, 2014), 3. Mostly, law was understood to be somehow absent. There were linear and ruptural aspects to this account. Either the Great War signalled a period of recession or rupture between two relatively civilised epochs (the *ius European publicum* and the intensely institutionalised Genevan compacts that followed the war), or the war was a continuation of a lawless 19th century of secret treaties, a-legal wars. In both cases, 1919 operates as a hinge; new fully legalised world order or a 19th century with institutions. For a variety of chronologies see David Kennedy, 'The Move to Institutions', 8 *Cardozo Law Review* (1987) 841–987.

(in comedy, in literature, in music) and the experience of ironic disjuncture goes on to become a feature of late-modern international law; indeed, by the end of the century, a calling card of critical international law. During the Great War, then, the clash between Edwardian convention and industrial horror gave rise to a form of ironic modernism.[36]

This emerges in its two modern variants: as a situational state involving the juxtaposition of two contradictory thoughts or circumstances or traditions (one sometimes obscured) and as a mode of thinking and speaking about these states (according to Sloterdijk, cynicism too became a mass phenomenon after the Great War).[37] Fussell's description of the transition of the pre-war values of the late Edwardian period into the poetic and demotic detachments of the trenches is mirrored, to an extent, in Isobel Hull's description of British popular attitudes to the war moving from the idea of a lawful war, with its arguments about securing a lawful peace and permanent system of international law, to the ironic, disabused attitude of a population that felt it had been hoodwinked into believing this was a war for law by a state that then blockaded and starved its enemy after the war (hence the dual image of a Germany guilty of making war and a Britain guilty of making peace).[38]

A more situational irony was in play too in the humanitarian field, where the Commission on the Responsibilities of the Authors of the War provided an exaggerated account of German crimes. When it came to aggressive war, there was the problem of Article 227 of the Treaty of Versailles, where

36. On modernism in international law, see work by Nathaniel Berman and Rose Parfitt: Nathaniel Berman, '"But the Alternative Is Despair": European Nationalism and the Modernist Renewal of International Law', 106(8) *Harvard Law Review* (1993) 1792–1903; Rose Parfitt, 'Empire Des Nègres Blancs: The Hybridity of International Personality and the Abyssinia Crisis of 1935–36', 24(4) *Leiden Journal of International Law* (2011) 849–972. Isobel Hull has written, too, against both of these views (n 35). Her 'Great War' is full of law but it was also a war *over* international law with an allied vision of cooperative institutionalism at war with a German theory of necessity (understandably often mistaken for—though Hull seems very wedded to the idea of keeping them apart—lawlessness). But this, in turn, produces a strange conjunction of effects. On one hand, there was a cultural and social experience of dissonance and disaffection produced by trench warfare trauma. On the other hand, international law entered a profoundly unironic moment of reform, legal pacifism, and institutionalism in Geneva at the League of Nations, where an earnest belief in progress and technique took institutional form in the face of revanchism, a mini-imperial revival, an unwillingness to renounce racial categorisation, and a continuation of rather vicious colonial expeditionaryism. Some of the atmosphere of the Genevan period is captured in *Grand Days* (1993), the first book in Frank Moorhouse's trilogy about the League and its aftermath. See also *Dark Palace* (2000) and *Cold Light* (2011).
37. Sloterdijk (n 16) 4.
38. To paraphrase *The Nation*, 15 March 1919, 732, cited in Hull (n 35) 5.

a provision designed to secure the place of law at the heart of international diplomacy ends up gesturing back to a whole repertoire of pre-legal forms (political morality, sanctity), thereby embracing the very language it was attempting to transcend. These juridical interventions marked the beginning of a phase of peacemaking that seemed to repeat, in a language of legal modernism, the very Edwardian solemnities that were subject to such ironic ridicule during the war.

In Fussell's *Great War*, the laughter of the Tommies is more potent and meaningful as a way of understanding and articulating the experience of trench warfare than are the lethal bromides of Kitchener and his General Command. Meanwhile, in San Cristobel, A. H.'s captors conduct a struggle between the claims of solemnity and the laughter of the Gods. These splits are reflected in the cultural products around the Great War and the Holocaust (two of modern international law's foundational catastrophes). Often the response to such events is styled as fastidious documentation (Raul Hilberg, *Shoah*), autobiographical moralising (Elie Weisel) and dramatic realism (Steven Spielberg, Leon Uris). But atrocity and violation have also been re-described in an entirely different tradition marked by (a deadly serious) laughter, literary playfulness and the commemoration of forgetfulness. In this tradition we find rigorous modernism (Brecht, Kiefer), comic despair (Roth, Bellow, *Catch 22*, Charlie Chaplin's *Great Dictator*, maybe even Roberto Benigni), sardonic dissent (the discordant notes in the Barbie Trial, Arendt's reportage in Jerusalem, Wilfred Owen's 'S. I. W.') and mordant observation (say, Gary Shteyngart in Manhattan, Michel Houellebecq in Paris).[39]

This cleavage is played out, too, in the wider culture around crimes against humanity. War crimes trials and commentary about them are conducted with a becoming and respectful gravity (a word, after all, found everywhere in its preambular flourishes and doctrine). The field recycles and recombines documentation, outrage and representation in a tone of absolute reverence. But there remains a gap between our intuitions about what justice can be or might become, and the sometimes tawdry circumstances of its institutional exercises. One way to illustrate this divide is to juxtapose the inflated claims made for international criminal justice (ending

---

39. And Milan Kundera (reminding us that forgetting has been dominant in the 20th century: 'until everyone has forgotten everything'). See Milan Kundera, *The Book of Laughter and Forgetting* (Faber and Faber, 1996).

impunity, expressing a revulsion for violence) with the tawdry events surrounding Saddam Hussein's execution or the bathetic demise of Slobodan Milošević in a Scheveningen prison or von Ribbentrop 'struggling in the air for twenty minutes', as he is hanged in Nuremberg.[40] There is certainly irony when a procedure designed to condemn violence ends in the mass execution of political enemies or long-term, and, sometimes, punitive incarceration (e.g. Hess in Spandau). But, more generally, and to paraphrase Fussell, every war crimes trial constitutes an irony of situation because its subject is so melodramatically disproportionate to its form, or the gravity and scale of the offences under scrutiny are ill-matched to the proceduralism and solemnity of the criminal trial, and, in the end the gap between our illusions and experiences and the languages of law that are created to give expression to these illusions and experiences cannot be bridged. In the case of international law's 'supreme crime', the Commission established at Versailles to determine 'authorship' of the Great War in fact rejected the whole idea that wars could be authored. There was, for them, an ironic lack of proportion between the scale and magnitude of war, and the smallness and specificity of criminal trial (not to mention the idea of authorship itself). And this unbridgeable gap between the minute rituals of legalism and the sweeping totalities of war forms part of the ongoing critique of 'aggressive war' as a category of crime. As Justice Pal put it at Tokyo: 'the historic causes of the war simply defy legal judgement'.

Pal alerted us to a further ironic gap between the forcible acquisition of territory for some four centuries by the European powers and their rather sudden decision at Tokyo and Nuremberg to render the forcible acquisition of territory a crime (at the very point when they had, for the first time, been its victims). Azar Gat's biblical study on war through the ages presents a picture of the causes of war as complex and unchanging and our efforts to deter them through legal mechanisms fundamentally otherworldly.[41] In short, and this was very much Justice Pal's view, the personalisation of responsibility for war is likely to be arbitrary, counter-intuitive, ahistorical, accidental—and subject to the operation of irony.

These ironic disjunctures are present too when it comes to crimes *in* war. The introduction of the term 'genocide' into the idioms of war and atrocity is usually credited as a major breakthrough in the history of international

---

40. On von Ribbentrop's execution, see Rebecca West, *A Train of Powder* (Virago 1984) 77.
41. Azar Gat, *War in Human Civilisation* (Oxford University Press, 2006).

law. At last, there was a word capable of capturing the special violations (Arendt's 'crimes unprecedented in history') inflicted on the Armenians, the Herero, the Gypsies, the Jews, the Slavs. The International Military Tribunal (IMT) was famously wary of Raphael Lemkin's new term, but it has by now entered the popular lexicon (as a term of abuse) and the legal order (as a defined criminal act).

There are obvious dangers, though, in transmuting the unspeakable into the routine. To hear lawyers speak about genocide (Was there 'intent'? Were the people cruelly massacred 'a substantial part' of the group? Was the group a group?) is to confront the possibility that the human heart loses some of its capacity for indignation when evil is judicialised. The minutiae of legal technique sit uneasily alongside the sheer range and depth of the violation being re-described. In 1945, when the horror of the Second World War was made fully visible, there was a sense that existing legal categories hardly seem adequate. By the 1990s, the categories had expanded and the language of mass criminality was ascendant and ubiquitous. But had law, by now, explained too much? Was there now an ironic disjunction between the technical requirements of law and the moral response to mass atrocity?[42]

International law, then, operates within the chasm between our commitments to human dignity, progress, rationality, law and civilisation and the experience of blood, war and atrocity that provokes ironic (and comic) gestures. These ironic disjunctures, we might say, begin their postwar lives, with the adoption of the Nuremberg Charter on the very day that the second nuclear bomb is dropped on Nagasaki. But the efforts to regulate these weapons, too, have been subject to the operation of irony. The idea that the use of a one-megaton weapon capable of destroying a city of 10 million people and the surrounding areas *and* terminating life in this zone for hundreds of years, could be a 'violation of the Charter', as the General Assembly once announced, sounds tonally dissonant.[43] Raimond

---

42. There are further incompatibilities that I cannot explore fully here. So, on one hand law's formalism demanded certainty, singularity and resolution in the face of a world that seems too messy, unfocused and political for this sort of law. But on the other hand, and in a contrasting conception of legality, law's inconclusive and open-textured anti-formalism sat uneasily with a diplomatic world that required (through legalised retribution) bright-line, moralising distinctions between perpetrators and victims.
43. UNGA Res. 1653 (XVI) (24 November 1961); UNGA Res. 33/71 B (14 December 1978); UNGA Res. 34/83 G (11 December 1979); UNGA Res. 35II52D (12 December 1980); UNGA Res. 36192 I (9 December 1981); UNGA Res. 45/59 B (4 December 1990); UNGA Res. 46/37D (6 December 1991).

Gaita has written about the ways in which rights language fails to capture certain types of wrongdoing, and to put this rather awkwardly, does injury to certain kinds of injury. He gives the example of a woman who suffers a terrible torment at the hands of a state and argues that to speak of her rights as having been 'violated' sounds painfully inadequate as a characterisation of the acts perpetrated on her and the wrongs suffered by her.[44]

Along with this problem of misdescription, there is, in relation to nuclear weapons, an additional tendency to engage in what I want to characterise as 'over-legibility'. So, for example, the ICJ, when it was asked in the *Nuclear Weapons* case to declare whether the use and possession of such weapons would be lawful, made nuclear obliteration legible by discussing it in terms of proportionality, discrimination and self-defence. In most cases, it turned out it would be disproportionate to end planetary life, discriminatory to immolate the world's toddlers, and a breach of the Geneva Convention to render blind the inhabitants of Amsterdam. Is this the right language to describe these horrors?

And there is a further difficulty in applying law to horror: the problem of the exception. Would putting an end to human civilisation be a breach of Article 2(4) of the United Nations Charter? Not necessarily. What about the right to self-defence, after all? Maybe the Security Council would authorise the end of the world in an appropriately worded resolution.[45]

In the end, the ICJ does two things it probably did not quite intend to do. It renders nuclear weapons legible, and it renders them usable. It establishes that the foundational nuclear norm in international law is the right to possess and use nuclear weapons and it makes the possession and use of such weapons comprehensible, and it does so through an (understandably) agonised prose that cannot quite make its mind up:

> In view of the unique characteristics of nuclear weapons, to which the Court has referred above, the use of such weapons in fact seems scarcely reconcilable with respect for such requirements. Nevertheless, the Court considers that it does not have sufficient elements to enable it to conclude with certainty that the use of nuclear weapons would necessarily be at variance with the

---

44. Raimond Gaita, in Raymond Gaita and Gerry Simpson (eds.), *Who's Afraid of International Law?* (Monash, 2017); See also, in general, Raimond Gaita, *A Common Humanity: Thinking about Love and Truth and Justice* (Routledge, 1999).
45. For a discussion, see Koselleck's discussion of absurd history in Reinhart Koselleck, 'Law, History and Justice', in Reinhart Koselleck, *Sediments of Time: On Possible Histories* (Stanford University Press, 2018) Chapter 8.

principles and rules of law applicable in international armed conflict in any circumstance. (para. 95)[46]

And this results in the dispositive, the *non-liquet*:

> However, in view of the current state of international law, and of the elements of fact at its disposal, the Court cannot conclude definitively whether the threat or use of nuclear weapons would be lawful or unlawful in an extreme circumstance of self-defence, in which the very survival of a State would be at stake.[47]

What we have is a kind of juridical cover, a form of lawful sleepwalking as international law reduces nuclearism to technique (self-defence, unnecessary suffering, specially affected states). It over-assimilates nuclear war. In this sense it resembles, with its lapses into bathos, its unironic attitude to apocalypse and its blithe legalisms, the insurance industry.[48] My insurance policy states that my home contents are uninsured—uninsurable—against 'nuclear activities and radioactivity, including the use, existence or escape of nuclear fuel, weapons, material or waste'. This includes 'nuclear pollution and contamination' (though the policy will also not cover 'gradual loss or damage' of any kind).[49] Frances Ferguson once said that the nuclear is 'what cannot be insured against'.[50] But perhaps it is also that which cannot be discussed, meaningfully, and without loss of immediacy and sense, in the ordinary vernaculars of international law.

In the end, adopting an ironic approach to the juridification of atrocity and nuclear terror is not 'just' a temperamental or intellectual choice, nor is it one unaware of the corrosive effects of irony in collective political action, nor does it deny the importance of solemn remembrance. Instead, irony and laughter work here as forms of moral vigilance. Given our commitment to neurotic over-consumption in the face of ecological catastrophe, this is not the moment to permit solemn self-satisfaction as we contemplate our efforts to eradicate only the most obvious examples of wrongdoing.

---

46. 'Legality of the Threat of Use of Nuclear Weapons' (Advisory Opinion), ICJ Reports 1996, p. 226, § 95.
47. Ibid. §105.
48. See also my 'Unprecedents', in Immi Tallgren and Thomas Skouteris, *The New Histories of International Criminal Law: Retrials* (Oxford University Press, 2019) Chapter 2.
49. 'General Exclusions', Comminsure Home Insurance, Product Disclosure Statement (2015) 76–78: https://www.commbank.com.au/content/dam/commbank/personal/apply-online/download-printed-forms/comminsure-home-insurance-pds-may2015.pdf.
50. Frances Ferguson, 'The Nuclear Sublime', 14(2) *Diacritics* (1984) 4.

And we must beware, too, of solemn edification. The lesson of 1939–1945 is that there is no lesson. By then, it was too late for lessons. The real lessons are found earlier, perhaps in 1932 or 1933, with the deformations visited on the body politic, the low-level humiliations endured by those marked as different, the cruelties of a monstrous economic order and the sometimes subtle violations visited on language. In order to absorb this lesson, we need to have (as Orwell and Joseph Heller had, as the soldiers in the Great War trenches had, as Wilfred Owen had and as Thomas Hardy had) a keen sense of irony.

After all, as Adam Phillips once remarked, 'people are only ever ironic about the things that they don't feel ironic about'.[51]

iv. ironic lawyers

No genuinely human life is possible without irony.

Kierkegaard

What might it mean to be ironic about the things we don't feel ironic about? And in the light of these ironic conjunctions, what is it to be an ironic (international) lawyer? To put this case in the negative: Is there a whole way of being associated with a field of study or professional domain that precludes critical enquiry or makes that critical enquiry very difficult to carry out?[52] This book is an exercise in trying to write and think differently about a field of argument saturated in moral resonance and crammed with all manner of historical imperatives. But the architectures of our professional life and its languages have the effect of sometimes closing down the very ways of thought, modes of expression or critical resources that might give us access to the experience of living in the world and changing it.[53] We then become isolated from the world upon which we are trying to, or purporting to, act.[54] So far, so familiar.

In particular, as we attempt to act and think, we might experience a form of two-sidedness (a two-sidedness associated with an experience of ironic

---

51. Adam Phillips, *Promises, Promises* (Faber and Faber, 2000).
52. Pierre Bourdieu, *Homo Academicus* (Polity Press, 1990).
53. Duncan Kennedy, 'Legal Education as Training for Hierarchy', in David Kairys (ed.), *The Politics of Law* (Basic Books, 1982) 54–75.
54. See Slavoj Žižek, *First as Tragedy, Then as Farce* (Verso, 2009) 4–6.

disengagement of the sort I have described above) when participating in the rituals of professional (international legal) existence.[55] Irony and joking seem to promise an explanation for, or at least a comic recognition of, this Borgesian doubling effect. The pervasive idea of having a 'critical faith' in international law or a chastened belief in its possibilities in the face of its failures is a form of doubleness: 'I can't go on, I must go on'. With work in this vein, the indictment is usually powerful, often lethal, the continued faith in the light of it, obscure, maybe inexplicable. The trenches at Vimy Ridge or the Somme were full of men who had utterly lost faith in the enterprise of war but continued to participate in it (and not always or often because of a compulsion from above). The public language of duty and patriotic ardour coexisted with a private idiom of sardonic—sometimes nihilistic—faithlessness. The circumstances are, of course, much less acute and dangerous for us as bourgeois international lawyers, but the predicament is similar.

In James Anderson Winn's book on the poetry of war, he describes irony as a 'way of encouraging the reader to consider several conflicting interpretations of war at the same time'.[56] In this sense, then, the absence of irony is a mark of an immature politics or a child-like desire for certainty. When we read short stories as a child or young adult, we expect a self-contained, narrative unit with an ending that resolves the conflicts built into that narrative. Most Hollywood films and many novels are like this. But, to take short-story writers as an example, we experience something quite different when reading say, Katherine Mansfield or James Baldwin. A variant of this short-story type is always two stories: the story told by the writer and the untold, never-to-be-told story that sits alongside or inside the written story. This two-storied-ness of life and work is important, partly reflecting a split between our private and public selves.[57] There is a sense in such work of a script no longer being adhered to. At the Prague Show Trials, the accused's testimony would be tracked by a silent tape-recording of the testimony recorded (in conditions of coercion) at an earlier point. The tape would rarely be played (there was no need; the accused was already reading from a script prepared in advance by the prosecuting authorities).

---

55. Deborah Cass has discussed this form of doubling (n 6).
56. James Anderson Winn, *The Poetry of War* (Cambridge University Press, 2008) 11.
57. See David Kennedy, 'Autumn Weekends', in A. Sarat and T. Kearns (eds.), *Law in Everyday Life* (University of Michigan Press, 1995).

But on one or two occasions, the accused would depart from the script and begin a denunciation of the proceedings. His microphone would then be switched off and the official tape-recorded version of the testimony would be substituted for his actual testimony. There must have been a brief moment, then, and before the latter trailed away, when the amplified recorded speech competed with the supplemental human testimony.[58] More recently at the International Criminal Court (ICC), there was the spectacle of Al Mahdi's apology for having engaged in crimes against humanity.[59] The fact that this was delivered using almost exactly the same tropes as those in Fatou Bensouda's opening statement put me in mind of *L'Aveu* (*The Confession*), a film about the Czechoslovak show trials in which the defendants repeat the language of the prosecutors just as compliantly.[60] In another scene, a defendant is busy parroting the official fabrications when his trousers fall down. This is a reference to Freisler's prosecution of the Hitler assassination conspirators but, in the film, it provokes a laughter which is terrifying and seems to spring from the dark, messy unconscious of punitive legalism itself.[61]

To take a less sinister, more familiar, everyday example of this doubleness, think of how we witness or experience speeches in an administrative setting (or elsewhere for that matter). There is often another, second, franker and comically subversive speech running alongside it. That second speech is an annotated version of the one being delivered but unspools only in our private ruminations. Sometimes this 'private' alternative speech becomes a collective experience. Everyone in a particular community is hearing the same alternative speech. The Dean farewells a colleague she is known to have despised for years. Let's say it is a matter of common knowledge that the Dean has a low opinion of the departing colleague's scholarship. The Dean's comments about this scholarship, of course, will be undercut, perhaps obliterated, by the silent collective speech 'heard' by everyone in the room. The other speech will tend to emerge in some form or other. These are the 'Freudian slips', universally recognised as such.[62] So, the Dean, in my example, might praise her colleague's 'unjustly neglected scholarship' (this

---

58. See chapter iv, for further discussion.
59. *Prosecutor v. Al Mahdi*, ICC-01/12-01/15 at https://www.icc-cpi.int/mali/al-mahdi.
60. *L'Aveu* (1970; dir. Costas-Gavras).
61. At Nuremberg, too, there were ruptures. Indeed, Hermann Goering may have introduced what later came to be characterised, in the Barbie Trial, as the strategy of rupture.
62. As Adam Phillips (n 51) has pointed out, we don't have Freudian slips, we *make* them.

can be translated by the audience directly into 'justifiably neglected scholarship') because, as Pierre Bourdieu remarked in *Homo Academicus*, almost every apparent encomium can be adapted in this way: 'of great practical benefit' become 'theoretically unsophisticated' or 'politically craven', 'accessible' is a synonym for 'reductive', 'theoretically engaged' a useful stand-in for 'irrelevant' or 'unnecessarily abstruse'.[63]

International law's double-ness, its dual identity, is a familiar aspect of its work from Carr's 'utopia and realism' to Jouannet's welfarist and liberal conceptions of international law.[64] Critical writing in international law has long had to reckon with the discipline's unhappy historical record, while at the same time trying to retrieve a usable political programme from this record. The idea of critical faith—the sense that we are working with fatally corrupted and damaged materials as we construct our cities on the hill and our utopic visions—remains a haunting motif. We confront these effects through doubling and irony. But, as ever, there are pitfalls. Irony can be an enemy of deep moral sensibility, an anti-politics. At some level, then, to be an 'ironic jurist' is to be unserious: to Lettermanise everything in a bid to avoid being outflanked. Irony would be tiresome and corrosive in this guise (though it would not be entirely without its uses). In the end, this ironic end-of-times mode is a perfect match for—indeed may be parasitic on—certain contemporary political styles.[65] It is also, of course, an implicit call to leave politics behind, to detach oneself from the conditions of life, to accept the existing dispensations. Žižek gives the example of Michael Palin's travel shows on BBC2, in which the narrator dribbles on in the soothing ironic tones of the Englishman abroad while screening out all the traumatic material.[66] This chapter, then, ought not to be read as a call for ironic distance or jocose cynicism in the face of a wildly asymmetrical distribution of life chances.

In Jonathan Lear's *A Case for Irony*, irony is, instead, revealed as a serious way to confront the world.[67] For Lear, Kierkegaardian irony requires

---

63. On euphemism and reversal in the academy, see Bourdieu (n 52) 204–209.
64. See Cass (n 6).
65. Scholars are perpetually trying to mash together the far right and the sceptical left. See Tom Farer, 'Diplomacy and International Law', in Andrew Cooper et al., *Oxford Handbook on Modern Diplomacy* (2013) Chapter 27.
66. He calls this a form of 'postmodern racism'. See Slavoj Žižek, *Living in the End Times* (Verso, 2011) 3–4.
67. Jonathan Lear, *A Case for Irony* (Harvard University Press, 2014) .

the leading of an ironic life. What sort of life would this be? According to Kierkegaard, it would be Socrates' life. While the 'entire contemporary population' of Greece was busying itself with merely living life, Socrates was permanently and continually questioning the meaning of this life.[68] I take Lear (and Kierkegaard) to be distinguishing the Socratic life from three potentially overlapping non-Socratic Athenian types here. The first are people with an ironic sensibility who are not leading an ironic life. Such people, perhaps, were the Athenian Letterman; they used turns of speech and displayed verbal virtuosity but did not really reflect with any depth on their position or vocation.[69] A second Athenian was the labourer or businessman who leads an unexamined life, simply (in both senses of that word) going about his days while being 'led down cemetery road'. These two categories of individual can be readily distinguished from Lear's Socrates, but a third figure is less easily understood as different. He is the politician or philosopher or *homo academicus* who *does* reflect on questions of purpose or honour; he possesses what contemporary Kantians call 'practical identity' (a sense of abstract selfhood against which he can judge his immediate preferences, inclinations, appetites). For Lear, this person is leading an examined life but falls short of the Socratic ideal.[70] The reason for this has something to do with the 'closed' nature of certain thought systems. Within these systems we may reflect on their imperfections and their contradictions—we often will want to offer critique—but, we do not, or cannot, take a meaningful step outside the system. In this way, reflective engagement simply leads to further intellectual and spiritual confinement.[71]

The truly ironic lawyer, for Lear, experiences a gap between pretence (the accumulation of our identities, the aspirations we advertise) and the deeper ideals embedded in the roles we play (as international criminal lawyers, as fathers, as sisters and so on). For Lear, this experience is 'uncanny'. The familiar ideals are returned to us in an unfamiliar guise.[72] It is these very ideals, and practical identity itself, that are placed into question when we adopt an ironic perspective on our own lives.

---

68. Ibid. 5.
69. *Kierkegaard's Journals* (Princeton University Press, 2007–2020) *passim*.
70. See e.g. Stephen Grosz, *The Examined Life* (Vintage, 2013).
71. Lear (n 67) 7.
72. On the uncanny, see Sigmund Freud, *The Uncanny* (Penguin, 2003 [1919]).

As a practitioner of international law, then, we might engage in a number of roles at the same time. A person may well spend time defending or prosecuting accused war criminals as well as writing critical essays on the failure to accord defendants fair trial rights. This person might also make some larger claims about justice, about what it means to practise justice in her world or this world. The ironic moment occurs when this person is struck by a disruptive sense of what justice or her practical identity entails: not, what I can do to be a better international lawyer (and 'better' has a meaning much wider than, say, 'more proficiently') but, instead, what is it to *be* an international lawyer?[73] Doing *what* better? And to what purpose? And what are the near-inescapable moral, temperamental and political constraints operating upon me when I attempt it?

Lear's view is that this is a form of erotic uncanniness: a combination of longing for a different sort of practical identity and a sudden sense of instability in the experience of one's present practical (professional) identity. This, too, is what distinguishes corrosive ironising in the earlier example of the Greek 'Letterman' from the experience of irony, or irony as an 'existence-determination', as Kierkegaard's alter ego, Johannes Climacus, described it. In the former, disillusionment leads to detachment; in the latter, desire provokes vertigo.

A key attribute of the ironic experience is the existence of some attachment or affection for a way of living or a practical identity: being a professor or a defence lawyer or a shopkeeper or a writer. The 'falling short' can have a depth only if there is a prior (ongoing) commitment. Irony, then, is a form of questioning about questioning, an existential uncertainty about life and professional identity. The ironist is distinguishable from the social critic (trying to improve a social or professional practice) or the ironic observer (sitting slightly above the field, all the better to comment wryly upon it). 'Uncertainty' in these cases, just becomes one more critical badge of honour. Universities, in particular, have institutionalised these forms of reflection: forms that stop well short of the 'uncanny'.

In the case of Learean irony, there is in the end uncertainty even about one's uncertainty ('you seem very certain in your ambivalence', as someone said to me from the floor of the Institute of Contemporary Arts, after I had spoken on international law and the Iraq War). Lear is setting a very high

---

73. Lear (n 67) 15.

standard here (perhaps the best we can do is to fail better). But a certain coming to terms with the irony of situation seems important. The ironic jurist has to remain above all *attentive*, or mindful. In Hannah Arendt's original *Eichmann* essays for *The New Yorker*, she describes Eichmann as 'thoughtless'; he had a stock of clichés and standard phrases to keep reality at bay. We all do, according to Arendt. How not to be Eichmann, then? Roughly speaking, this might involve keeping things in mind. Keeping things in mind, rigorously, is not just engaging in reform-minded criticisms of the present international or national or local order (one of the *least* critical interventions one can make these days is to parrot the thought that justice is selective or partial—apparently tough-minded-criticism becoming lazy justification) or bemoaning the state of the world. It might involve a renunciation of the absolute and the unqualified and especially a refusal to find oneself perpetually on the side of the angels. It might require taking an ironic distance from the existing (and by this time naturalised) arrangements, which I discuss in chapter vii ('gardening, instead'). Sometimes, laughter will be necessary as a way of exposing a taboo or deploying surplus libidinal energies or expressing the inexpressible: an uncovering of the underpinnings of a progressive-humanitarian international legal order coexisting comfortably with mass, abject and remediable misery. It might involve electing the agonising—sometimes, comic—uncertainties of the ironic jurist over the solemn and definitive judgments of international 'justice'.

v. contrapuntal laughter: blasphemy and rebellion

In the spring of 2019, I attended a festival of twenty-minute plays in the small English market town of Halesworth in Suffolk. There were plays about Brexit, about relationships, about the rural–urban divide. This was an often quite affecting bourgeois theatre that confirmed the gap between our ideals and our practices. The final play was about three dogs playing on the beach. But in their 'play', the rest of the programme seemed to be rendered absurd and irrational, perhaps beside the point. The dogs were—at the same time—relentlessly material (defecating, slobbering, naked, promiscuous), irreverent (playfully cynical about their masters) and philosophically alive to their predicament (liberally quoting Diogenes).

Diogenes has been described as the 'anti-Socrates', an originator of a plebeian, Banksyan street philosophy in which high-flown rhetoric is constantly assailed by low-born materiality—in which universal ideals are undercut by everyday squalor or the mechanisms of the human body—and a counterpoint to the sobrieties and absolutes of Platonism. Diogenes was famous for his theatrical, scatological responses to the discursive mannerisms of his more renowned contemporaries. Is there a Diogenean international law? A cheekiness from below? This, I suggest, would be less an ironic self-questioning and more a disgusted materiality (the materiality of silence, for example) or an instinctive contrapuntal laughter.

In *A Critique of Cynical Reason*, Peter Sloterdijk offers up—insists upon— Diogenean *kynicism* as a response to the failures of the enlightenment, the condition of postmodernity that comes in the wake of that failure, the prevailing norms that govern this condition and the appearance of cynicism as a mode of practice in contemporary administrative life.[74] For Sloterdijk, Diogenes and his corporeal cheekiness was one sort of answer to the relentlessly serious 'engineers of human souls'.[75]

blasphemy

But laughter might have its darker sides too, and I want to begin with these before returning to Diogenes. Such laughter could offer us moments of revelation: a daemonic laughter that discloses the undiscloseable. This is laughter that brings to the surface the hidden pathologies of a particular practice, a moment in which the unsayable is said and cannot be unsaid, the nasty laughter of the repressed unconscious self: in the present instance, international law's comic *id*. This darker, blasphemous laughter has emerged at different points in the history of international politics, a return of the

---

74. Sloterdijk (n 16). Kynicism is posited here as a cure for cynicism (the cynicism of contemporary disaffection, or moral nihilism, or exploitative doubleness). See also, for an analysis of this condition focusing on the relations between [cynical] aesthetic formations and flexible capital accumulation, and positing 1972 as the beginning of the time–space compression that is the mark of postmodernity, David Harvey, *The Condition of Postmodernity* (Blackwell, 1990).
75. Some of Sloterdijk's views are distinctly outré. His provocations directed at West German humanism and bourgeois life have now become a populist orthodoxy; his talk of uber-humans and genetic reform, meanwhile, have caused alarm in Germany. See his *Rules for the Human Zoo* (1999).

repressed.⁷⁶ For Freud, as we have seen, laughter was the unconscious expression of long deadened Diogenean urges to ridicule, to explode the limits of, to deconstruct.

V. S. Naipaul describes viewers in the Caribbean, just after the war, watching footage taken by soldiers liberating the camps in 1945 and responding with grotesque laughter.⁷⁷ Whether such events took place or not, what would it suggest about the laughter of the subaltern if they had? Perhaps such laughter could be read as a kind of pre-political or pre-verbal reaction to a global order organised—solemnly and in the name of a rule of law and justice—along fantastically unequal and unjust lines. What would an audience of West Indians, in 1945, think of the distressing footage emerging from post-war Europe? It's impossible to tell. They might be tempted to laugh into the horror of it all, or, in a way that failed to distinguish victim and perpetrator or see it as a comeuppance for western civilisation. If this could be done in the name of European high culture, then could European empire any longer be taken seriously? In a similar vein, after suffering a lifetime of bombing from above and repression on the ground, might not people laugh secretly, blasphemously, at the slow disintegration of the Twin Towers and the desperate, falling men and women. Such laughter is grotesque and cruel, of course, but at the same time recognisable.⁷⁸

In *Crime and Punishment*, Raskolnikov talks about being tempted by the devil into his own double murder.

> 'Funny, isn't it?' he asks.
> 'Don't laugh, blasphemer!' exclaims Sonia.⁷⁹

During war crimes trials, this sort of explosive laughter erupts the bounds of trial (just as the acts themselves were said to explode legal categories (Jaspers)).⁸⁰ As Immi Tallgren has shown, the Nuremberg Trial itself relied at one point on a film of the camps as a way of provoking reaction from the accused, and, in a double-cinematic moment, the reaction in the courtroom

---

76. Or, for Sloterdijk, the persistence of ancient urges in the context of contemporary life that is thought to have eradicated them. See Thomas Meaney, 'Dr Zeitgeist', *The New Yorker*, 19 February 2018, 3.
77. Naipaul had described elsewhere how British and Dutch slavery had turned the Caribbean into 'a giant concentration camp'.
78. I take this to be a global version of the laughter schoolboys might suppress at a funeral.
79. Fyodor Dostoevsky, *Crime and Punishment* (Penguin, 1982).
80. Ibid.

to this film footage of the liberation of the camps was itself filmed.[81] And this double-cinematic moment was an inversion, both literal and figurative. The film, intended to shame the persecutors, was shown upside down and made them laugh instead; and this blasphemous laughter then became somehow confirmation of their moral disability and guilt. But it was also a laughter surely that emerged from the dark heart of the Nazi project, not Diogenean self-ridicule but Freudian self-revelation. In Arusha, at the International Criminal Tribunal for Rwanda (ICTR), it is alleged that some judges laughed during the cross-examination of a witness in the *Butari Trial* (which involved accusations of sexual assault and rape).[82] This incident, denied by the ICTR, has come to represent a masculine privilege that remains at the core of war-making, even after the civilising effects of the Geneva Conventions and the various advances in the international laws of sexual assault. It is a laughter ringing down from history in which rape was treated variously as a reward for conquest, the infliction of an injury on the male sovereign, a breach of honour and chivalry or part of the generalised commission of harms on the body of the enemy.[83]

rebellion

Off to the side of this blasphemous laughter is the kynical comedy of Diogenes, itself a response to more conventionally understood 'cynicism'. International law has always been fairly certain about its relationship to cynicism: cynics are people (unscrupulous politicians, rogue regimes) engaged in 'the abuse and circumvention of international law' (to quote a recent conference title). To accuse someone or something of 'abusing' international law might be to argue that he or it has ignored or infringed some

---

81. Immi Tallgren, unpublished paper, on file with author.
82. The *Global Policy Monitor* reported on 3 December 2001, the day after the alleged incident, that three judges and a defence lawyer had laughed while a young prosecution witness and rape victim has testified. See 'UN judge laughs at rape victim', *Global Policy Monitor* (2001). An enquiry undertaken by Navi Pillay, the Tribunal President, concluded that the laughter had not taken place.
83. I am using law in the expansive sense of agreed norms operating during periods of warfare—from the Greek Confederacy's war with Troy ('Did he not take the girl I won? Did none of my fair weather friends agree? That she was mine by rape and conquest?'—Achilles to Patroclus), in Christopher Logue, *War Music: An Account of Books 16–19 of Homer's Iliad* (Faber and Faber, 1988), through to the Tokyo War Crimes Trials (where even Justice Pal describes sexual assault at Nanking as 'misbehaviour', in Robert Cryer and Neil Boister, *Documents on the Tokyo International Military Tribunal* (Oxford University Press, 2008), 1342.

principle or rule of international law. But I think more is being asserted than this. Abuse or circumvention implies a certain deviousness, or cunning—perhaps taking an international legal norm and subjecting it to an unacceptable or bad faith interpretation or manoeuvring around a prohibition of international law by over-enlarging the exceptions to that prohibition or even refusing to sign up to something or other.[84]

To think like this is to believe in international law, and here I don't just mean belief in a set of norms or institutions or practices but also faith in a sometimes barely articulated conglomeration of ideas called 'international law'. It is this, sometimes free-floating, abstract set of ideas that the circumventers and abusers are busy circumventing and abusing, even when technically their arguments might make sense, or, at least, pass Tom Franck's laughter test. The international law loyalists opposed to this cynicism then hold that it is not enough to pass the laughter test, one has to pass the virtue test too.

Not everyone believes in international law in quite this way. Such people are more inclined to ask: what might it mean to abuse an already chronically elastic legal norm? Might it not be, on occasion, a good idea to circumvent a legal norm? How cynical was it to call for intervention in Rwanda in defiance of agreed commitments?

But alongside this split between believers and non-believers, the idea of circumvention and abuse also I think presents us with a world divided between right-thinking internationalists and a variety of 'low, dishonest' nativists (represented by, say, Boris Johnson or Jair Bolsonaro). These are the cynics no longer committed to international law or even internationalism, and willing to somehow use and abuse international law (even in a 'limited and specific way') for their own unseemly ends. I inhabit the virtuous half of this divided world on my journeys from my home in the liberal-bourgeois London heartland of Hampstead to my workplace at the staunchly Europeanist LSE and then on holidays to Left-Remain-Nationalist-Internationalist Scotland.

This idea about international law as a cosmopolitan, oppositional strategy is very important to the self-image of many international lawyers who see

---

84. I always found it curious that the detentions on Guantanamo Bay, the invasion of Iraq and the 'failure' (this was the word usually employed) to ratify the Rome Statute, were all lumped together as evidence of the second Bush administration's 'cynical disregard' for international law.

themselves as engaged in a noble task to bring law to the international, or international to the law, or to tame the Great Powers or humanise war, or to juridify trade and so on. And all this good work is perpetually undermined by forces beyond our control, by the abusers and circumventers, cold-hearted calculators, Machiavellians, the recalcitrants, the withdrawers, so-called realists, the *cynics*. Richard Goldstone's autobiography *For Humanity* is a prime exhibit of this tendency. Goldstone works for humanity and international law, the doubters working against him (the former British PM Ted Heath, Inkatha, the Serbs) are, well, in a way enemies of humanity. That is why international lawyers always seem more charged and excited during periods of oppressive rule: Reagan v. International law, Bush v. International Law, Putin v. International Law. Think about international law's period of public fame in the UK when Tony Blair invaded Iraq and launched a thousand law review articles and opinion pieces. International lawyers never seem more vitalised than while swimming in a sea of cynics.

But what about the cynicism of international law itself?

I gave my last anti-war paper in 2002: a jeremiad against the Iraq War (condemning, especially, the 'misuse' of international law by the Coalition of the Willing). In that speech, I was guilty of a different form of cynicism, or what Sloterdijk called 'enlightened false consciousness'.[85] Sloterdijk's definition of cynicism, quite different from Learean irony, involves knowing the gap between one's abstract commitments and embedded practices and going on as before as if nothing has changed: in other words, to continue acting as if international legal rules could somehow determine ethical choices or furnish a knock-down legal argument to resist war, having spent a decade arguing (jurisprudentially, politically) against this view of legality. My 2002 audience was delighted. Sometimes, I wonder if I ever delighted an audience again.

This cynical intervention into the Iraq War then became the subject of an unpopular collective *mea culpa*, in which a group of international lawyers tried to understand our own cynicism as a response to the even more cynical uses of international law by the Blair Government. (In the end we were out-cynicalled. I remember the moment of realisation. Tony Blair was on the radio being interviewed about the Iraq War, it was late 2003, and the occupation was unravelling badly. The interviewer had cornered Blair: the intervention had been a disaster, British forces were being outflanked

---

85. Sloterdijk (n 16) 5.

in Basra, the country was dividing along ethnic lines, terrorism was on the rise, no weapons of mass destruction had been found. Blair agreed with all of this. But he said, smooth as you like, that there were, you see, 'thirteen Security Council resolutions' authorising the war. It just had to be done. When it came to justifications for the war, international law was the last man standing.)

To go back to the sorts of arguments we might make and not quite fully believe in, I will not say too much more about this form of cynicism because it is so familiar to us as international law practitioners and it has become a way of life for us as consumer-citizens. We are deeply embedded, complicit, amid unliveable lives, busy protesting endlessly about our very own *modus vivendi*. Likewise, international law goes on despite its groundlessness or its faithlessness, its cruel optimism.

Irony has been one way in which we have experienced this practice. But it is the specific experience of it as cynical that Sloterdijk is describing, and the play of kynicism, laughter and sensuality, its counter-strategy. Because the practice of international lawyering is so very tightly circumscribed—dress codes are rigidly adhered to, narrowly defined conventions of paper-presenting and question and answer-giving are quickly inculcated—it is hard to find a physics of play anywhere near it (there is a handful of masterful performers, the odd appearance of a suckling child, but that's about it). What shape might the revolt from below take? In his introduction to *Critique of Cynical Reason*, Andreas Huyssen lists three kynical modes: 'satirical laughter, defiant body action and strategic silence'.[86] I will discuss 'strategic silence' later in chapter vii. 'Defiant body action', meanwhile, might involve not attending overseas conferences (those air-miles), refusing to shake the hands of political enemies, departing noisily from tedious keynotes by poorly selected dignitaries but, in truth, the prospects are limited. How to escape then?

In the wake of techno-totalitarianism or robot empire or ecological self-destruction, the survivors, if they can speak, might ask: why an international criminal court? Was that really a thing? Did it ban poverty? Planetary overheating? Nuclear annihilation? Were there really 500 university courses on international criminal law and not a single subject on 'Diogenes and International Legal Kynicism'? How was the international legal order

---

86. Andreas Huyssen, "Foreword" to Sloterdijk (n 16).

organised, and why did it permit so much horror? Who allowed this to happen and what were they doing, as it happened? Did no one get up and simply scream, Munch-like, at the sheer absurdity of it all? I have often wondered how many of my students each year at LSE get arrested. Did no one think to disable some bombing equipment at an RAF base? But it is difficult to find either the ironic jurist or the Rabelasian kynic in us: a certain, but small, amount of self-questioning goes a long way. Ironic lawyering takes an enormous lifetime of effort while blasphemous laughter is professionally self-cancelling. A few especially insouciant or outrightly narcissistic types do not even go this far. For the rest of us, there is the 'chic bitterness' that provides an 'undertone' to our activities.[87]

One route out might take the form of a disinhibited truth-telling, a refusal to participate in the crazed rituals of international legal life, a grasp of—then performance of—the materiality of existence, a shamelessness, a bohemian renunciation of bourgeois comforts in favour of creature comforts, a 'rejection of the superstructure'.[88] But the Diogenes I want to invoke here is the existentialist who sits in his tub asking Alexander the Great to stop blocking the sun, the Diogenes whose (anti)biopolitics is a form of scatology and, especially, the Diogenes for whom laughter was an instinctive rebellion against social super-norms. The constraints on this form of laughter are powerful, of course—a Diogenean set of performances would surely result in social death and professional disenfranchisement.

But the spirit of Diogenes is present in extra-juridical moments of revelation. At Tokyo, at Nuremberg, in The Hague, there have been moments of laughter and physical comedy that operate as marginalia to the trials themselves and yet reveal something about these trials that is unavailable from a reading of the interlocutory findings or the judgments. The sheer physicality of the subconscious was, for example, on display in Tokyo in 1946 when Shumei Okawa, the Japanese propagandist and a famously disruptive presence—cutting an agitated figure during his trial and fidgeting endlessly—slapped Tojo over the head in a piece of slapstick comedy that prefigures the later hanging of Tojo. Tojo's symbolic decapitation mirrored the judicial decapitation of the Japanese military and political elite by the Allies.

---

87. Sloterdijk (n 16) 5.
88. Ibid. 164.

In the end, Okawa's giggling presence proved too much for the Court, which removed him declaring that he was 'unable to defend himself' but not before his pre-war activities had been used as evidence to establish a conspiracy to commit crimes against peace. In a 1924 book, he had predicted a war between East and West. As the Judgement puts it: 'he had organised a Patriotic Society which advocated the liberation of the colored races and the moral unification of the world', adding that he often lectured to the Army General Staff along similar lines.[89] One might say that he was being prosecuted for trying to end racial discrimination and advocating a form of cosmopolitanism. Just prior to his removal, Okawa had remarked: 'The trial is not the realisation of justice but the continuation of war'. This brilliantly Clausewitzian but ultimately blasphemous formula anticipates later critiques of the trial and of international criminal justice itself. Okawa had argued that Japan's imperial war was not an aggressive war at all but an act of pre-emptive self-defence. The Soviets, in particular (later to preemptively attack Czechoslovakia) declared the doctrine to be disreputable. Meanwhile, half a century later, Okawa's insanity was to become George W. Bush's foreign policy. Okawa is the Shakespearean Fool: a madman speaking obscure, subterranean sense in a senseless world.

Okawa produces here a Diogenean theatre of decapitation uncovering the violence of lawful solemnity and offering, at the same time, a verbal critique of the trial's foundations. And this physical response to legal solemnity is provoked not just by critique but also by trauma. Shoshana Felman has written about the disruptive caesurae—the forbidden testimonies—that might produce surplus legal meaning during war crimes trials.[90] Both she and Laurence Douglas—in his book on memory—recount an incident where a witness in the Eichmann Trial, K-Zetnik, is called to the stand.[91] The witness opens his mouth and begins: 'This is a chronicle from the planet of Auschwitz ... the inhabitants of that planet had no names. They did not love, nor did they die, by the laws of this world'.[92] The witness, who cannot bear witness, then collapses into silence and is taken to hospital where he (only just) recovers from a paralytic stroke (he lives on well

---

89. International Military Tribunal for the Far East (IMTFE) Judgement, Cryer and Boister (n 83) 111–112 [48, 516].
90. Shoshana Felman, *The Juridical Unconscious* (Harvard University Press, 2002) 132.
91. Laurence Douglas, *The Memory of Judgement* (Yale University Press, 2001).
92. *The Eichmann Trial Proceedings* (1962) vol. 3, session 68 (1961).

into his eighties). As a lawful gesture, this testimony may lack meaning; the witness does not testify to anything usable. But as a literary moment (K-Zetnik is, himself, a novelist) his collapse has been frequently read as a vivid comment on the impossibility of testimony—a moment in which the legal-rational slips into incomprehension and the literary can grasp for meaning only for a few short minutes. Here Dinur, or Dineer, to give him the names used by Hannah Arendt and others, is operating at the very outposts of the unconscious, giving a literal and figurative (lack of) voice to the unspeakable horrors of the Shoah: an unstrategic silence. His collapse is a Diogenean return to the physical.

★ ★ ★

Irony and comedy are threads running through international law's encounters with the world. Sometimes there is ironic disjuncture: Eichmann's blank passivity and his hyperactive murderousness; Speer's urbane pleas of innocence and his entanglement in Nazi racial politics; Slobodan Paljak's very public suicide with the curtain being immediately drawn and the International Criminal Tribunal for the former Yugoslavia (ICTY) itself being described as a 'crime scene'. At other times, these ironic gestures provoked a destabilising laughter. In this chapter, I have tried to introduce, by way of sketch, and in turn, an ironic and then a kynical international law or, better, an ironic international lawyer (the self-doubting, agonistic jurist) and a kynical international lawyer (the defiant, disinhibited, lawyer-rebel). These figures seem, to me, to be characters who confront the world with a close-to-tearful laughter or a physical exclamation but most of all, a desperate wish to see it different.

Not everyone will agree, of course.

When Raskolnikov confesses his double murder he asks Sonia—'You think it's funny?'—before answering his own question:

> 'Well, yes, the funny part about it, Sonia, is that that's exactly how it was'. Sonia did not think it at all funny.[93]

---

93. Dostoevsky (n 79) 429.

iv

'bluebeard on trial': the experience of bathos

i. 'before': precedent as bathos	92
ii. 'never before': unprecedenting	96
unprecedenting past atrocity	98
unprecedenting past trials	101
critical precedents	104
iii. 'never again': re-precedenting	107

In the previous chapters, I made several promises. One was to apply some familiar literary devices to international legal projects in order to reveal something about why these projects so often begin with hope and end in disappointment. In this spirit, and here, I want to build on the ideas of irony circulated in chapter iii by examining the field of international criminal law through the device of bathos and the way it seems to organise the relations between the juridical convention of precedent and the politico-legal rhetoric around 'unprecedentedness'. This work on bathos picks up a theme present in the opening three chapters, too, where the languages of international law operate to both liberate us (from, say, incivility or brutishness) but also confine us in a prison house of linguistic restraints. As James Boyd White said, 'the lawyer is a user of words but like all such people, he

IV. 'BLUEBEARD ON TRIAL': THE EXPERIENCE OF BATHOS

must use them in a world of unexpressed and inexpressible experience'.[1] What happens when international legal languages begin to articulate what had long thought to be inexpressible, or unprecedented, experiences? Here, international (criminal) law, borrowing from Peter Gabel, could be understood as a form of 'alienated legal thought', a levelling down of longing.[2]

But in this chapter, I also want to offer another way of doing international law in the redemptive, practical vein that I said would be present throughout the book and which I said would involve offering some sort of answer to the perennial questions about what ought to be done. Here, I ask how we might construct a workable sentimental-juridical response to the remembrance of political violence.

Extreme political violence has generally been understood as a breach of international law's cardinal norms. This idea has been articulated through a variety of legal disciplines. In the international law on the use of force, a state is held 'responsible' for unlawful intrusions into, or annexations of, another state's territories. International human rights law, meanwhile, purports to shield individuals and groups from the repressive appetites of states themselves. In this chapter, I want to examine human rights law's 'corollary' field, international criminal law, a subsystem of international law dedicated to putting on trial those individuals most responsible for grave acts of political violence.

The history of international criminal law has been a largely stylised affair.[3] Landmarks and projects are remembered, misremembered (Nuremberg), and sometimes barely remembered at all (Tokyo, Versailles, Moscow 1937, the post-war critique of criminalisation). There are gaps (periods, say from 1948 to 1993, in which, it was said, nothing much happened); and there is an—often perfunctorily rendered—prehistory (the *von Hagenbach* trial—recruited by Telford Taylor to show that prosecution of defeated enemies before international tribunals 'was almost but not wholly unprecedented'—Leipzig,

---

1. James Boyd White, *The Legal Imagination* (Wolters Kluwer, 1973).
2. The phrase comes from Marius Pieterse, 'Eating Socioeconomic Rights', 29(3) *Human Rights Quarterly* (2007) 796–822, at 893. See also Martin Heidegger, Zollikon Seminars: Protocols—Conversations—Letters, ed. Medard Boss, trans. Franz K. Mayr and Richard R. Askay (Northwestern University Press, 2001) 49–50.
3. See e.g. M. Cherif Bassiouni, Crimes Against Humanity in International Criminal Law (Martinus Nijhoff, 1992).

Napoleon on Elba).[4] Meanwhile in its judicial-doctrinal life, the establishment of an international criminal law has necessitated a sometimes half-hearted search for a history of largely inadequate 'precedents' in the context of the punishment of acts that are also said to be 'unprecedented' or absent from history, and in the shadow of a suspicion that the criminalisation of such acts is itself 'unprecedented'.[5]

Putting all of this together, we might say that what we have is a law of unprecedentedness to which it could be useful to apply a counter-history of unprecedents or unprecedenting or, even, re-precedenting. This idea of 'unprecedents' (a neologism that, I admit, some people may find unattractive), then, ought to make visible some pathologies, elisions, repressions, around—and in one instance a possibility inherent in—international criminal law.

★ ★ ★

When German artists scanned history for monumental forms that could be revived or recuperated in the attempt to memorialise the Holocaust, they experienced past monuments as perpetually disappointing, incommensurable or 'overtaxed'.[6] In a similar vein, the idea of international criminal law (indeed law itself) as a somehow anti-climactic response to atrocity goes back at least to Karl Jaspers (in his correspondence with Arendt) and the idea that the Holocaust 'exploded the limits of the law'.[7] In the first part of this chapter (i. 'before': precedent as bathos'), then, I ask what it might mean to build precedent on the unprecedented; or to ground the unprecedented on precedent (or precedents that are not quite precedents). Here, as I say, international criminal law can be understood as a discipline performed in the style of *bathos*.

---

4. See e.g. Kevin Jon Heller and Gerry Simpson, The Hidden Histories of War Crimes Trials (Oxford University Press, 2013); Telford Taylor, Nuremberg and Vietnam: An American Tragedy (Bantam Books, 1997).
5. For a general history, along these lines, see Steven Ratner and Jason Abrams, Accountability for Human Rights Atrocities in International Law: Beyond the Nuremberg Legacy (Oxford University Press, 2000).
6. Julia Kristeva captures some of this sense in Black Sun: Depression and Melancholia (Columbia University Press, 1989): 'As if overtaxed or destroyed by too powerful a breaker, our symbolic means found themselves hollowed out, nearly wiped out, paralysed' (223).
7. See e.g. Hannah Arendt, Eichmann in Jerusalem: A Report on the Banality of Evil (Penguin 1994 [1963]) 253–279.

The second set of unprecedents encompasses historical events, legal proceedings or maverick figures that are written out of the official or semi-official histories of international criminal law (ii. 'never before': unprecedenting'). In the case of prior atrocity, these can precede (sometimes immediately) 'unprecedented' atrocity, and are occluded by the juridical memorialisation of the later atrocities. What we end up with is, in this instance, not so much a quest for precedents that must always seem deficient but instead an effort to manoeuvre past the historical precedents that do exist and are uncomfortably (because they feature the wrong sort of victim, or saintly perpetrators) close (historically, politically) to that which is being claimed as 'unprecedented'. Here there is a different sort of bathos in operation where the revelation of past atrocity serves to render the 'unprecedented' as unexceptional.

In the case of those legal proceedings that are seen as unappealing precursors, acts of unprecedenting ensure that these are seen either as unnatural siblings or are ignored altogether. Finally, there are those writers whose early critical scholarship has been actively 'un-precedented' by the rush to find the right sorts of precedents rather than the wrong sort of critique.

The chapter ends on a more hopeful, impressionistic note by calling international criminal law into a relationship with unadvertised or self-effacing acts of remembrance that could nonetheless be understood as part of the field of memory (the 'never again' field) in which international criminal law is located (iii. 'never again': re-precedenting'). Here the chapter offers a sort of shadow history of an international criminal law that didn't happen (or, at least, was not enacted through 'tribunality'). These unprecedents become something else altogether: not so much a hidden history of obscure trials, then, but a buried history of non-trials that might help reveal the conditions of possibility for the trials we do have: a de-memorialisation, perhaps even an embrace of bathetic memory.

So, this chapter concerns itself with the relationship between precedents (the lawful) and the unprecedented (the sublime) and the production of bathos in the exchange between the two, with three acts of unprecedenting in the field of international criminal law and, finally, with the possibility that some form of re-precedenting could be achieved through (anti-)monumentalism. Could monuments and, especially, the disappearing monuments of the German post-war style, act as both a form of remembrance, a prompt for a sentimental life of international law and as a reminder to think about what goes missing when we remember in trial or in stone?

i. 'before': precedent as bathos

It was a characteristic of early international criminal law that a search for precedents coexisted alongside obsessive declarations of 'unprecedentedness'.[8] The 'unprecedented' provided a moral and diplomatic basis for the invention of the field and its various novel doctrines. It is unprecedented outrage that engages—perhaps establishes the existence of—a 'conscience of mankind' so vital to the spirit behind these original tribunals. 'Crimes against humanity' (as legal category) are more or less unheard of before the 20th century because, the story goes, crimes against humanity (as sequence of brutal acts), too, were unheard of before that point. Meanwhile, the German invasion of Belgium in 1914 was the first 'crime against peace', because it was understood to be (or reconstructed as) the first invasion to violate an existing politico-legal code prohibiting undeclared, out-of-the-blue, acts of war.

But in an uncertain, bootstrapping move, the atrocity that has never been experienced before must, at the same time, be situated in a trajectory of juridical activity in response to analogous historical acts. And so international criminal law is dotted with a quest to discover precedents for the unprecedented.[9] This search for analogy becomes, I argue, a form of bathos, but it exists alongside various pronouncements declaring the absence of any need for such precedents in the case of sublime violence.[10]

In literary theory, bathos is used to describe a falling off, or a mismatch among various acts included in the same category but not quite belonging

---

8. James F. Willis, Prologue to Nuremberg: The Politics and Diplomacy of Punishing War Criminals of the First World War (Greenwood Press, 1982); 'International Military Tribunal (Nuremberg), Judgment and Sentences', 41(1) *American Journal of International Law* (1947) 172–333.
9. Sometimes these are literary: see e.g. Shakespearian precedents in Antonio Cassese, 'On the Current Trends towards Criminal Prosecution and Punishment of Breaches of International Humanitarian Law', 9(1) *European Journal of International Law* (1998) 2–17; Theodor Meron, 'The Humanization of Humanitarian Law' 94(2) *American Journal of International Law* (2000) 239–278, at 243.
10. Sara Crangle, Prosaic Desires: Modernist Knowledge, Boredom, Laughter, and Anticipation (Edinburgh University Press, 2010); Sara Crangle and Peter Nicholls (eds.), On Bathos (Bloomsbury Academic, 2010).

(or belonging in the same way) to that category, or a 'descent from the sublime to the ridiculous'.[11] This is usually intended to produce an ironic effect whereby the outlier is revealed as inadequate to the concept being illustrated or is comically incongruous: thus the t-shirt that lists the great cities of the world alongside the wearer's own small town: 'London–New York–Paris–Glenuig', or a verse that combines an injunction to the Gods to 'annihilate space and time' with a winking side-request that they also 'make two lovers happy'. This latter is from Alexander Pope who is said to have been the first to discourse on the idea of bathos in his *Peri Bathous, or the Art of Sinking in Poetry* (1727), where he explores depth and depthlessness through a series of vicious reviews of his contemporaries whose striving for the sublime but lack of profundity, he suggests, produces unintentionally ridiculous consequences.[12]

The sublime here refers to a literary encounter with the vast and metaphysical that exceeds the rules and constraints of hitherto existing literatures.[13] These are the terms, too, under which the engineers of international criminal law envisaged their role. Sublime atrocity did away with need for the old limitations. The Preliminary Peace Conference at Versailles begins, in this vein, with a speech by the President of the French Republic, Raymond Poincaré. War, for Poincaré, was a 'cataclysm' that had 'overwhelmed the universe'.[14] At the Imperial War Cabinet, too, Lloyd George is impatient with the existing norms: 'with regard to the question of international law, well, we are making international law'.[15] Meanwhile, at Nuremberg, the wrongdoing was so fearsome that the Allies did away with the usual legalistic conventions:

> The Tribunal shall not be bound by technical rules of evidence. It shall adopt and apply to the greatest possible extent expeditious a non-technical procedure, and shall admit any evidence which it deems to be of probative value.[16]

But if this sublime violence provokes an absence of restraint—a requirement that the existing order be abolished—at the same time, it gives rise to

---

11. Dinah Birch and Margaret Drabble (eds.), The Oxford Companion to English Literature (Oxford University Press, 2009) 103.
12. Crangle and Nicholls (n 10).
13. Birch and Drabble (n 11) 962.
14. Department of State, United States, Papers Relating to the Foreign Relations of the United States (US Government Printing Office, 1919) 159.
15. David Lloyd George, *The Truth about the Peace Treaties*, 1st edition (Victor Gollancz, 1938) 100.
16. Charter of the International Military Tribunal (1945), Article 19.

a falling off, a quest for norms that must inevitably be unequal to the task of capturing sublimity: the search for precursors always threatening a toppling over into anticlimax, an experience of bathos.

This combination of sublime violence and depthless evil is a signature of commentary on the Eichmann Trial where Eichmann's shallow wrongdoing provokes in Arendt a sense that the whole proceeding is '*stinknormal*, indescribably inferior, worthless'.[17] Indeed, in her *New Yorker* essays, Arendt contrasts Eichmann's thoughtlessness with the baroque evil of a Richard II or the imaginative, cunning will to destroy of someone like Iago. Eichmann is the very embodiment of bathos. He enters the District Court of Jerusalem with the audience anxiously awaiting the monster's entrance. Instead, 'everyone's next door neighbour' arrives.[18] Arendt is confronted with a ghost who 'minute by minute fades in substance'.[19] Eichmann's personification of bathos is given a spectral twist in Arendt's writing. He becomes more and more ghostly, his presence increasingly anticlimactic: the effort to implicate him in the cold-blooded murder of a Hungarian Jewish boy the last gasp of this failed effort to bring Eichmann to monstrous life.[20]

But if Eichmann is a disappointment, his precursors are even more so. Unprecedentedness haunts the pages of Arendt's book on Eichmann. As Ayça Çubukçu has pointed out, Arendt was determined to think of the Holocaust as utterly unprecedented, a system of atrocity in relation to which existing precedents were 'incompetent'.[21] For Arendt, the assault on the Jewish people in Europe was part of an effort to remove a race of human beings from the Earth. This was not simply a quantitative matter of scale and intensity (it was *not* about the 6 million dead) but rather a qualitative leap into a world in which human status itself was threatened.[22]

This was the essence of the crime that was not a crime.[23] According to Arendt, the precedents for such crimes could be found neither in existing international law (its 'well-known coins' of superior orders and act of state

---

17. See Elisabeth Young-Bruehl, Hannah Arendt: For Love of the World (Yale University Press, 1982) 329–331. Arendt came to regard the trial with less distaste as the proceedings continued. See Arendt (n 7) 331.
18. David Cesarani, Eichmann: His Life and Crimes (Random House, 2005) 257.
19. Ibid.
20. Hanna Yablonka, The State of Israel v Adolf Eichmann (Schocken Books, 2004) 240.
21. Ayça Çubukçu, 'On the Exception of Hannah Arendt', 15(3) *Law, Culture and the Humanities* (2015) 684–704.
22. Ibid.
23. Eichmann was no 'ordinary criminal', the Holocaust no 'ordinary crime', Arendt (n 7) 246.

were manifestly not up to the task) nor in general criminal law (these were not 'ordinary' crimes).[24] The Holocaust was for law, then, a Badiouesque event, exploding its epistemological and juridical surroundings and demanding new law.[25] But both at Nuremberg and in the Eichmann Trial, the respective courts initiated a bathetic search for precedent. At the International Military Tribunal (IMT), genocide is collapsed into wartime excess or is wrapped into crimes against peace (a crime containing 'the accumulated evil of the whole'). So, the Tribunal is concerned to pluck precedents from history in order to support the application of crimes against humanity or the crime of aggression to the defeated Nazis. Later, in Jerusalem the unprecedented is buried by the District Court 'under a flood of precedents'.[26]

The precedents themselves seem measly and strained: incommensurate to the task. The abduction of Eichmann is set alongside some US Supreme Court decisions in which suspects were snatched from Illinois by troopers based in Michigan. Pirates are plucked out of a history of pain and human misery in order to represent 'enemies of mankind'. The District Court of Jerusalem conjures an image of Adolf Eichmann as a Jolly Roger who happened to be placed in charge of a Europe-wide extermination programme (rather like the later case involving the Paraguayan Police Chief who takes Jose Filartiga to the station and inflicts unspeakable horrors on him as punishment for his father's political activities, and becomes a 'latter-day pirate').[27] But in the end, as Arendt remarks, the world's press had not gathered in Jerusalem to see Bluebeard on trial.

Indeed, it becomes hard to think of international criminal law in a non-bathetic mode. In 1919, the Commission on the Responsibility of the Authors of the War offers up a startling list of German iniquities. These, surely, are the most horrible, indeed, unprecedented, violations that human beings could commit? But this list is odd because it contains a built-in bathos. The atrocities resemble a musical hall joke where grave offence is punctuated by trivial violation as if man's inhumanity to man could be captured in the failure of an occupying authority to deliver the mail. But

---

24. Ibid. 135.
25. On the application to international law of Badiou's idea of the event, see Gerry Simpson, 'Paris 1793 and 1872', in Fleur Johns, Sundhya Pahuja and Richard Joyce (eds.), Events in International Law (Routledge, 2011) Chapter 7.
26. Çubukçu (n 21); Arendt (n 7) 263.
27. *Filartiga v. Pena-Irala* (1980) 2d Cir. 630 F.2d 876; Eugene Kontorovich, 'The Piracy Analogy: Modern Universal Jurisdiction's Hollow Foundation', 45(1) *Harvard International Law Journal* (2004) 183–237.

then, maybe, the juridification of war itself is an exercise in bathos. Siegfried Sassoon's 'butchered, frantic gestures of the dead' become, in the eye of the law, 'serious violations of the laws of war'. One senses very clearly here the dropping away.

International criminal law's institutional history, too, is constructed around this sort of bathos.[28] The proposed trial of the century at Versailles becomes a smattering of local proceedings in Leipzig; the post-war hesitancies of the Great Powers becomes a 'customary international law' found by the House of Lords in *R v. Jones* [2006] in a sequence of interwar failures (a draft convention for this, a mutual pact with one signatory for that, a treaty to end all wars except those the signatories want to fight); the late 20th century sees a history of little old Nazis (beloved by their grandchildren) staggering to the dock to account for one of the greatest genocides in history; the International Criminal Court (ICC), established in a flush of pomp, ceremony and the promise of transformative justice, begins with the jailing of a relatively minor figure like Lubanga for having deployed child soldiers.[29] Meanwhile, the persistent deployment of phrases such as 'crimes against humanity' or 'genocide' or 'gross violations of human rights' transforms juridical innovations into slogans, the life drained from them. In the end, it all begins to resemble a scene in Don DeLillo's *White Noise*, where Professor Gladney is being celebrated by a junior colleague for having invented Hitler Studies:

> 'You've established a wonderful thing here with Hitler', he tells Gladney. 'You created it, you nurtured it ... He is now your Hitler. I marvel at the effort. It was masterful, shrewd and stunningly pre-emptive. It's what I want to do with Elvis'.[30]

The history of international criminal law is a history best understood as bathetic, a history of Elvises recruited as precedents for Hitlers.

ii. 'never before': unprecedenting

At noon, on 20 November 1918, Lord Curzon is urging the Imperial War Cabinet to support a trial of the Kaiser: 'The supreme and colossal

---

28. See 'Commission on the Responsibility of the Authors of the War and the Enforcement of Penalties', *14*(1–2) *American Journal of International Law, Supplement* (1920) 95–154, 107, 112–125 and Annex II, 127, 135–154.
29. *Lubanga Case (The Prosecutor v. Thomas Lubanga Dyilo)* Case No ICC-01/04-01/06.
30. Don DeLillo, White Noise (Viking Press, 1985) 11–12.

nature of his crime seems to call for some supreme and unprecedented condemnation'.[31]

Thus does international criminal justice begin, with a reference to an unprecedented violence that finally provokes—and must give rise to—the establishment of legal order.[32] On one hand though, and this has been the subject of the first section of the chapter, this violence is situated in a pattern of history, a trajectory of such acts (each more 'unprecedented' than the next but each requiring a gesture to precedent). The most recent atrocity in this historical sequence becomes the moment when failure to act or constitute law becomes unforgivable. On the other hand, and this is the subject of the first part of this second section, the proximate historical juncture is one of a kind, a never-before-seen moment of human savagery. So, the slogan of international criminal law—'never again'—needs to be supplemented by the slogan 'never before'. In this sense, international criminal law imagines itself to be constructed around one point in time, that is, the 'never before, never again' moment: the unprecedented atrocity, wrenched from history, that ends all atrocity. This requires a screening out of previous atrocities in the name of unprecedenting. Humanity must be rendered innocent. And this unprecedenting occurs in relation to two other 'pasts' of international criminal justice as well. In one case, awkward trial precedents are forgotten or obscured. In the other, there is the unprecedenting of what we might think of as early anti-anti-impunity advocates. These three acts of unprecedenting are the subject of the rest of this section of the chapter.

---

31. *Imperial War Cabinet 37, CAB 23/43* (1918).
32. Though this might first be an only liminally lawful order. For Arendt, the unprecedented aspect of the Eichmann case was the kidnapping of the suspect in Buenos Aires by Israeli agents (though she also believed that the special nature of Israeli sovereignty and especially the imperative to think of the Jewish diaspora as a proto-sovereign collective, was unprecedented and misunderstood). Arendt gives the kidnapping a very detached seal of approval: 'Those who are convinced that justice, and nothing else, is the end of law will be inclined to condone the kidnapping act' (Arendt (n 7) 265). This is because of the absence of a satisfactory lawful alternative. But this cannot become a precedent. Indeed, it is a 'desperate, unprecedented and no-precedent setting act' (ibid.). This raises the obvious question: why cannot this be a precedent for similar desperate, now re-precedented acts? The conditions of necessity can bear repetition, after all. (There is a darker explanation for Arendt's unprecedenting act here. 'What are we going to say if tomorrow it occurs to *some African state* to send its agents into Mississippi and to kidnap one of the segregationist leaders there?'. See ibid. 264.) In 1949, Ethiopia (unsuccessfully) asked Italy to extradite various individuals responsible for the invasion of Abyssinia. See C. Miglioli, *La sanzione nel diritto internazionale* (Giuffrè, 1951) 69 (quoted in Danilo Zolo, *Victors' Justice* (Polity, 2006) fn 60).

unprecedenting past atrocity

In 1944, Georg Schwarzenberger wrote, in his book *Totalitarian Lawlessness*, '[T]he human mind revolts at the idea of covering these deeds with an all-forgetting mantle of oblivion'.[33] And yet, one international law counter-history is a history of this 'revolting idea' in action. The legal-diplomatic demand has traditionally been for amnesia not remembrance. The history of international criminal law is, in a way, a history of trials not convened, prosecutions not initiated, investigations not begun: not a rising to the occasion but a falling away.[34] Impunity might be understood as international criminal law's state of nature. As Malcolm Bull once said, 'states didn't mind their citizens dying as long as another state didn't do the killing'.[35] International criminal law was the law of impunity. One gets a sense of this in, say, the treatment of Napoleon after the Napoleonic Wars. His time on Elba—now regarded as a too merciful interregnum—was an impunity that represented, also, a form of mature politics. But more than this, if a reader picks up, say, a history of the Concert of Europe 1815–1914 and reads its passages on war crimes trials or looks for a reference to ending impunity, well, such references are simply not there. Nobody, bar a handful of bloodthirsty Prussians, was interested in trying Napoleon for atrocities or invasion.

Recently, I read some of the documents emerging from the Congress of Vienna and my initial impression was that these read as if they had been edited in some way. There are ellipses where there should be trials. Instead of thunderous calls for retribution we have a gentler language of diplomatic nicety: 'The object of this union is as simple as it is great ... calm and consistent in its proceedings, it has no other object than the maintenance of peace'.[36]

---

33. Georg Schwarzenberger, International Law and Totalitarian Lawlessness (Cape, 1943) 57.
34. This is true even of the contemporary scene. See Leslie Vinjamuri and Jack Snyder, 'Trials and Errors', *28*(3) *International Security* (2003) 5–44.
35. Malcolm Bull, 'State of Exception', *26*(24) *London Review of Books* (2004) 3–6.
36. See *Declaration of the Five Cabinets*, Aix-la-Chapelle, 15 November 1818. Or maybe a better way to put this is to notice that where there was anti-impunity, it involved not legalised retribution but either diplomatic censure (states indicating disapproval by withdrawing certain privileges and by declaring diplomatic staff *persona non grata*) or exemplary punishment. It's not as if the pre-modern treatise can't be quite bloodthirsty. Lawrence, for example, is sanguine (sanguinary, in fact) when it comes to the treatment of unauthorised combatants (those whose crime is fighting back against an occupier). The laws of war, he avers, allowed the summary execution of such individuals. See Thomas Lawrence, The Principles of International Law, Part 2 (D.C. Heath, 1985) 332–333.

IV. 'BLUEBEARD ON TRIAL': THE EXPERIENCE OF BATHOS

The high-point of impunity—perhaps, also a turning point—came when Hitler celebrated, and provoked the end of, this impunity with his famous question: 'Who remembers the Armenians?' This was, more or less, the sort of amnesia demanded by the Treaty of Munster back in 1648:

> That there shall be on the one side and the other a perpetual ... Amnesty, or Pardon of all that has been committed since the beginning of these Troubles ... but that all that has pass'd on the one side, and the other ... during the War, shall be bury'd in eternal Oblivion.

International law was—to restate the point—the law of oblivion.

So, at least one political-historical project for international criminal law would be aimed at detecting the history inscribed in the legal form but read out of it, the blood in the code—even a code as bloodless as the *Draft Code on Crimes Against the Peace and Security of Mankind*.[37] This might be a history of atrocity or preventable deaths actively forgotten or subject to un-remembering.[38] I have written elsewhere about this in relation to Jacques Vergès' rupture strategy during the trial of Klaus Barbie and the various acts of un-remembering conducted at Nuremberg, so here, in the interests of time and space, I will go back to one of the origins of international criminal law for an act of un-remembering, one subject to the historical laws of irony.[39]

---

37. Michel Foucault, Lectures at the College de France 1975–1976, 21 January 1976 (Picador, 2003) 56. About half way through this lecture, Foucault re-describes the idea that becomes critical international criminal law: '[This discourse] is not interested in passing judgement on unjust governments, or on crimes and acts of violence, by referring them to a certain ideal schema (that of natural law, the will of God, basic principles and so on). On the contrary, it is interested in defining and discovering beneath the forms of justice that have been instituted, the order that has been imposed'.
38. Stanley Cohen, 'State Crimes of Previous Regimes: Knowledge, Accountability, and the Policing of the Past', 20(1) *Law and Social Inquiry* (1995) 7–50; Carlos Nino, Radical Evil on Trial (Yale University Press, 1996); Ed Morgan, 'Retributory Theater', 3(1) *Journal of International Law and Policy* (1988) 1–64, at 62 (noting, in respect of the Demjanjuk trial, that 'in describing dramatically ... the nightmarish events that occurred (what now seems to be) a lifetime ago, the victims are given another chance to purge the past and celebrate its having passed'); Shoshana Felman, 'Theaters of Justice: Arendt in Jerusalem, the Eichmann Trial, and the Redefinition of Legal Meaning in the Wake of the Holocaust', 27(2) *Theoretical Inquiries in Law* (2000) 465, at 498 ('it is this revolutionary transformation of the victim that makes the victim's story happen for the first time and happen as a legal act of authorship of history').
39. E.g. Gerry Simpson, 'The Conscience of Mankind and Its Discontents: A Counter-History of International Criminal Law', in Phillip Kastner (ed.), The Handbook of International Criminal Law (Routledge, 2018) 11–27. See also Jose E. Alvarez, 'Rush to Closure: Lessons of the Tadić Judgment', 96(7) *Michigan Law Review* (1998) 2061.

It begins, again, with Raymond Poincaré, announcing, at the opening of the Versailles Peace Conference: 'Humanity can place confidence in you, because you are not among those who have outraged the rights of humanity'.[40] But humanity here included the Belgians, French and British, each of whom were, by this time, responsible for three centuries of sometimes violent, certainly racially-inflected, Empire.

Later at Versailles, a list is produced of German outrages, but this list has both a strangely proleptic and backward-looking quality; what is being described is not unprecedented violation but both historical massacres and yet-to-be witnessed atrocity. The Allies—busy documenting German 'crimes', seeking to bring them into existence as 'crimes'—inadvertently describe a set of atrocities that do not occur in Europe until the 1940s. The Great War atrocities, meanwhile, were inflated, sometimes fabricated. Indeed, the bayoneted Belgian babies of occupation mythology have become a byword for war propaganda (this did not stop the once-estimable UK newspaper, *The Daily Telegraph*, from putting on its 1990 front page a story about the Iraqi invaders throwing Kuwaiti babies out of incubators—a story subsequently shown to be false). There was no evidence for the atrocities reported by the Allies of maimed Belgian children, their hands hacked off by German soldiers. Elsewhere, though, there was plenty of evidence of this practice: 'the reference—a Freudian one perhaps—was to the policy of documenting killings in the rubber region of The Congo. This was, of course, forgotten, or remembered as humanitarian'.[41]

Though the Imperial War Cabinet meeting on 20 November 1918 began at noon, there was a lot to get through.[42] The main line of business was the disposition of the Kaiser. What were the representatives of humanity going to do about this outlaw? But first, there were some minor matters to take care of. Lloyd George: 'there are two or three questions we are not clear about . . . Palestine, East Africa . . . questions of that kind . . . We have not quite settled either in our minds *what sort of government we will set up* in Mesopotamia'.[43] It was ever thus. Here are the representatives of civilisation, just prior to elaborating the idea that aggressive war would be a crime

---

40. *Documents, Paris Peace Conference* (n 14) 159.
41. Adam Hothschild, King Leopold's Ghost (Mariner Books, 1998) 296.
42. Imperial War Cabinet Meeting 37, 20 November 1918, at http://filestore.nationalarchives.gov.uk/pdfs/large/cab-23-43.pdf.
43. Ibid. 2 (emphasis added).

against humanity, reordering their imperial outposts, themselves, as Justice Pal remarked at Tokyo, the result of three centuries of aggressive war.

I went back recently to the National Archive documentation from this meeting. How did the Imperial War Cabinet get from its own imperial consolidations and restructurings to the enemy's crimes against humanity? After all, they each seemed to be grounded on precisely the same combination of non-consensual territorial acquisition and mass violations of human rights. Was there a hint of self-consciousness? What was the hinge?

Between the surprisingly cursory discussion of Palestine, Syria and Iraq and the lengthier debate about the Kaiser there is one short announcement. A telegram is read out from the Association of Universal Loyal Negroes of Panama. It reads:

> Negroes throughout Panama send congratulations on your victory and in return for services rendered by the negroes throughout the world in fighting ... beg that their heritage wrested from Germany in Africa may become the negro national home with self-government.[44]

This is passed over in silence—and with it a counter-history of international criminal law that might have something to say about the massacre of the Herero or Leopold's psychopathic occupation of the Congo. The discussion then moves on to the Kaiser's terrible crime of making war on Europe and the shock this delivered to the conscience of mankind. Not all deaths, it seems, are given precedential value.[45]

unprecedenting past trials

But it is not just un-prosecuted atrocity that constitutes a counter-history of international criminal law. Precursor trials, too, are forgotten.

Usually, the history of war crimes trials passes over the interwar years in silence. This was a period in which the efforts of progressives seem to be directed at social and economic change, or minority rights treaties or welfare or the sort of softer internationalism found in Geneva. But are the Moscow Show Trials, perhaps, the missing link between Versailles and Nuremberg?

---

44. Ibid. 6. See also UK National Archives, Document No CO 323/800, Foreign Office Correspondence Folios 41–54.
45. Judith Butler, Precarious Life: The Powers of Mourning and Violence (Verso, 2006); Gerry Simpson, 'Linear Law: A History of International Criminal Law', in Christine Schwöbel (ed.), Critical Approaches to International Criminal Law (Routledge, 2014) 159–179.

Moscow 1937 is an embarrassing antecedent after all. Judith Shklar defines show trials as the liquidation of political enemies using legal procedure.[46] Stalin knew all about that, but, in this, he does not seem too far removed from Lloyd George and Lord Curzon. Establishing a tribunal for the specific purpose of liquidating or punishing an enemy? This is what the Imperial War Cabinet was debating in 1918.

Of course, in many very important respects, the Moscow Show Trials were very unlike the Nuremberg War Crimes proceedings, but the idea that people's justice or humanity's justice or a sense of justice can somehow dispose of the need for proper procedure or legal precedent represents a sort of sibling (and bathetic) dark side to these trials. A show trial is one in which it is obvious that the guilty are guilty, the mere performance of a justice already delivered elsewhere. Vishinsky, the Soviet Prosecutor at Moscow, was also at Nuremberg. During dinner with the judges at Nuremberg he raises a toast 'To the defendants, they will all hang'. This was before the trial had begun. Roosevelt, too, was worried about acquittals and his concerns made their way into Article 19 of the IMT Charter (1945).

But then maybe these trials are as much about political spectacle as they are about legal propriety. For Hannah Arendt, a show trial is a 'spectacle with prearranged results' or the obliteration through compulsive staging of 'the irreducible risk' of acquittal.[47] The point of the trial is the trial itself: its ramifications, its warnings, its effluxions of terror.

George Orwell, for example, understood this. In *1984*, Mrs. Parsons lives with her two little daemonic children at Victory Mansions; her drains are blocked, as they often are, and she calls Winston Smith down to help her unblock the sink. The two children torment Winston, calling him a Eurasian spy, threatening to vaporise him and shouting 'Goldstein' as he leaves the flat. Mrs. Parsons is apologetic; the children are furious, she explains, because she failed to take them to the hanging:

> Some Eurasian prisoners, guilty of war crimes, were to be hanged that evening ... this happened once a month and was a popular spectacle.[48]

It strikes me as important to think about trials in this way; not as depoliticised programmes of management but as slightly wild-eyed theatres of

---

46. Judith Shklar, *Legalism* (Harvard University Press, 1964) 149.
47. See also Otto Kirchheimer, Political Justice (Princeton University Press, 1961).
48. George Orwell, *1984* (Penguin, 1974 [1949]).

revenge: human rights with a vengeance. As one of the observers of the Moscow Show Trials eerily put it: these were 'dramas of subjective innocence and objective guilt'.[49] This objective guilt was repeatedly enunciated in the months preceding the major trials at Nuremberg and Tokyo, where the Nazis were described as the world's worst criminals and where the defendants were chosen on the basis of political impact. The show trials, themselves, continued into the 1950s, most famously in Prague, where the purpose was not to determine guilt or innocence, nor, even, to remove political opponents, but rather to create them. The trials there were initially conceived as trials of fairly low-level *apparatchiks*. Under pressure from Moscow, President Gottwald found a higher-level defendant, Otto Sling, a district party secretary. Under torture, Sling implicated Rudolf Slansky, the General Secretary of the Czech Communist Party, in a fantastic and implausible conspiracy. Finally, the Soviet advisers had a defendant of sufficient seniority. The Czechs were initially shocked and bemused. What about the evidence? One Soviet legal adviser, soon himself to be purged, reminded the Czechs that he had been sent to stage trials not to check whether the charges were true.

As for the existence of legal norms. Again, this didn't matter. The instincts of the proletariat would stand in for what Kyrlenko, one of the Moscow prosecutors, called 'bourgeois sophistry'. And this recalls, too, a Nazi law of 28 June 1935 referring to the need to punish criminals and deviants according to 'the sound perceptions of the people'. Ten years later, though, President Roosevelt was worrying about acquittals on technicalities, and Robert Jackson—pressed on the existence of crimes against humanity or aggression—replied by saying 'We can avoid these pitfalls of definition if our test of what is a crime gives recognition to those things which fundamentally outrage the conscience of the American people'.[50] The victims of war crimes had become the people in general. Legalism remained the only viable solution. This became, at trial, the idea of 'shocking the conscience of mankind'.[51] Moscow is one sort of precedent for this sort of meta-legality. The need for supreme law in the face of sublime violence in turn produced a bathetically lawless origin.

---

49. Maurice Merleau-Ponty, *Humanism and Terror* (Beacon Press, 1969), 202.
50. Robert Jackson, *Report to the President,* 7 June 1945, section 5.
51. This section is partly drawn from Simpson (n 39).

critical precedents

The third act of unprecedenting I consider in this section concerns a largely forgotten unprecedented hidden history of critique in international criminal law.

In the post–Second World War era, there was a period of resistance to criminalisation, when books by Rebecca West (*A Train of Powder*), F. J. P. Veale (*Advance to Barbarism*), Montgomery Belgion (*Victors' Justice*) and Freda Uttley (*High Cost of Vengeance*) rejected the assumptions of Tokyoberg retribution and opened up the way for later figures like Shklar and Arendt.[52] The period 1946–1949 is the moment, too, of the great anti-anti-impunity dissent of Justice Pal. I have written elsewhere and extensively about Pal, and the Australian poet, Barry Hill, has published a monumental study of (among many, many other things) Pal and Tagore, so I will leave him for the time being.[53]

There is one particular moment, though, I want to focus on here, and that is the period 1949–1950, when the Bishop of Chichester, George Bell, appealed to the House of Lords for an end to the punishment of German war criminals, and Maurice Hankey published the first full treatment of anti-anti-impunity in his *Politics, Trials and Errors*.[54]

Bell is one of the most interesting church figures of the mid-century. During the Second World War, he offered his home to a number of Jewish refugees, he protested against the carpet-bombing of Germany and he was in close contact with members of the German resistance before and during the Stauffenberg plot. He was an ardent supporter of German rehabilitation after the war and saw the later war crimes trials both as damaging distraction and unseemly vindictiveness. When I encountered Bell in my reading, it seemed natural to me that he should be against both the trials (with their concomitant executions) and the bombings. He was a member, if you like, of the anti-death league.[55]

---

52. See also J. P. Veale, Advance to Barbarism (C. C. Nelson, 1953); Montgomery Belgion, Victors' Justice: A Letter Intended to Have Been Sent to a Friend Recently in Germany (lulu.com, 2017); George (n 15) 94–114.
53. Barry Hill, Peacemongers (University of Queensland Press, 2015).
54. Maurice Hankey, Politics, Trials and Errors (Pen-In-Hand, 1950).
55. The reference is to Kingsley Amis' novel, *The Anti-Death League*. As many people have pointed out, there can be a merging or, at least, alignment of humanitarian and military sensibilities and languages in contemporary international law and military policy. In this way, responsibility to protect and international criminal law can be understood as a shared project of exemplary punishment. David Kennedy is essential here. See Of Law and War (Princeton University

At 5.20pm on 5 May 1949, Bell spoke in the House of Lords against anti-impunity. For Bell, merciful treatment of our enemies is the test of 'our reputation of justice and humanity'.[56] When it comes to justice, he goes on to say: 'it is very difficult for a defeated foe to appreciate the justice of punishing such crimes ... when similar charges could be brought against one or more of the allies'. This is a familiar enough charge of victors' justice.[57] But what is now strikingly unfamiliar is Bell's powerful language of clemency (he calls for a 'permanent clemency programme'), the explicit pleas for 'general amnesty', the concern for the well-being of the imprisoned Nazis in Spandau, the reminder that anti-impunity can result in seventy-six trials, sixty-seven death sentences and no acquittals (the case of the Yugoslav war crimes trials), the belief that there must be some end to penal process (this is not *infinite* justice) and, finally, a recognition of the impossibility of trying even a fraction of offenders (even anti-impunity is always a form of mediated impunity, or a landscape of bathetic impunity dotted with the occasional sublime trial).

Very little of this mood survived the enthusiasm for international criminal justice. During the 1949 debates, Bell was defended by Maurice (Lord) Hankey, a former Secretary of the Imperial War Cabinet and member of the 1939–1940 War Cabinet. Hankey's attack on the policy of unconditional surrender and anti-impunity is extremely robust. This policy produced, according to him, 'a sadistic orgy of competitive frightfulness ... frantic war crimes on one side, and, on the other, unlimited bombing'.[58] In addition to this, he elaborated the problems of decontextualisation, over-individualisation and bad history that were hinted at in 1919 and became a form of critique by the early 21st century.[59] The debate in the House of Lords continued into the night of 19 May, but this time concerned the Tokyo War Crimes Trials. Hankey was traduced by several speakers as unpatriotic. It was claimed that

---

Press, 2006) and Dark Side of Virtue: Reassessing International Humanitarianism (Princeton University Press, 2005) especially.

56. *HL (Hansard)* (1949) vol. 162 cc.
57. General Montgomery had said, too, that Nuremberg made the waging of unsuccessful war a crime.
58. *HL (Hansard)* (1949) vol. 162 cc, 11.
59. Karen Engle, Zina Miller and Dennis Davis (eds.), Anti-Impunity and the Human Rights Agenda (Cambridge University Press, 2016); Christine Schwöbel (ed.), Critical Approaches to International Criminal Law: An Introduction (Routledge, 2016); Frédéric Mégret, 'The Politics of International Criminal Justice', 13(5) *European Journal of International Law* (2002) 1261–1284.

he had defamed the Soviet judges at Nuremberg and over-concerned himself with the irrelevant history of the 1920s. By the time he rose to respond at the end of the debate, it was too late. Hankey ended by saying: 'The House is so empty now that it is no good my challenging ... I shall not reply to the other speakers because they have all gone'.[60]

Little wonder, then, that Hankey wrote *Politics, Trials and Errors* as a response to his absent interlocutors. The victors' justice argument remained front and centre, but Hankey had the added advantage of immediacy and proximity. He visited Rotterdam at Christmas, 1948, and discovered two wastelands—one inflicted by the Germans at the beginning of the war, the other visited upon the city by the Allies during the liberation of Western Europe.[61] He noticed that the Universal Declaration on Human Rights (UNDHR) and the IMT Charter work against each other (Article 10 of the UNDHR requiring independent and impartial judicial enquiries and Article 11 prohibiting the imposition of retroactive law). He wrote as political leaders were tried and executed in the Eastern Bloc under conditions of imperfect justice and by tribunals composed entirely of former enemies.[62] Hankey argued (borrowing from Pal) that international criminal law seemed too often unconcerned with the methods of liquidation. According to Pal, the usurpation of 'lawful authority' resulted in a reversion to a period in which the victor could do as he pleased with the vanquished. And commentators have pointed out that the complementarity provisions in the Rome Statute work in a similar manner. When it comes to local jurisdictions, the ICC worries about impunity but not about punitiveness. There is much greater outrage that Libya has refused to release Saif Gaddafi to the Court than there was about the slaying of his father, allegedly by a French agent.

At the end of his book, Hankey—by now in full anti-punitive flight—calls for a sort of Armistice Day but not, he goes on, a day of remembrance but rather one when 'prisoners would be released and reunited with their families and the politics, trials and errors of the war would be effaced for ever more'.[63] Recalling the Treaty of Munster 300 years before, he suggests that this be called a 'Day of Oblivion', a day of un-remembering.

---

60. *HL (Hansard)* (1949) vol. 162 cc., 21.
61. Hankey (n 54) 126.
62. I have written elsewhere about Rudolf Slansky. Hankey writes about Nikola Petkov, the leader of the Bulgarian Agrarian Party, executed in September 1947 in a trial resembling, for Hankey, the Tokyo War Crimes Trials.
63. Hankey (n 54) 145.

iii. 'never again': re-precedenting

But oblivion is not always quite the appropriate response.

In post-war Germany, a new style of Holocaust commemoration began to emerge. James Young called its exemplars 'anti-monuments'.[64] A common feature of the anti-monument was a material absence or radical fragility intended to restate historical memory as ruptural, tentative, and suspect. So, some monuments simply were not 'there'. Others were designed to slowly disappear. Still others refused orthodox memory or solidity or inscription by permitting and encouraging plebeian engagement with the anti-monument (e.g. graffiti). Often, what was being marked, of course, was the absence of something (Jewish children, say, in Munster), and the marking of this absence could only be itself achieved through some sort of gap or slow, physical recession.

This chapter has tried to come to terms with historical absence and remembrance in the field of international criminal law by sketching the outlines of an anti-history, maybe an anti-monumental history, a history grounded in bathetic disjunctions, a recognition of international law's amnesiac inclinations: one kind of literary international law.[65] International war crimes trials can be thought of here as international criminal law's official or semi-official monuments. The absence of trial might indicate, for lawyers especially, a past without a history; a history lacking a permanent juridical marker might suggest a past hardly worth remembering. But perhaps the act of not-prosecuting or not remembering needs to be understood, too, as a form of international criminal law. Monuments, as we know, do not simply fail to remember: they actively 'unremember' that which is not commemorated.[66] So, just as monuments unremember acts of history, trials sometimes erase those 'crimes' not juridified. The contemporary history of German

---

64. James E. Young, '"Memory and Counter-Memory" 9', 1 *Harvard Design Magazine* (2017), at http://www.harvarddesignmagazine.org/issues/9/memory-and-counter-memory>.
65. On (a different) monumental history, see Friedrich Nietzsche, The Advantage and Disadvantage of History for Life (Standard Publications, 2008 [1874]).
66. In Alan Bennett's play, *The History Boys*, we hear Tom Irwin say:

    And all the mourning's veiled the truth. It's not 'lest we forget', it's 'lest we remember'. That's what all this is about—the memorials, the Cenotaph, the two minutes' silence. Because there is no better way of forgetting something than by commemorating it. Alan Bennett, The History Boys (Faber, 2004).

anti-monuments might get us thinking about how to think about absence and memory while resisting the call for more and more trials.[67]

Rather like the UN forces at Pusan during the Korean War, international criminal lawyers have become adept at defending a tinier and tinier beachhead of justifications for their project of criminalising atrocity. The standard rationales for sending people to jail in reasonably functional domestic carceral systems seem somehow inadequate or puny or not fit for purpose when applied to the world of international crimes.[68] So, lawyers have sought out alternative justifications or rearranged the existing ones.[69] We have had the recuperation of expressivist justifications for international criminal law or didactic jurisprudences or arguments that convictions at least remove malefactors from the political system.[70] Dissatisfaction with carceralism itself has resulted in a focus on other mechanisms for delivering justice or providing redress. This goes back to the attention given to reparations in the human rights system and the focus on victims and victim-redress in the field of international criminal law itself.[71] Meanwhile in the field of transitional justice, there is a commitment to the pursuit of consolation through non-punitive mechanisms within the broader context of establishing decent, post-traumatic societies.[72] This emphasis brings in its train a set of problems, inevitably, but it also opens up space to think about succour in a more expansive, perhaps, better way.[73]

---

67. On the turn to objects and materiality, see Jesse Hohmann and Dan Joyce, International Law's Objects (Oxford University Press, 2018), esp. Hohmann, 'The Lives of Objects', 30–47.
68. For more on this, see Immi Tallgren's influential 'The Sense and Sensibility of International Criminal Law', 13(3) *European Journal of International Law* (2002) 561–595. I am excluding the United States (where around a million African-American men are imprisoned) from this group.
69. Mirjan R. Damaska, 'What Is the Point of International Criminal Justice?', 83(1) *Chicago Kent Law Review* (2008).
70. On expressivism, see Mark Drumbl, Atrocity, Punishment and International Law (Cambridge University Press, 2007); on didactic jurisprudence. See Lawrence Douglas, The Memory of Judgement: Making Law and History in the Trials of the Holocaust (Yale University Press, 2005).
71. See United Nations General Assembly (UNGA), *Basic Principles and Guidelines on the Right to a Remedy and Reparation for Victims of Gross Violations of International Human Rights Law and Serious Violations of International Humanitarian Law* (adopted 21 March 2006), Articles 15(3), 53 and 75 of UNGA, *Rome Statute of the International Criminal Court* (last amended 2010, 17 July 1998). See Carla Ferstman, 'The Reparations Regime of the International Court of Justice', 15(3) *Leiden Journal of International Law* (2002) 667–686. On restitution, see Article 23, *Statute of the International Criminal Tribunal for the Prosecution of Persons Responsible for Genocide and Other Serious Violations of International Humanitarian Law Committed in the Territory of Rwanda* (1995).
72. Ruti Teitel, Transitional Justice (Oxford University Press, 2000).
73. On 'succour', see Mark Drumbl, 'Succour', unpublished essay on file.

The problems are well documented. There are difficulties of proportion. Is reparation equal to the task? Is (monetary) compensation tasteless, or depoliticising or just plain inadequate?[74] Might it not simply divide communities into those victimised by kinetic violence and those harmed by structural wrongs? The danger with reparation, indeed victimicity itself, is that it might create a class of people who are victims but nothing else.[75] Then there is the difficulty of scale: so many victims, so little in the trust fund. In 2008, the Victims Trust Fund had, in its account for all victims of crimes 'within the jurisdiction of the Court', about half the money recently paid for the house two doors down from my apartment in London. Finally, though hardly exhaustively, there is the problem of hitching compensation to international criminal law. Is reparation then dependent on some prior finding of individual responsibility: life chances determined by the vicissitudes of someone-else's criminal responsibility?[76]

One response to all of this is to incorporate the symbolic or didactic responses to atrocity into the heart of the discipline. The beachhead is small (war crimes trials fail to deter, punish or rehabilitate, but they can be defended by reference to their capacity to symbolise loss, or register in important ways the pain of others), but on the other hand it could be expanded (by including within the remit of international criminal justice, other acts that perform precisely these symbolic tasks).

Linda Keller and Fred Mégret have issued pleas to think about shrines or memorials or bridges as forms of reparative justice or acts of juridical remembrance.[77] Mégret has pointed to sites of conscience as ways to preserve memory and offer solace.[78] Monuments can 'provide places of mourning, remembrance and contemplation for victims and their relatives'.[79] As well as this, they can help attribute responsibility, provide a sense of acknowledgement of suffering and collectivise victimhood. As Mégret points out in his essay, the idea of building monuments has taken root in international

---

74. See Alma Begicevic, *'Money as Justice'* (Melbourne University, unpublished dissertation, 2018).
75. See chapter ii.
76. For a more comprehensive engagement with the problems of reparation, see Frédéric Mégret, 'Of Shrines, Memorials and Museums: Using the International Criminal Court's Victim Reparation and Assistance Regime to Promote Transitional Justice', *SSRN* (2009) 12–18.
77. Linda Keller, 'Seeking Justice at the International Criminal Court: Victims' Reparations', *29(2) Thomas Jefferson Law Review* (2006) 189–219, at 210–212.
78. See also Martha Minow, Between Vengeance and Forgiveness: Facing History after Genocide and Mass Violence (Beacon Press, 1998).
79. Mégret (n 76) 24.

institutions and in the decisions of courts themselves (in particular the Inter-American Court of Human Rights).[80] And sometimes these court decisions are very explicit about how the monument should be constructed, where it should be positioned, who should be consulted in its design and whether and what accompanying text should be included.

Recently I wrote about the trial, execution and memorialisation of the English nurse, Edith Cavell.[81] The Cavell case seems to represent a kind of origin for international criminal law: a precedent but also an opportunity for some re-precedenting. A few weeks after Edith Cavell's execution, an Edith Cavell War Memorial Committee was formed.[82] It was composed of the usual aristocratic worthies, including Viscount Burnham, the owner of the *Daily Telegraph*. The Committee wrote to Cavell's family asking them how they would like to see Cavell commemorated.[83]

The (Nietzschean) reply duly arrived: 'no monuments'. The family asked that the money be used to build a nursing home for retired nurses instead.[84]

One response to monumentalism (trial, stone, conviction, hanging) is to move towards a form of non-punitive restitution (a nursing home, reparations, money). Another is to engage in anti-monumentalism (the critique of international criminal law, the rehabilitation of historical antecedents for

---

80. See e.g. *Case of the Moiwana Community v. Suriname, Series C No. 124, Inter-American Court of Human Rights (IACrtHR)* (15 June 2005); *Case of Myrna Mack Chang v. Guatemala, Series C No. 101, Inter-American Court of Human Rights (IACrtHR)* (25 November 2003).
81. See Gerry Simpson, 'Human Rights with a Vengeance: One Hundred Years of Retributive Humanitarianism', 33(1) *Australian Yearbook of International Law* (2016) 1–14.
82. See my 'OS Grid Ref. NM 68226 84912 & OS Grid Ref. TQ 30052 80597', in Dan Joyce and Jesse Hohmann (eds.), *The Objects of International Law* (Oxford University Press, 2018). On the pervasiveness and working methods of the Committees in designing such memorials at the time, see Jay Winter, Sites of Memory, Sites of Mourning: The Great War in European Cultural History (Cambridge University Press, 1995) 86.
83. For a discussion of the way in which monuments might help injured and hurt communities, see Vasuki Nesiah, 'Overcoming Tensions between Family and Judicial Procedures', 84(848) *International Review of the Red Cross* (2002) 823, 841.
84. According to Nietzsche, monumental history has a motto: 'let the dead bury the living'. And so he said: 'away with the monuments!' See Veronica Tello, Counter-Memorial Aesthetics (Bloomsbury, 2016). In a non-Nietzschean frame, international law has its own law of monuments, the international law of cultural property. The earliest instances were *The Athens Charter* (1931) and *The Venice Charter* (1964): the latter was inspired by another planned destruction, that of the Nubian Temples during the building of the Aswan Dam in 1959. This time, development not fundamentalism was the culprit. See François Hartog, Regimes of Historicity: Presentism and Experiences of Time (Columbia University Press, 2015) 183. Meanwhile, the destruction of the Buddhist Temples and the partial destruction of Palmyra can be reread not as wanton acts of destruction but very deliberate political-religious acts of self-assertion we might place in a lengthy tradition of similar acts of 'terrorism' from Moses and the destruction of the Golden Calf to the disfigurement of ninety-three carved relief sculptures of the Virgin Mary in Ely Cathedral during the Reformation.

this critique, an interrogation of monumental histories recruited to bolster imperial refurbishments, the anti-statue). In the latter register, we have the fourth plinth in Trafalgar Square, where modern artists have, in a series of irreverent sculptural gestures, consciously worked against the grain of state solemnity conveyed by the lions standing on the other plinths (and against the phallic-monumentalism of Nelson's Column at its centre), or the horizontality of Maya Lin's anti-figurative Vietnam War Memorial in Washington DC.

Meanwhile, Germany's relationship to its past has been restated in an equally ruptured series of national monuments—or 'counter-monuments'.[85] One of the many examples of these German anti-memorials is the disappearing black pillar designed by Jochen and Esther Gerz.[86] Another model is found in Horst Hoheisel's suggestion that the Holocaust be remembered through the destruction of the Brandenburg Gate and its replacement with the remaining dust and some glass plates.[87] Anti-monumentalism adopts many different positions, of course, but in its essentials, it incorporates a suspicion of official memorialisation (noting an inverse relation between public commemoration and private reflection) and scepticism about the monument's claim to authority (as national memory or patriotic obligation). As James Young has pointed out, these tendencies took root in the period after the Great War, when monumental statuary came to be regarded as a betrayal of the experience of slaughter in the trenches.[88] The best examples—though monumental in their own austere and blank manner—are the two famous Luytens monuments to the fallen at Thiepval and in Whitehall where the Cenotaph almost accidentally inaugurates this tradition.[89] Cavell's monument was constructed precisely in this period and operates both as patriotic and cosmopolitan self-assertion, as well as modernist doubt: a combination appearing on its face and in the story of its construction.[90]

---

85. As Neil MacGregor's Germany: Memories of a Nation (Penguin, 2014) states in its first sentence: 'Monuments in Germany are different from monuments in other countries' (ix). I would like to thank Helmut Aust for alerting me to this.
86. Young (n 64).
87. Ibid.
88. Ibid.
89. For a discussion and celebration of Luytens, though with no mention of the Cavell monument, see Winter (n 82) 102–108.
90. My essay, 'OS Grid NM 68226 84912/TQ 30052 80597', in Hohmann and Joyce (n 67), plays this combination of faith and doubt off against the relationship between extra-curricular violence and legalised retribution that is a defining characteristic of international law.

Can we not imagine a history of reckoning that takes it cue from this sort of thing: a re-precedenting that uncovers the hidden history of war crimes and war crimes trials? Perhaps it would be a disappointed, chastened, bathetic history of trials that slowly disappear from view or a history of trials that never occurred?[91] Or a history of international criminal law that chooses to emphasise transcript over judgement (the Milošević Trial as the presence of testimony not the absence of decision), or absence over presence (why remove Okawa from a Tokyo courtroom in 1946?) or incarceration over trial (*Spandau* as a sublimated history of the Nuremberg Trials).[92] Or a history of international criminal law that is not international, criminal or law.[93]

To borrow a term of Charles Peguy's, memorials are 'inscriptive history'. Péguy contrasted memory (moving horizontally) with history (vertically imposed by experts or monument builders).[94] And so, a few years ago, I stepped out of the side entrance of the National Portrait Gallery in London, crossed a busy intersection leading up to Soho, and found myself, on the north-east corner of Trafalgar Square, in a tiny square opposite St. Martin's Church. In the centre of the square: a monument. It is made out of Cornish Granite, designed by Sir George Frampton. Edith Cavell stands in white marble above the monument with a single word engraved over her head: HUMANITY. The words of her final letter sent on the eve of her death, 'I realise that patriotism is not enough', were omitted from the monument.[95]

The words were added later in smaller script, at a time when patriotic feelings had waned a little.

In Virginia Woolf's *The Years*, Eleanor and Peggy pass through Trafalgar Square. They see the Edith Cavell monument. They glance at the figure of a woman in a nurse's uniform holding out her hand.

> Eleanor was shocked for a moment ... 'The only fine thing that was said in the war', she said, aloud, reading the words cut on the pedestal.[96]

---

91. David King, The Trial of Adolf Hitler: The Beer Hall Putsch and the Rise of Nazi Germany (W.W. Norton, 2017); William Schabas, The Trial of the Kaiser (Oxford University Press, 2019); George Steiner, *The Portage to San Christobal of A. H.* (University of Chicago Press, 1999).
92. The prison at Spandau is now a shopping centre.
93. Truth and Reconciliation Commissions are an obvious example of this, but the conditions of possibility for these events is usually the impossibility of some other mode of responsibility. So, in the South African case, the emblematic moment might be the unsuccessful application from an unnamed Indian woman to receive an amnesty for her apathy. Jacqueline Rose, On Not Being Able to Sleep (Princeton University Press, 2003) 2016–2017.
94. Hartog (n 84) 32, 130.
95. Diana Souhami, *Edith Cavell* (Quercus, 2010) 409–419.
96. Virginia Woolf, The Years (Harcourt, Brace, 1937) 336; Souhami (n 95) 18, 420.

V

an uncertain style: after method in international legal history

i. historical precincts	113
ii. international law/international history	120
arrangements of time	121
anachronism	125
greatness	128
iii. after method	135
iv. at Tate Britain	143

'Ah ... yes ...'. Lord Kessler's faint smile and tucked-in chin suggested an easily mastered disappointment. 'And what is your chosen field?'
'Mm. I want to have a look at *style*', Nick said.
Lord Kessler appeared uncertain.

Alan Hollinghurst, *The Line of Beauty* (2004)

i. historical precincts

In some respects this book can be viewed as an arrangement of encounters between something we seem to want to call 'international law' and a number of sentimental-literary ways of thinking or practices—some heretic (gardening, comedy), some tangential (bathos, friendship)—about the world.[1] These encounters might even be labelled 'interdisciplinary', though

---

1. I thank Megan Donaldson for her meticulous and informed reading of this chapter. Andrea Bianchi, Matthew Craven, Ayça Çubuçku, Justin Desautels-Stein, Emily Kidd White, Martti Koskenniemi and Tom Poole also read and commented on this chapter. I thank them. An

that would be a pity. This chapter, unusually, is a reflection on an already constituted encounter between two actual disciplines: (global) history and (international) law. In it, I want to take stock of this encounter and suggest that the methodological stakes of this encounter have been overstated. Instead, I argue that something more instinctive— perhaps inexpressible—is happening when we read a piece of historical or legal-historical work and that this instinctive response is entangled with our experience of this reading as literary rather than methodological.

So, this chapter is a very indirect intervention into the continuing debates about how to conduct oneself in the field of global legal history and especially how to think about doing history *after* method (or in the aftermath of the methodology debates). I am happy to wear, for these purposes, the too-seamless origin myth assumed by these questions; after all, it is not as if many of the international lawyers who wrote history in the past did not think about method. What *has* happened, though, is that there is now a new, probably more systematic, certainly more self-aware, discipline-wide orientation towards thinking about historical method. In the aftermath of this change, it has become at least less likely that international legal histories will be written with blitheness about, or resistance to, or disregard for, method. Part of this orientation has required an engagement with, and a taking seriously of, techniques of studying the past found in other fields ('History' would seem to be a good place to begin), but another part of it has provoked a series of thoughts about what it might mean either to have a historical method that is distinctively legal (one that perhaps learns from the protocols found in other fields but at the same time breaches some of the apparent prohibitions stipulated in those same fields) or to study a context that is somehow linguistic or structural or is, itself, 'a legal context'.[2]

But while much of the chapter describes international law's encounter with method and how the field might look after that encounter, I want to end by issuing a plea concerning the limits of method. Maybe this plea is

---

early version of this chapter was presented at the 'Thinking through the International: History, Politics, Law' workshop at Clare College, Cambridge, 16–17 May 2016.

2. On 'legal' contexts, see Justin Desautels-Stein, 'International Legal Structuralism: A Primer', 8 *International Theory* (2016) 201. For a defence of the idea of a distinctive legal method, see also Anne Orford, 'On International Legal Method', 1 *London Review of International Law* (2013) 166.

just another array of questions: Is there method that is not method? Or is method all method? Or, what lies beyond method (or 'after method') that makes a particular piece of history or legal scholarship attractive to us? The simplest way to put this is to say that when I read international law or fiction, or watch a film, I quite often have a sense—sometimes within minutes—that I am in good or bad hands. And a consideration of this sense cannot be exhausted by an attention to method (or 'method' does not seem quite the right word to capture our intuitions about these things, or, if you like, our intuitions about intuition).[3] I am not certain how I would describe this quality—I have settled on literary virtue (absent the strong moral implication), but sometimes it appears as a species of writerly ethics, sometimes as a 'way of seeing' and, no doubt, sometimes it really does map quite neatly onto a set of methodological prescriptions.[4] Warning: for those who don't share this experience (or think the explanations for it are banal), the last part of the chapter will have been in vain.

I spent time in Brisbane some years ago (at a conference on the history of international society) and noticed that it had a cultural precinct.[5] There were signs everywhere announcing the position of the visitor or resident in relation to culture (e.g. 'you are three kilometres from the cultural centre', or 'veer left for the cultural precinct'). It was not clear to me what was being said about the rest of the city. Perhaps this was an intimation that other parts of Brisbane were an acultural sphere of capitalist expansion (a free fire zone of unplanned skyscrapers and anonymous shopping malls). On the other

---

3. On substituting style for method while at the same time articulating a resistance to the idea of adjudicating among international legal 'methods' on the grounds that method can hardly capture the diversity of ways of being and seeing within a particular collective orientation (e.g. 'Critical Legal Studies'), or because to do so would be to already accept the liberal-consumerist premise of a marketplace of approaches from which to choose an appropriate method or because the questions being asked of (or solutions sought from) methods—at least those understood in this way—are fundamentally instrumental, see Martti Koskenniemi, 'Letter to the Editors of the Symposium', *American Journal of International Law* (1999) 351–361.
4. Style might be a promising contender but it has over-inclusive and under-inclusive associations. For an example of the former, see David Kennedy's 'The International Style in Postwar Law and Policy: John Jackson and the Field of International Economic Law', 10(2) *American University International Law Review* (1995) 671–716 (where the word 'style' refers to a whole doctrinal-theoretical approach to the field). In the latter vein we have the idea that style might refer to a prose style, narrowly understood, e.g. a tendency to write in regimented subject–verb–object sentences, a liking for judiciously-selected adverbs, a passion for sparkling adjectives. For a discussion of style as persuasion, see Andrea Bianchi, *International Law Theories: An Inquiry into Different Ways of Thinking* (Oxford University Press, 2016) 299–301.
5. The conference led to Tim Dunne and Christian Reus-Smit (eds.), *The Globalization of International Society* (Oxford University Press, 2017).

hand, it was apparent that more organic and unofficial cultural centres had appeared all over the city in the interstices of the de-cultured city (in lanes, along railway lines, in disused building sites).

This all reminded me of Rem Koolhaas' generic city, a contemporary city (no longer situated in history) that recreates its own historical district (Vancouver's 'Gastown', say); Koolhaas calls this place 'Lipservice'.[6] For a long time, international law, too, had its historical district: the place—most often the chapter of a book—a reader went to do or acquire (or pay lip service to) some history; a chapter often usefully titled 'History of International Law'. Doctoral students, in imitation of this, would wonder if their dissertations ought to have 'a history chapter'. This chapter might then act as an overture to the main body of the thesis. Except very often it wasn't an overture because the motifs did not reappear. What followed, instead, was a historyless present. At various points in its history, then, international law has occupied this historyless present, a moment where either there is no discernible encounter with history—not even 'a memory of a memory' (Koolhaas, again)—or where the history recounted is so attenuated as to constitute a form of historylessness or where the historical periods referred to are stripped of 'everything that makes them different; so that they all look more or less like our own'.[7]

In recent years though, the history of international law has come in from the cold and become a vibrant field of multidisciplinary scholarship.[8] This (re)turn to history has been hotly pursued by a serious sensitivity to method

---

6. Rem Koolhaas, *Generic City* (Sikkens Foundation, 1995). See also François Hartog, *Regimes of Historicity*, trans. Saskia Brown (Columbia University Press, 2015 [2003]).
7. Bertolt Brecht, *Brecht on Theatre*, 3rd ed. (Bloomsbury Methuen Drama, 1964 [1948]) 3, quoted in Koolhaas (n 6) 1256. We can think of the San Francisco Conference (and the exclusion of the League of Nations secretariat from the conference) as an example of the first, the history included in some textbooks as an example of the third.
8. A smattering from a variety of fields: Sundhya Pahuja, *Decolonising International Law: Development, Growth and the Politics of Universality* (Cambridge University Press, 2011); Lauren Benton and Lisa Ford, *Rage for Order: The British Empire and the Origins of International Law, 1800–1850* (Harvard University Press, 2016); Benjamin Allen Coates, *Legalist Empire: International Law and American Foreign Relations in the Early Twentieth Century* (Oxford University Press, 2016); Arnulf Becker Lorca, *Mestizo International Law: A Global Intellectual History 1842–1933* (Cambridge University Press, 2015); Matthew Craven, *The Decolonization of International Law: State Succession and the Law of Treaties* (Oxford University Press, 2007). Meanwhile, Philippe Sands' book about the Nuremberg War Crimes trials, published in 2016, made international legal history a literary event in the United Kingdom. See Philippe Sands, *East West Street: On the Origins of Genocide and Crimes against Humanity* (Vintage, 2017).

or a new-ish historiographical self-awareness.[9] Now, every sub-field has its history and then its counter-history, and then its anxiety that perhaps all these previous histories were methodologically suspect or even inept—a mere writing down of some things that happened and then some other things that happened but weren't noticed the first time round.[10] We now seem to be in a third stage where even unusually sophisticated accounts of international legal episodes or developments are the subject of criticism on the grounds of flawed or unconvincing or insufficiently contextualised historical method. And this attention—mostly sympathetic, robust, friendly—has come both from within the discipline (e.g. Peevers) and from outside it (e.g. Hunter, Keene).[11]

So, my title refers to a loss of methodological innocence. (In fact, I originally entitled the chapter 'never such innocence again'.[12] But that title was

9. See e.g. Thomas Skouteris, *The Notion of Progress in International Law Discourse* (TMC Asser Press, 2010). In the field of history itself, Marc Bloch was already noticing an explosion in interest in historiography in 1941 that in turn provoked a tendency to 'worry about the value and nature of history'. See Marc Bloch, *The Historian's Craft* (Manchester University Press, 1941). Bloch, by then a resistance fighter, was shot on 16 June 1944 by forces under the command of Klaus Barbie. Two key interventions in the field of historical method (though the topic is vast) are Quentin Skinner, *Visions of Politics, Volume 1: Regarding Method* (Cambridge University Press, 2002) (See also 'A Reply to My Critics' in J. Tully, *Meaning and Context* (Princeton, 1989) 231–288) and Hayden White, 'Historicism, History, and the Figurative Imagination', 14(4) *History and Theory* (1975) 48.
10. In the history of international criminal law, which I will turn to later in the chapter, we had in the first mode, M. Cherif Bassiouni, *Crimes against Humanity: Historical Evolution and Contemporary Application* (Cambridge University Press, 2011) and Geoffrey Robertson, *Crimes Against Humanity: The Struggle for Global Justice*, 3rd ed. (Penguin, 2006); in the second, Kevin Heller and Gerry Simpson (eds.), *The Hidden Histories of War Crimes Trials* (Oxford University Press, 2013); and in the third, Immi Tallgren and Thomas Skouteris (eds.), *The New Histories of International Criminal Law: Retrials* (Oxford University Press, 2019). See, generally, Matthew Craven, 'Theorising the Turn to History in International Law', in Anne Orford and Florian Hoffmann (eds.), *The Oxford Handbook of the Theory of International Law* (Oxford University Press, 2016) 21–37.
11. See e.g. Charlotte Peevers, 'Conducting International Authority: Hammarskjöld, the Great Powers and the Suez Crisis', 1 *London Review of International Law* (2013) 131–140; Ian Hunter, 'Global Justice and Regional Metaphysics: On the Critical History of the Law of Nature and Nations', in Shaunnagh Dorsett and Ian Hunter (eds.), *Law and Politics in British Colonial Thought: Transpositions of Empire* (Palgrave Macmillan, 2010) 11–29.
12. This is from Philip Larkin's poem 'MCMXIV', where he describes men lining up—as if on a bank-holiday weekend—to join the slaughter. But even this poem about memory and history is misremembered. From its title and subject it looks very much as if these are verses are about a national loss of innocence. But Larkin ends with the line, 'Never such innocence, Never before or since, As changed itself to past'. This might act as warning to those of us who want make the sort of sweeping periodisations about historical method I have just made. In a very obvious sense lawyers, far from being innocent of method, have made a fetish out of it. US Supreme Court judges, for example, have built whole jural identities around the adoption of historical methods ('originalism', 'intentionalism').

no more original than the present one, and anyway this 'innocence' is often experienced as a sense of guilt or culpability around the failure to ask questions, or the right questions, about our relationship to the historical material we study.) Whatever happens now must happen in the wake of this period of methodological restlessness. Why *this* material in *this* way from *this* position with *this* attitude and *this* method? Why *this* writer?[13] Of course, there is no guarantee that some international legal histories won't trundle on in blissful ignorance or innocence in the same way that popular history seems immune from the methodological preoccupations of academic historians or historians of political thought. History as 'one damned thing after another' will continue to be written just as international law as 'one damned rule after another' will continue to be practised.[14]

In this chapter, I want to argue that this moment of self-consciousness offers an opportunity for international lawyers to maintain or consolidate a sensibility about the world that I want to think of as literary rather than technical.[15] And this split between the literary and the technical partly reflects the experience of reading the literature on intellectual international history or international intellectual history (the diction is David Armitage's),[16] or historical method. Here one encounters at the same time an array of techniques for doing better history (richer contexts, a watchfulness around anachronism, a vigilance about the relationship between polemic and description) but also (and this is more true of some traditions than others) and alongside this, a sense that the most compelling or resonant histories possess literary virtues or writerly sensibilities that might be hard to domesticate as a form of 'method'. Of course, there is a whole tradition (White, Ankersmit, Jenkins)

---

13. According to Hayden White, R. G. Collingwood used to say that the histories one wrote were a function of the kind of man (sic) one was. See Hayden White, *Metahistory: The Historical Imagination in Nineteenth-Century Europe* (Johns Hopkins University Press, 2014 [1973]) 434. Martin Wight made a similar point about political theory. See Martin Wight, 'An Anatomy of International Thought', 13(3) *Review of International Studies* (1987) 221–227.
14. A phrase variously attributed to Toynbee and Henry Ford but found in a fruitier version in Alan Bennett's play *The History Boys* (Faber & Faber, 2008).
15. It is important that I am not understood to be arguing for a politically neutered form of literary history, or a history 'the study of which is at once gratifying to the liberal curiosity' (John Westlake, Introductory Lectures, *Collected Papers*, ed. Oppenheim (1914, at 395). For examples of syntheses of the literary and legal, see Ed Morgan, *The Aesthetics of International Law* (University of Toronto Press, 2007). For a more general philosophical treatment, see also Martha Nussbaum, *Love's Knowledge: Essays on Philosophy and Literature* (Oxford University Press, 1990) and *Poetic Justice: The Literary Imagination and Public Life* (Beacon Press, 1996).
16. David Armitage, *Foundations of Modern International Thought* (Cambridge University Press, 2012).

that wants to think of history as having fictive power (as having *only* fictive power).[17] I am not incurious about this debate, but this chapter is mostly about a gnawing sense that when it comes to method, something other than 'method' is at stake.

To put this more concretely, when we are acquainting ourselves with a prospective new friend, we would not ask 'What form of the novel do you prefer?' but instead the more common (and less pretentious): 'What novels do you read?' So that asking which methods produce the most invigorating or politically radical or truthful histories of international law might be like asking someone what forms of the novel she admires instead of noticing the book she carries in her handbag.[18] I would not want to push this too far. Clearly, we all have powerful aesthetic preference for certain methods of novel writing. No one can prefer Camus, Joyce and Woolf, or Roberto Bolaño and Tom McCarthy without admitting that, as a matter of general method, plot and character might be peripheral to what is necessary to the success of a novel.[19]

My hunch is that we might understand the relationship between historians of international political thought (I am just going to call them 'historians' from now on) and international lawyers in terms of both method and writerly ethic, and that what unites some of us might be a shared aesthetic around international law in history, whatever the specifics of the methodologies that divide us.

I will begin by describing the experiences (bad and good) of interdisciplinarity and then discuss some of the special problems (related to time, context and 'greatness') lawyers face when they face history (and here, taking my cue from Jennifer Pitts' idea of conceptual frames, I want to think about the sorts of historical worlds international lawyers inhabit and reproduce as a result of their predispositions).[20] All of this will lead to a plea for

---

17. See e.g. Hayden White, *The Content of the Form: Narrative Discourse and Historical Representation* (Johns Hopkins University Press, 1987); Frank Ankersmit, 'Historiography and Postmodernism', *History and Theory* 28 (1989) 137–153; Keith Jenkins, *Re-thinking History* (Routledge, 1991).
18. For a creative reading of Nietzsche's understanding of 'truthfulness', see Bernard Williams, *Truth and Truthfulness* (Princeton University Press, 2002) 12–19.
19. The modernist movement in literature is associated with a move away from plot and character towards language and form while, in history, modernism—though it provokes a suspicion about traditional historical narrative—turned *towards* plot as a way of rethinking history (*via* White's 'emplotment' techniques: see e.g. White (n 13) 5–7. See e.g. Roberto Bolaño, *Nazi Literature in the Americas* (New Directions, 2008), Tom McCarthy, *C* (Vintage, 2011).
20. Jennifer Pitts, 'Law of Nations, World of Empires: The Politics of Law's Conceptual Frames', in Annabel Brett, Megan Donaldson and Martti Koskenniemi, *History, Politics, Law: Thinking Internationally* (Cambridge University Press, 2021, forthcoming).

a post-method in which these worlds can be opened up to acts of contestation and reimagination.

ii. international law/international history

Some dialogue across fields produces stasis. At interdisciplinary conferences and meetings, it is not uncommon to experience a kind of need coming off the other discipline. Among international lawyers, one becomes a type of international lawyer (an institutional engineer, a woman with fancy ideas about Hannah Arendt, a dyed-in-the-wool textualist, a post-positivist, a man in exile from the Department of English Literature). Among strangers, one becomes merely an international lawyer: the Ambassador for Customary International Law. There is a rabbi in Philip Roth's *The Plot against America* who knows everything but doesn't know anything else. And sometimes I have felt like that rabbi at, say, international relations conferences. I am expected to know everything about international law but nothing about anything else. My method is legal (I read cases and am obsessed with textual detail), theirs is political (they know what's going on in the world). So, as David Kennedy pointed out years ago, what is produced is an emaciated account of both fields, a co-dependency.[21] This is obviously not a good thing.

I encounter familiar feelings, too, in reading the depictions of international law found in other fields. Delight that international law is present (why this delight?) followed by undelight that the picture of international law remains somehow undercooked or not quite recognisable. Sometimes, again, international lawyers are reduced to a bunch of people worrying about 'norms' or obsessing about the relationship between moral precept and positive rule or busy pointing to *De jure belli ac pacis* rather than Westphalia or Utrecht as the genesis of our discipline.[22] Occasionally, people are just downright rude. Here is a mid-century writer praising another historian: 'when he described institutions, they were not the petrified fictions of the lawyer'.[23]

In another vein, international lawyers are thought of as innocent (indeed, this innocence has become part of our own self-image): innocent about

---

21. David Kennedy, 'The Disciplines of International Law and Policy', *Leiden Journal of International Law* 12 (1999) 9–133.
22. See also Armitage (n 16) 4–13.
23. Preface to Bloch (n 9) x.

power, innocent about politics and innocent, perhaps, about method. While researching this chapter, I mentioned to an anthropologist I know that I was writing on historical method and began to talk excitedly about Ginzburg, Koselleck, emplotment and anachronism. She replied: 'oh yes, we did that in a first year course on method at graduate school'. And there is something to this: it took a long time for international law—a thoroughly historical field, after all—to come to terms, in any overt way, with work on the philosophy of history or historical method. Standard histories of international law can happily get by without mentioning Skinner or Hartog or Hayden White.[24]

There is another interdisciplinary story to be told though. From the intellectual history and international relations side has come a serious engagement with international legal history that leaves behind, indeed seeks to disturb, some of the commonplaces of the interdisciplinary space to produce defamiliarising and unorthodox depictions of the field.

Amid all this promising work, the encounter with international history and with 'method' has exposed again at least three special problems for international law: one related to the arrangement of time (or what Scott thinks of as the relations between temporality and history), a second concerning the relationship between anachronism and context in international legal history, and a third involving the idea of 'greatness' (or, more specifically, ideas about individual greatness, Great Powers and great crises).[25]

arrangements of time

Marc Bloch once remarked on the way in which historical periods always arrive neatly as 'centuries',[26] before going on to condemn the tendency of

---

24. I would not want to push the innocence of international law too far. David Armitage—and this insight goes back to Martin Wight, at least—talks about the way in which political theory has somehow only belatedly turned its attention from the internal arrangements within states to questions around the boundaries of political life. But, this, of course, is the prose international lawyers have been speaking all their lives; sometimes, it turns out, we are in the vanguard. See Armitage (n 16) 3–5. But there is, also, a prose about prose that others have been speaking for a long time, a prose that forty years ago, Andrew Linklater deployed to announce another, earlier, 'new turn' for political theory. See Andrew Linklater, 'Rationality and Obligation in the States-System: The Lessons of Pufendorf's Law of Nations', 9 *Millennium* (1980) 215–228. Examples of this might include Michael Walzer's *Just and Unjust Wars* (Basic Books, 1977) or John Rawls' *Law of Peoples* (Harvard University Press, 1999) or Richard Tuck's *The Rights of War and Peace* (Oxford University Press, 1999).
25. David Scott, *Omens of Adversity* (Duke University Press, 2014).
26. Bloch (n 9) 183.

synchronic histories to narrate 'pell mell events whose only connection was that they happened around the same time'.[27] International law has been prone to centurise its history. One-hundred-year slices of human existence are presented as hermetic moments in time, sheared off from their immediate predecessors and precursors. Whole centuries go missing (the 18th century, for a while, seemed lost: a Vattelian stop-gap between a Westphalian 17th century and a 'scientific' or 'positivistic' 19th century). The 19th century itself has been a victim of this general inclination to press different events or circumstances into the service of one-hundred-year histories. The Congress of Vienna is collapsed into the Berlin Conference or the men of 1873 with insufficient regard for the way in which developments in the century cut against one another or seem radically discontinuous.

This centurising reflex has tended to accompany, too, an historical method through which history is endowed with a purpose. For Henry Wheaton, in his *History of the Law of Nations*, history is used to show how far international law has advanced from its primitive, unsystematised and ancient origins.[28] In Thomas Lawrence, a similar arc is traced from incomplete, fragmentary origins to legalised political order.[29] Of course, a great deal has been written about this progressivist account of international legal history.[30] From the perspective of contemporary international lawyers, the (centurised) 19th century has played a constitutive role in these sequential histories. It is the century that came before: before the modern, before the transformation, before institutions. In the standard narrative, it is embryonic; here are the inchoate, half-baked beginnings of everything we are now familiar with: tiny fragments of arbitration (*Alabama Claims*), the hesitant opening moves towards an international *humanitarian* law (Brussels, St. Petersburg), early signs of an institutionalist spirit (the Universal Postal Union).

---

27. Ibid. 23.
28. Henry Wheaton, *History of the Law of Nations in Europe and America* (Gould, Banks, 1845) 1–14. For a useful discussion, see Walter Rech, 'International Law, Empire, and the Relative Indeterminacy of Narrative', in Martti Koskenniemi, Walter Rech and Manuel Jiménez Fonseca (eds.), *International Law and Empire* (Oxford University Press, 2016) 57–80.
29. Thomas Lawrence, *The Principles of International Law* (D. C. Heath, 1895) 52–54.
30. See Skouteris (n 9). See the debate, too, about the relationship between humanitarian project and progressivist historical method in Martti Koskenniemi, 'Review of Ruti Teitel's Humanity's Law', 26(3) *Ethics and International Affairs* (Fall 2012); Ruti Teitel, 'Response', 27(2) *Ethics and International Affairs* (Summer 2013).

A post-method sensibility, then, requires us to remember that we *are* remembering the 19th century and, sometimes, bringing into being the idea of it *as a* century. So, recent history has reminded us that though the 19th century is remembered as an era of 'sovereignty' it was, in the first quarter of the century alone, a period in which sovereignty was revived as a reaction to Napoleonic expansion but then seriously compromised by an interventionist ethic arising out of the Holy Alliance's preoccupation with revolutionary constitutionalism. After method, the 19th century has become many centuries: a 'long' 19th century beginning with the French revolution and ending with the Treaty of Versailles, or a 'short' 19th century framed by 1815 and the emergence of a public law of Europe and the Franco–Prussian war, or a 19th century of plural colonialisms, or a 'last five minutes' (Kennedy) of the Hague Peace Conferences or the professionalisation of international law, or the humanisation of war project.[31] Or the 19th century is imagined *as* the imagined 19th century: the illusion of sovereignty, positivism, philosophy, unmoored jurisprudence, the international legal order before pragmatism and so on.[32]

Meanwhile, smoothly linear chronicles of history—perhaps even the relationship between time and history itself—have been disrupted and disarticulated in recent accounts.[33] To take the 19th century again, it has been posited in anti-linear readings as a moment of discontinuity rather than the incomplete prelude to the modernisation and renovation of international law in the early 20th century. The centrality of the colonial encounter in the 19th century has, of course, been emphasised by contemporary international lawyers (Tony Anghie, Liliana Obregón Tarazona).[34] Their scepticism about international law's roots in a sovereignty-founding moment at Westphalia (or Utrecht) or in a slow rise to civilisation through law, is as

---

31. On professionalisation, see Casper Sylvest, 'International Law in Nineteenth-Century Britain', 75 *British Yearbook of International Law* (2004) 9–70. On international law as professional activity, see Jean d'Aspremont, Tarcisio Gazzini, André Nollkaemper and Wouter Werner (eds.), *International Law as a Profession* (Cambridge University Press, 2017).
32. In this regard, the 'after method' period stretches back at least as far as David Kennedy's 'International Law and the Nineteenth Century: History of an Illusion', 65 *Nordic Journal of International Law* (1996) 385–420.
33. David Scott, *Conscripts of Modernity: The Tragedy of Colonial Enlightenment* (Duke University Press, 2004) 1–20.
34. E.g. Liliana Obregón Tarazona, 'The Civilized and the Uncivilized', in Bardo Fassbender and Anne Peters (eds.), *The Oxford Handbook of the History of International Law* (Oxford University Press) 917–939.

pronounced as that of Carl Schmitt or Wilhelm Grewe, and the dark implications of 19th-century colonialism are present in Anghie and in Schmitt (though the darkness has to be read into the latter).[35]

But the 19th century is an outlier, too, in the work of someone like Charles Alexandrowicz who, *partly*, refuses this line of progressive development in favour of what he calls a 'historicized international law',[36] in which the colonial period is an exception or gap in the universalisation of international law.[37] Alexandrowicz's method is not dissimilar to that of Grewe and Schmitt, in one sense at least. He emphasises the way in which the European powers rewrite the history of international law itself (in Alexandrowicz's case by forgetting the prior existence of non-European civilisations and states in order that these occluded peoples might be 'admitted' to a newly-assembled family of nations).[38] His response is to produce an archive partly cleansed of what he thinks of as international law's Eurocentrism. This choice of archive can be seen as an embrace of a shared predicament (his appreciation of the continuities between Polish self-assertion and wider anti-colonial struggle) and an accident (on being appointed to a chair in India, he found himself with access to Indian records) as well as a political gesture (Alexandrowicz was committed to the idea of international law as a global, egalitarian, universal family of nations, a project in relation to which the 19th century, far from being constitutive, was an aberrant period of European exceptionalism). The idea, then, was to fashion a new temporality, one that would, in turn, close the gap between 1815 and 1945.[39] The sacred cows (Westphalia

---

35. Schmitt's nostalgia for empire is clear from the language he uses when referring to it as 'heroic' or 'great'. The problem of 19th-century empire, for Schmitt, was not that it was a form of land appropriation but that it marked a decline from, or 'epilogue' to, the 'great' imperial enterprises of the 16th and 17th centuries: Carl Schmitt, *The* Nomos *of the Earth in the International Law of the* Jus Publicum Europaeum, trans. G. L. Ulmen (Telos Press, 2006) 336–342, at 226. For Anghie, the problem of international law in this period lies not in its failures but its successes.
36. David Armitage and Jennifer Pitts, '"This Modern Grotius": An Introduction to the Life and Thought of C. H. Alexandrowicz', in David Armitage and Jennifer Pitts (eds.), *C. H. Alexandrowicz: The Law of Nations in Global History* (Oxford University Press, 2017) 1–31, at 15.
37. For Alexandrowicz, history *was* method. For him, precisely, studying the contemporary alone was a guarantee of irrelevance. Part of international law's problem in 1963, say, was that it was refusing to take its own history seriously in favour of 'a lifeless repetition of historical slogans'. See C. H. Alexandrowicz, 'Some Problems in the History of the Law of Nations in Asia', reproduced in David Armitage and Jennifer Pitts (eds.), *C. H. Alexandrowicz:* Law of Nations in Global History (Oxford University Press, 2017) 76–82, at 76.
38. Though Alexandrowicz states that this 19th-century development was a political initiative whose 'juridical significance was negligible': ibid. 81.
39. Armitage and Pitts (n 36) 20–21.

was unimportant compared to, say, a treaty signed by the Ottomans and France in 1535;Vienna, a wrong turn) were slain.[40]

It would be wrong, though, to think of Alexandrowicz's method as entirely anti-progressive. For him, the commercial spirit (via Kant and Cobden) would, after all, inevitably prevail over systems of cultural superiority and sovereign exclusion. The method, then, is a form of positivism (he relies heavily on the voluntary compacts of legal persons) but the theory is anti-positivistic and teleological (these legal persons are not all sovereigns, positivism's 19th-century exclusions are repudiated and there is a strong commitment to the idea that 'the principle of universality of nations was and is inherent in a law derived from reason and not based on human will alone').[41]

anachronism

Alongside this desire for *telos*, a certain variety of international law has been conducted in an unselfconsciously anachronistic mode. The idea—sometimes 'a magpie history'—is to find antecedents and map them onto contemporary circumstance or to take ideas and reify them across centuries.[42] Alongside this is a 'mania' to find the origins of something or other.[43] In this way, Pufendorf's 'state system', reduced to a mere precursor, is read directly and seamlessly onto the UN Charter inter-sovereign order or 19th-century 'society'.[44] This is a compulsion in an area I work in—international war crimes law—where the field of history is configured as a galaxy of free-floating precedents. 'The past is a foreign country and, look, they do things the same way there', whether it be banning poison-tip arrows (rather like chemical weapons) or offering immunity to visiting diplomats (cue reference to *The Iliad* or Shakespeare) or deploring bad behaviour (surely an early incarnation of 'crimes against humanity'). This hyper-anachronism is especially prevalent in judicial doctrine, where it becomes a search for

---

40. Ibid. 19.
41. Alexandrowicz (n 37) 79.
42. The phrase is Richard Rosecrance's. See George Lawson, 'The Eternal Divide? History and International Relations', 18 *European Journal of International Relations* (2012) 203–226. See also Armitage (n 16) 29–30.
43. The word is Marc Bloch's.
44. For Pufendorf's discussion of state systems, see Samuel von Pufendorf, *Of the Law of Nature and Nations* (Clarendon Press, 1934 [1672]) 1043–1051.

'historical validation'.[45] So, a post-war court at Nuremberg was happy to announce that 'aggression' had been a crime since 'time immemorial' (in the *Ministries* trial) while the District Court of Jerusalem, in 1961, styled Adolf Eichmann as a 'latter-day pirate', as if he had merely plundered some merchant vessels on the high seas.[46] Sometimes anachronism is presented as necessity. In an infamous Australian decision from 1971, one with international legal history at its core, a court affirmed that Australia was 'desert and uncultivated' (i.e. *terra nullius*) in 1788, at the time of the British invasion, even while conceding that it in fact wasn't.[47] Here, law insists not just on anachronism (*terra nullius* has meant many different things at different times) but on the necessity of inaccuracy or legal fiction.[48]

In international criminal law, as we shall see later, the search for origins, or 'usable history', is part of an effort to establish the authority of a new and insecure legal project. In this way, categories like 'aggression' or 'piracy' move through time in an uncomplicated, acontextual manner that is surely red meat to a certain sort of historian of political thought on the lookout for facile homologies. Of course, international lawyers are not alone in adopting this approach to history. Similar commitments to anachronism are found in the work of structural realists in political theory for whom international history is marked by the repetition and recurrence of timeless dilemmas (to appease or not to appease, that is always the question) or is imagined as a timeless zone of the tragic.[49]

More recently, however, after method, international legal history has been obliged to defend (often robustly) its commitments to anachronism.[50] And with this development has come an understanding that the debate over anachronism is partly a political struggle over the meaning of history and the requirements of the present, and perhaps not so much a 'choice of method'. So that the typical response to the problem of anachronism—a turn to context—should itself be understood as a political choice or a series

---

45. Armitage (n 16) 10.
46. See Hannah Arendt, *Eichmann in Jerusalem* (Penguin, 1994 [1963]) 263–265, 276.
47. *Milirrpum v. Nabalco Pty Ltd* (1971) 17 FLR 141 (the 'Gove land rights case').
48. Gerry Simpson, '*Mabo*, International Law, *Terra Nullius* and the Stories of Settlement: An Unresolved Jurisprudence', 19(1) *Melbourne University Law Review* (1993) 195–210.
49. Reinhold Niebuhr, *Moral Man and Immoral Society: A Study in Ethics and Politics* (Scribner's Sons, 1948 [1932]).
50. See n 2.

of Russian-doll political choices (which context?) embedded in the larger decision to make 'context' (with its pre-existing methodological biases, its scholarly tradition) important so that contextualism becomes both political decision and indeterminate method.

Meanwhile, the deployment of deliberately acontextual reasoning can also have a political potency, whether it involves taking the 'war on terror', and its accompanying ensemble of governing practices, and assimilating them to, say, 19th-century imperialism,[51] or showing how the Anglo-American defection from the UN collective security system resembled the clash between papal authority and secular natural law, or pointing to resemblances across time between mandate and international administration or noticing some parallels between the Moscow Show Trials and the work of the international tribunals. Though these comparisons might be methodologically suspect, the claim will be made that they do important heuristic or political work, which a fully contextualised (whatever *that* might entail) reading of the historical circumstance would blur or undercut.

Indeed, an influential form of international legal history thinks of apparently innocuous contemporary practices and doctrines as being implicated in imperial, or more overtly violent, logics of the past. Thus, does every apparently progressive or neutral legal norm of the present have its avatar in some more facially political or exploitative norm in the past. Concepts are wrenched from history as part of a provocative political project.[52] In the end it may be that, as Josef Engel puts it, 'every historical judgement is an analogical judgement'.[53] To be a lawyer is to spend one's day making analogical judgements. What historians might think of as 'a lack of context' (the absence of culture, event, social surroundings), might simply be a different sort of context: a linguistic context, a textual context, a legal context.[54]

---

51. Antony Anghie, *Imperialism, Sovereignty and the Making of International Law* (Cambridge University Press, 2005).
52. There is, at the same time, a need for a certain amount of wariness around the insistence that this or that engagement with Baldus or Lorimer is important because it might tell us something about the porousness of borders today or about the origins of self-defence. Here, history might feel too instrumentalised.
53. As quoted in Alberto Toscano, 'The Spectre of Analogy', 66 *New Left Review* (2010) 152–160, at 153.
54. This idea of legal context is discussed in Desautels-Stein (n 2).

greatness

A context that international law has struggled with, and against, is the context of 'greatness'. At least one methodological imperative inherited from other fields is a suspicion of history as a history of Great Men and their activities (Terry Eagleton calls this sort of work 'philistine') or as a sequence of crises or as a mere effect of Great Power politics.

The epilogue to *War and Peace* is an essay denouncing the historical method of the novel itself. At one point, Tolstoy remarks:

> The theory of the transference of the collective will of the people to historical persons may perhaps explain much in the domain of jurisprudence and be essential for its purposes, but in its application to history, as soon as revolutions, conquests or civil wars occur—that is, as soon as history begins—that theory explains nothing.[55]

The novel, of course, plays the chamber politics of Russian aristocratic life against the deeds and misdeeds of historically significant figures as well as fictional heroes and anti-heroes. One interpretation of *War and Peace*, then, is that the novel struggles against its author's theory of history. The centrality of great historical persons, for Tolstoy, is essential to the success of a piece of literature (the structural novel was to come later) and essential in 'the domain of jurisprudence', but as history it explained nothing.[56]

The discipline of international law has conducted a similar internal struggle with the concept of 'greatness' in its accounts of history and its chosen methods. There is a method of international legal history, for example, that will continually refer back to a set of lightly interrogated facts or 'realities' as the authentic or ultimate ground of international law or historical development.[57] And this history is sometimes written in a dismissive tone: a jeremiad against the blindness or idiocy of those who would base their

---

55. Leo Tolstoy, *War and Peace* (Penguin, 1999 [1869]) 1282.
56. Turgenev was not convinced by Tolstoy's venture into historical method: 'The historical appendix, on the other hand, which has brought the readers to such a pitch of frenzy, is nothing but puppetry and charlatanism': Turgenev, 'Letter to Annenkov', 14 February 1868, quoted in Henri Troyat, *Tolstoy* (Penguin, 1970) 418.
57. See, for example, Grewe's objection to the Nuremberg trials. Such 'models', he argued, 'could only impress zealots and starry-eyed idealists who were blind to . . . the realities of world politics' [as if Nuremberg was not an expression of those 'realities']: Wilhelm G. Grewe, *The Epochs of International Law*, trans. Michael Byers (De Gruyter, 2000) 667. On the relationship between 'reality' and 'fact', see e.g. Richard Rorty, *Contingency, Irony, and Solidarity* (Cambridge University Press, 1989) 7–8; White (n 13) 41–53.

historical accounts on something other than the realities of history. There are contemporary manifestations of this, but the modern exemplars of this form of hegemonic determinism are two otherwise quite distinct (and distinctive) German scholars, Carl Schmitt and Wilhelm Grewe.[58]

It was Michael Byers' translation of Wilhelm Grewe's *Epochs of International Law* that brought this, in some respects eccentric, work into the mainstream of Anglo-American international legal history. The reviews were often favourable. One early reviewer called it 'consistently sound' (it isn't), while Marc Weller declared that *Epochs* would 'certainly entice people who are not experts in international law and history to read and enjoy it' (it didn't).

Grewe's method is macro-historical, periodising, pseudo-scientific and 'realist' but at the same time concerned with the styles (of governorship, of scholarship) that gave each of his epochs their own spirit.[59] Like almost everyone who has ever written histories of international law, he seeks to bring theory and practice together (though it is clear here that practice will tend to dictate the kinds of styles available to be deployed within different moments of international legal history). So, for Grewe, international legal history was catalogued as a sequence of Spanish, French, British and US–Soviet epochs, in which the international law of the period was an expression of the dominant power's style of global leadership.[60] Throughout *Epochs* there is both an elevation of theory (the style of scholarship predominating at any one time) but also a preference for 'facts' (the idea of a European sovereign state system or the balance of power or the institution of permanent diplomacy) over 'theories' (of late-mediaeval universalism or papal authority).[61] Accordingly, concrete political systems conditioned by the style of the dominant power were to be preferred over the ahistorical, autonomous legalisms of contemporaries like Hans Kelsen (a section of *Epochs* is entitled 'Legal orders corresponding to changes in the state system').

---

58. J. S. Watson, 'A Realistic Jurisprudence of International Law', 30 *Year Book of World Affairs* (1980) 265–285.
59. Grewe (n 57) xii, 6.
60. Though this did not mean international legal scholarship was 'nationalised'. The Spanish Age produced Grotius, the French Age failed to give rise to a single great French international lawyer. On the idea of international law as a native or foreign language in the contemporary scene, see Anna Dolidze, 'How Well Does Russia Speak the Language of International Law?' *Open Democracy* (2015), https://www.opendemocracy.net/od-russia/anna-dolidze/how-well-does-russia-speak-language-of-international-law.
61. And especially facts that are then converted into, or acknowledged as, legal forms. See Grewe's discussion of the Treaty of Utrecht and the balance of power: (n 57) 282.

Of course, a wealth of revisionist scholarship has suggested that the 'fact' of Westphalian sovereignty was just one more narrative retrospectively imposed by 19th-century post-Napoleonic positivism or a (mis)representation of the summits in Munster and Osnabruck.[62] Equally, when Grewe, in his rendering of Cold War International Law, demands that we attend to 'the realities of State practice, the actual behaviour of powerful States', we might ask what this 'actual behaviour' is and why it is the stuff of international law.[63] In the end, the self-conscious methodological realism of Grewe is open to the objections of another realism, the structural realism of someone like Kenneth Waltz, who once said 'explanatory power is gained ... by moving away from "reality", not by staying close to it'.[64]

Having said all that, this sweeping macro-history—to be set against the work of, say, Carlo Ginzburg (recently revived in conference papers delivered by Thomas Skouteris)—at least permits (or doesn't prevent) Grewe from asking the sorts of questions that became the basis for a later historical turn.[65] Indeed, there are commonalities between Grewe and later legal historians who want to think of international law as having been shaped or constituted in its encounter with colonialism or Great Power preference. And, of course, Grewe is an important figure for the purposes of this chapter because his history is attentive to styles (of hegemony). Grewe's 'style' is both broader and narrower than the style I discuss here: it encompasses the politics, method and constitutional presuppositions of the dominant imperial powers, but not the deeper methodological questions about how histories get to be written, far less whether method exhausts the sorts of questions that could be asked about such historical writing. However, Grewe's emphasis on style nevertheless demands an attention to the ways in which international law is written (its presiding languages, national forms and so on) that is not always present in international legal history.

The centrality of the concrete, the imperial, and 'the real' mark out Grewe and Carl Schmitt as contemporaries and co-sympathisers though the Schmitt of *Der Nomos*, at least, is more gnostic than Grewe with his

---

62. See e.g. Benno Teschke, *The Myth of 1648* (Verso, 2003).
63. Grewe (n 57) 640.
64. Kenneth Waltz, *Theory of International Politics* (McGraw Hill, 1979) 7.
65. In particular, asking whether a particular international legal order operates as a Christian order, an occidental order, a civilised order or a universal system of law.

discussion of, say, the 'katechon' (or the etymologies of the 'nomos' itself).⁶⁶ But alongside all of this is the obsessive quest for the 'concrete' grounds of political order.⁶⁷ Here, again, as with Grewe, and the post-war US political realists, it is assumed that there exists an underlying order or set of relations or real social circumstance obscured by something less real (the legal order, or liberalism or parliamentary democracy or some aesthetic or ethical superstructure).⁶⁸

But what are we to make of this longing for 'concreteness'? It appears repeatedly in Grewe's work and Schmitt's and, in the field in general, it represents a kind of methodological *telos* in its various sociological (New Haven), statist (positivism) and naturalist (the quest for a secure, secular basis—'conscience of mankind') variants. In Schmitt's case, the concrete is everywhere. The 'exception' produces a moment of revelation in which 'the power of real life breaks through the crust of a mechanism that has become torpid by repetition' while the friend–enemy distinction clears away the normative or supervening or spiritual in order to fully illuminate and make plain the political and the real (little wonder that a de-theologised—maybe even depoliticised—version of Schmitt's thinking became the basis of US Cold War realism).⁶⁹ Meanwhile, *The* Nomos *of the Earth* is, itself, a story of physical appropriations of land, sea and air.⁷⁰ This craving for the tangible, or the underlying, is of course a feature of the social sciences in general but for Schmitt and Grewe it is a style encrusted into method. The concrete relations are always somewhere (often out of reach) underpinning everything and to be juxtaposed to the abstractions of certain kinds of legalism, but

---

66. Though this is a minority position, I suspect. For Rob Howse, the international legal writing has been much less influential than the two founding texts of Schmittianism (*Concept of the Political* and *Political Theology*), each of them free of most of this mysticism.
67. On etymology, see Schmitt (n 35). On the *Katechon*, see 59–62. For a fresh reading of the *Katechon*, see Richard Joyce, 'International Law and the Cold War', in Matthew Craven, Sundhya Pahuja and Gerry Simpson (eds.), *International Law and the Cold War* (Cambridge University Press, 2019) 27–48.
68. This sort of thinking is all over a certain kind of American realism; see e.g. Hans J. Morgenthau, 'Positivism, Functionalism, and International Law', 34 *American Journal of International Law* (1940) 260–284.
69. Carl Schmitt, *Political Theology*, trans. George Schwab (University of Chicago Press, 2005) 15.
70. In his Author's Foreword, Schmitt quotes Goethe: 'All petty things have trickled away, [/] Only sea and land count here'. In fact, Schmitt's gloss on this betrays an anxiety about his method. As he puts it, these references to sea and land and concreteness should not indicate that he is taking an 'elemental-mythological approach'. He goes on: 'this would not do justice to the essentially jurisprudential foundations of the book, which I have taken much pains to construct': Schmitt (n 35) 37.

their restatement as a series of synonyms sometimes feels more like theological yearning than social science.[71]

These gestures to political reality are suspect, of course. For all the reasons given by White and Ankersmit, but also because, in the case of Grewe, the author himself it seemed could only bear so much reality.[72] As others have pointed out, *Epochs* manages to offer a millennium-long political history of international law without saying very much at all about the war it was written in the midst of. So, while Grewe can sound like Ian Hunter or Quentin Skinner when he demands that we 'acknowledge the concrete intellectual historical position of a Vitoria, a Gentili or a Grotius',[73] he manages to avoid this sort of positioning when he celebrates the work of Schmitt.[74] In both Schmitt and Grewe, there is a concrete context that remains enigmatically out of sight, and this is also the shadow of a predicament hanging over the chosen method. Grewe, for example, retained his chair in international law throughout Hitler's reign. This leads to some peculiar historical ellipses beginning with Frowein's biographical account of Grewe, which reads as if Grewe began his academic career in 1945.[75]

---

71. In the sense, and perhaps *only* in this sense, the work comes to resemble concrete poetry: the concreteness of form producing an eventual abstraction of thought. See e.g. Emmett Williams, *An Anthology of Concrete Poetry* (Something Else Press, 1967).
72. Grewe could not quite consistently stick with his method, in any case. See his reliance on the judgements of international courts or academic literature in establishing the continued existence of a universal international order: Grewe (n 57) 648.
73. Ibid. 2, 70 *passim*.
74. This contrasts with, say, Rob Howse, who insists that Schmitt himself believed arguments have to be read as 'polemical or situational'. See Robert Howse, 'Schmitt, Schmitteanism and Contemporary International Legal Theory', in Anne Orford and Florian Hoffman with Martin Clark (eds.), *Oxford Handbook of the Theory of International Law* (Oxford University Press, 2016) 212–230, at 213. Irony and bathos seem to be the presiding tropes when Grewe speaks about Nazi Germany. About the Third Reich he has this to say: 'The more these dictatorships deviated from the standard of civilisation, the more it was important to avoid breaking diplomatic links with them and to conserve the ties which bound them to the rules of international law' (585). The Holocaust and the war of aggression, meanwhile, are described in passive, sanitised terms: 'With the outbreak of war in 1939 . . . in land warfare the execution of hostages played a sad role as a reprisal against the activities of partisans' (626). Compare this to the views expressed by German émigré Georg Schwarzenberger in Georg Schwarzenberger, *International Law and Totalitarian Lawlessness* (Cape, 1943). If euphemism is the dominant style when it comes to the Second World War, hyperbole is the preferred mode in other instances; the occupation by Iranian revolutionary students of the US Embassy in Teheran is later described as a 'terrorist action' (641).
75. In frontmatter to Grewe (n 57). For a delicate appraisal of this period of German international law with some insights into the relationship between Grewe and Schmitt, see Bardo Fassbender, 'Stories of War and Peace: On Writing the History of International Law in the "Third Reich" and After', 13 *European Journal of International Law* (2002) 479–512, esp. 503–506.

This book is partly an exercise in understanding international law and politics (and history) as matters of taste or aesthetics, and in chapter ii, I write about the way in which the acknowledgements in a work of scholarship might work against the ideas being expounded in the text itself. In Grewe's case we have a lapse of taste that makes him think it is important to register that the publication and writing of *Epochs* were each impeded by 'the air raids' or that it might be matter of self-satisfaction that he had resisted the efforts of the (Soviet) authorities in the post-war era to modify his work.[76]

Grewe and Schmitt had an ambiguous (perhaps not so ambiguous in Schmitt's case) relationship to Hitler and his policies. In a great many popular accounts of the past, of course, such men *make* history and are themselves consequently made by a particular historical method (as Marx alleged Victor Hugo does to Bonaparte in *Napoleon le Petit*).[77] But a typical disciplinary training in international law will tend to lack many references to leading statespersons, these characters are perpetually offstage, lending their names to the occasional doctrine (Truman, Brezhnev, Monroe) or providing the odd moment of context (Stalin, Nehru et al.). On the other hand, in 1919, when a committee was established at the Versailles Peace Conference to consider the question of war crimes trials for the defeated German elite (including the Kaiser), the then-revolutionary idea was to make greatness the very subject of international criminal adjudication.

Labouring under a curious but revealing title, 'The Commission on the Responsibilities of the Authors of the War', the Commission's deliberations turned out to be stormier than anyone had anticipated. In effect, the Commission enacted a series of debates around opposing views of history, wrestling from the outset with the title it had been given (and the first of its tasks) and the whole idea of 'authorship'. In what sense is history or war authored? And who authors it? Or is 'authorship' the wrong metaphor?

This was not just a struggle over metaphor. The Commission eventually held that wars were not authored by Great Men (at least not in a way that would give rise to individual criminal responsibility). And this accords with

---

76. In the preface to the second edition (1984), Grewe says of post-war censorship: 'it was stipulated that a publication was now only possible under certain conditions which I was not prepared to accept. It had already been a remarkable accomplishment to avoid *any alteration* to the text by the censor during the Third Reich': Grewe (n 57) xi (emphasis added).
77. Karl Marx, *The 18th Brumaire of Louis Bonaparte* (International Publishers, 1969 [1852]) 8.

an international law that emphasises, as the motors of international diplomacy, the slow accretion of norms, or the intensification of a certain form of practice or the steady construction of institutions rather than the inclinations of statespersons. Since the field understands itself to be a practice of taming the instincts of Great Powers or the pathologies of Great Men, it makes sense to underplay these figures in its own history.

But international law can be understood also as the enactment of a Tolstoyan struggle between the institutional and diplomatic structure of international political life and the agency of Great Men. This latter tendency is reflected, first, in an intellectual history, or 'the study of past thoughts' (in Skinner's elegant formula), of an international law consisting in what Great Men *thought* at different times.[78] This is the history of international law from Gentili to Wolff and Vattel and then on to Oppenheim or Kelsen and beyond.[79] This tendency, in turn, has been buttressed and complicated by the increasing attention given to the biographies of international legal practitioners as part of a general biographical turn in the field.[80] Alongside all of this, we would have to register the histories written and authorised by international tribunals, which think of war and atrocity as an emanation from the evil minds of elite state and military leaders possessing 'individual responsibility' and 'criminal intent': international legal history *via* Milošević, Pinochet and Goering.[81]

Meanwhile, war crimes tribunals also write the history of international law as a line of great, defining crises from Nuremberg to the former Yugoslavia and the Rwandan genocide. This could be understood as both a departure from, and a confirmation of, existing tendencies in international law's historical

---

78. See Stefan Collini, 'What Is Intellectual History?', 35(10) *History Today* (1985) 46–48.
79. On recurring criticisms that history focused on a small aristocratic elite and their intellectual contribution constitutes a form of 'classism', see Armitage (n 16) 31–32.
80. See Andrew Lang and Susan Marks, 'People with Projects: Writing the Lives of International Lawyers', 27(2) *Temple International and Comparative Law Journal* (2013) 437–453; Armitage and Pitts (n 36) 21–23, 28–31. One thought, suggested by Carlo Ginzburg, is that we could usefully turn our attention to the *readers* of history. So, what is interesting in Keene's account is not so much that a number of treaties were created in a particular period but that we were read in different periods by different audiences in order to establish a certain way of doing international law ('one cannot just read the books; one must also understand the readers': Edward Keene, 'The Age of Grotius', in David Armstrong (ed.), *Routledge Handbook of International Law* (Routledge, 2009) 126–140, at 127)). For thoughts along these lines, see Carlo Ginzburg, *Threads and Traces: True, False, Fictive*, transl. Anne C. Tedeschi and John Tedeschi (University of California Press, 2012).
81. For a fuller discussion, see Gerry Simpson, 'Linear Law: The History of International Criminal Law', in Christine E. J. Schwöbel (ed.), *Critical Approaches to International Criminal Law: An Introduction* (Routledge, 2014) 159–179.

methodologies. On one hand, international lawyers go to the past in search of regularity, pattern and uniformity (a sequence of treaties, a practice 'consistent and universal'). But another way of writing international legal history will precisely think of it as a response to crisis ('Kosovo', 'Rwanda', 'Libya') or a history of post-war settlements (1648, 1713, 1815, 1919, 1945). And indeed, whole legal methods have been built round this sort of thing.[82]

Hilary Charlesworth and others have criticised this over-attention to crises and the deforming effects this has had on international legal culture, and that seems right. On the other hand, a certain sort of revolutionary moment—whether blueprint or singularity—might be understood as having transformed the ground on which judgement itself is made.[83] After method, we might approach this idea of crisis differently: as opportunity and danger. Just as concepts might be viewed as abstractions travelling freely across time *and* as situated sites of argument about the world so, too, events are no longer just happenings that arrive on our desks to be periodised or interred (Grewe, Schmitt, Wheaton) but are to be treated with wariness (Charlesworth) or as moments of possibility, and political (Badiou) or theoretical (Johns, Joyce and Pahuja) renewal.[84]

iii. after method

These special problems I have identified suggest that, in the end, individual methodological pre- and proscriptions can sometimes cut both ways.

---

82. W. Michael Reisman and Andrew R. Willard, *International Incidents: The Law That Counts in World Politics* (Princeton University Press, 1988); Burns H. Weston, Richard A. Falk and Hilary Charlesworth, *International Law and World Order: A Problem-Oriented Coursebook* (West Group, 1997). See also Grewe (n 57) and its dependence on the demarcation of epochs and the fixing of major turning points, e.g. at 28.
83. The language is from the Toscano essay (n 53), the theorising is from Alain Badiou's Polemics, trans. Steve Corcoran (Verso, 2012); the application to international law is found in Fleur Johns, Richard Joyce and Sundhya Pahuja (eds.), *Events: The Force of International Law* (Routledge, 2010). A relatively recent reference to the need to be attentive to 'Events' one might be living through is found in Martti Koskenniemi, 'Histories of International Law: Significance and Problems for a Critical View', 27 *Temple International and Comparative Law Journal* (2013) 215–240. For the idea of a crisis as a juridical moment of decision, see Reinhart Koselleck, trans. Michaela W. Richter, 'Crisis', 67 *Journal of the History of Ideas* (2006) 357–400, at 359–360. On the revolutionary moment as a vantage point from which to observe history at its most 'vivid', see Scott (n 25) 3.
84. There is a hint of arbitrariness in the choice of some events: 'the peace of Westphalia may be chosen as the epoch from which to deduce the history of the modern science of international law': Wheaton (n 28) 69.

Grewe's attention to 'context' might be viewed as underwhelming, selective and reductive, or it might act as a bold, sweeping antidote to Kelsenian legalism; Schmitt's anti-Weimar manoeuvrings will either seem deliciously prophetic or dismally authoritarian (or both); Alexandrowicz's pluriverse could be celebrated as a form of perspicacious anti-imperialism or dismissed as the product of a method borne out of serendipity rather than intellectual decision. Choice of method does not always (or, for some readers, very often) determine what we take to be convincing work. 'Fully' contextualised account is read as depoliticised antiquarianism. Anachronistic *faux pas* becomes playfully defiant, cross-historical gesture. Biographical retrieval is Great Man fetish. Finger-on-the-pulse contemporariness is 'discipline of crisis'.

So, *after method*, we might experience simply a greater awareness of the choices open to us along with an awareness that these are choices, and a sense that these choices are both methodological and political: decisions we make rather than decisions that are made for us (by context, by choice of field, by disciplinary tradition). 'Interest ... precedes method', as Catherine MacKinnon put it forty years ago.[85] So, the decision to write about the experience of the ordinary soldier in Tolstoy, or the working classes in E. P. Thompson or the pirate society in Marcus Rediker is a matter of method and politics.[86] In international legal history, such choices are constantly having to be made, whether these involve thinking from below (Rajagopal), writing history from a particular place (the Russian history of international law or the Ottoman experiences of legality), conjuring forms of micro-history (Eslava's Bogotá or Istanbul) or simply attending to a different archive (Alexandrowicz).

There might be, in turn, a more acute awareness that we *write* history. The master-theorist of history in this mode (though he denied that he wrote 'philosophy of history') is, of course, Hayden White. For White, style and method merge, and the method of discerning or describing history becomes the style of writing it. Style, no longer quite 'after' method, is always and perpetually with it. Or, better still, is the origin of it. Thinkers as diverse as Althusser and Alain have identified the metaphorical thought that provokes

---

85. Catharine A. MacKinnon, 'Feminism, Marxism, Method, and the State: Toward Feminist Jurisprudence', 8 *Signs* (1983) 635–658, at 636–637.
86. And position, of course. As Alexandrowicz notes, a certain distance from power or fashion has a habit of widening perspective and perspicacity. See his 'Doctrinal Aspects of the Universality of the Law of Nations', reproduced in David Armitage and Jennifer Pitts (eds.), *C. H. Alexandrowicz: Law of Nations in Global History* (Oxford University Press, 2017) 168–179.

or initiates the philosophical endeavour. But it is White who makes of this a virtuoso performance in identifying what we might, clumsily, call the stylishness of history. According to White, the poetic act—(less elegantly) part of a 'prefigurative' cognitive structure—is anterior to the particular analysis of field and object, indeed establishes the object and 'the modality of the conceptual strategies he will use to explain it'.[87] When it comes to these modalities, White identifies a number of different emplotments (I will discuss these a little more when I return to the history of international criminal law). Suffice to say here, White regards this not as a choice of method (to be applied to an object of study in order to produce the greatest correspondence between the past and the history of that past) but as a deep moral and aesthetic decision that predates archive and method.[88] No wonder, then, that in White's work there is a commitment to bringing out the writerly, literary, sentimental (or personal) aspects and dimensions of history-writing (it may be the case also, according to one writer, that histories written under such conditions—and with their 'sensitivity to narrative, literary form, and poetic technique'—mark a return to the better aspects of the idioms of 17th-century humanism).[89]

After method, or after the interdisciplinary methodological encounter, we might see, too, that it is very probable that what we have here are shared predispositions and virtues (maybe even tonalities) rather than shared methods. Sometimes these virtues might involve something as simple as the ability or inclination to read the small print alongside the larger structural changes. Marc Bloch wrote in 1941 that the best history features a sort of zooming and stretching, a moving back and forth between attention to minute detail and awareness of large-scale transformation. This may simply be a fidelity (or is it a form of infidelity?) to text and context. What did Grotius actually say here? And did he say it over here too? And did he fail to say it there? So, for example, in nuanced accounts across the three fields of international law, international history and international political theory, we end up with a picture of Grotius as a person concerned with private rights and private war (permitted where there was no existing public authority—say,

---

87. See e.g. White (n 13) xxx, 30.
88. Ibid.
89. Christopher N. Warren, 'John Milton and the Epochs of International Law', 24 *European Journal of International Law* (2013) 557–581, at 559.

the Dutch East Indies) or concerned to describe highly variegated forms of authority, or a Grotius in possession of a coherent historical consciousness as he amasses his eclectic material, rather than the cartoon figure of the disciplinary imagination who manages to invent sovereignty *de novo* and reconcile naturalism and positivism while losing control of his hodgepodge of historical sources.[90] In a way, then, to be *for* Grotius (or to retrieve the anomalies in Grotius) is to be against Grotianism. To approach Grotius is to be aware that one is approaching from a particular place—Whitean cognitive structure already *in* place—and to remember that this poetic, pre-analytic moment already screens out a number of Grotiuses (how many international lawyers think Grotius' extensive poetry is part of his international law or that Milton is a contemporary international lawyer whose work on marriage or circumcision might constitute a form of international law?).[91]

We might learn, too, from the best work in other fields that international law has power as an organising idea of international political life. Recent historical work has thickened and complicated international law's own critical project about this power by demonstrating that international legal ideas mattered hugely in determining how certain worlds were constructed, how certain practices were named and renamed, how certain possibilities were closed, perhaps forever.[92] The easy clichés of an international law somehow always on the outside of a politics or a social practice seem less present in such work. I remember saying to my college professor back in 1986 that I wanted to write my honours dissertation on the law of war crimes. In the afterwash of his disapproval, one phrase stuck out. He said there was little point in this sort of study since it was 'purely historical'. I pressed on with it, perhaps drawn to a subject that promised both 'purity' and 'history'. Later he warned me that 'nothing had happened since the Second World War and the Nuremberg Trials'. What did it mean for nothing to have happened? What was the nature of this absence? Wouldn't it be interesting to discover why something *hadn't* happened?

---

90. Edward Keene, *Beyond the Anarchical Society: Grotius, Colonialism and Order in World Politics* (Cambridge University Press, 2002) 38 (describing how Grotius is 'squeeze[d] . . . into a small box' in order to accommodate the demands of an early 19th-century adoption of unified sovereignty and to resist future Napoleonic ambitions).
91. On Milton, see Warren (n 89).
92. See e.g. Isobel Hull, *A Scrap of Paper: Breaking and Making International Law during the Great War* (Cornell University Press, 2014).

There has been a tendency among lawyers to believe that at different points of history nothing happened. Isabel Hull's recent book was, after all, an argument against the long-standing canard that during the Great War international law simply hadn't happened.[93] But we have also been given, or given ourselves, at various moments, the impression that nothing happened before 1603, or nothing in the first half of the 19th century or nothing during the Cold War.[94]

And after method, we might find the struggle over context and anachronism means that international legal work is productively reread. When I teach Tony Anghie's book on international law and empire, students say: 'Yes, we know this'. Well, the reason they know whatever it is they know is because of the book and the intellectual activity it provoked. It is striking to consider how outré Anghie's book was when it was first published (indeed, considered for publication). Now part of a new orthodoxy on the relationship between colonialism and international law, it was treated at the time as a methodologically suspect polemical intervention. It remains by far one of the most cited international law books by historians of international thought and by international relations scholars. Before the recent turn to method, though, it had acquired a kind of encrusted presence in the discipline. After method, we might find ourselves reading Anghie differently: first, paradigm shift, then monument (outside TWAIL-ish circles *Imperialism* ossified and came to stand for a few desultory propositions about 'empire' or 'colonialism' or 'positivism') and now site of interdisciplinary contention. Did the book underplay the variousness of colonial encounters, the immediate political circumstances of Vitoria or the sheer physicality of the extra-European world into which Europe ventured? Does it overstate the continuities between war on terror and 19th-century empire? Who knows? Methodological cross-hatching has reactivated the book—no longer a monument to be gingerly circumnavigated but part of a conversation about history and method.

Accordingly, after method, we might see how whole sub-disciplines understand themselves through the forms of writing and methods that are required in order for a set of ideas to join a conversation or be deemed

---

93. Ibid.
94. On the latter, see Matthew Craven, Sundhya Pahuja and Gerry Simpson (eds.), *Cold War International Law* (Cambridge University Press, 2019). On absence, see Fleur Johns, *Non-Legality in International Law: Unruly Law* (Cambridge University Press, 2013).

competent. I have already spoken about international criminal law's historical method, but it is worth considering in a little more detail how limited in ideological and stylistic range the field's *loci classici* were. A selection of the founding texts of the field would have to include Cherif Bassiouni's monumental works on crimes against humanity, Theodor Meron's essays calling for the humanisation of the laws of war, Antonio Cassese's bootstrapping articles on war crimes and Geoffrey Robertson's panoramic celebrations of the origins of international criminal law. What sort of histories do these efforts depend upon?

The first thing to note is that this is a very distinctive, early project with its own characteristic methods, and it generated a mass of mimetic work as the field began to establish itself. Hayden White's dictum that every field is constituted by what it forbids its practitioners to do is seen very clearly here.[95] And it is White, of course, who organises the writing of realist history into four genres: romance, comedy, tragedy and satire. The point in deploying White, here, is to think of these founding histories as acts of creation or ideological gestures and to try to work out how such acts are produced and how they aim to persuade and what a set of 'criteria of plausibility' might do to the range of thought available to us.[96]

In Whitean terms, then, to write as an international criminal lawyer is to write in the 'romantic' style—redemptive, eschatological, transcendent.[97] White's description of Jules Michelet's romantic style will be familiar to contemporary observers of international criminal law, with its perpetual 'striving to become':

> the historian must write his histories in such a way as to promote the realization of the unity that everything is striving to become. And ... everything appearing in history must be assessed finally in terms of the contribution it makes to the realization of the goal or the extent to which it impedes its realization.[98]

In the field of international criminal law, histories were initially written in precisely this style. Three methodological tendencies seem very obviously present in the histories of this discipline: a commitment to a prehistory of absence (compare this to the search for origins engaged in by international

---

95. Hayden White, *Tropics of Discourse* (John Hopkins University Press, 1985) 126–127.
96. Ibid. Foreword, xvii.
97. White (n 13) 8–9.
98. Ibid. 150.

tribunals); an appeal to an instinctive internationalism (whereas the past is a place where normative projects are dissolved in the politics of the domestic); and an incipient naturalism.

So, all precursors were simply a 'striving to become' an institutional system dedicated to ending impunity, preferably—and certainly at least in the shadow of—international courts. Everything local (the German trials in Leipzig after the Great War), merciful (any decisions to free or rehabilitate), experimental (Napoleon's exile on Elba and, then, St. Helena) or diplomatically subtle (the various decisions to accord immunity to high-ranking officials) was cast as ineffectual or insufficiently punitive, or simply formed part of a primitive prehistory of 'failure'.

This standard story begins with the disappointing non-hanging of Wilhelm II after Versailles, followed by the turning point (or 'promise') of Nuremberg, then a regrettable fifty-year gap in which international criminal law goes into abeyance, prior to the re-emergence of international tribunality in the Balkans and in Rwanda and the consummation of the project at Rome with the establishment of the International Criminal Court (ICC).[99] The normative commitments aimed at ending impunity. The institutional preferences were strongly in the direction of permanent international criminal jurisdiction. The politics was a thinly neo-naturalist, anti-sovereignist and anti-hegemonic humanitarianism. The 'method' was a combination of an episodic, selective and anachronistic 'magpie' history, with an exceedingly rigid periodisation, topped off with a kind of inevitabilism. The style was largely, as I have said, 'romantic,'[100] and the tone unvaryingly solemn, sometimes turgid; a seriousness of moral purpose weighing heavily on the prose. This method meant that historical counter-examples or anomalies or comic juxtapositions had to be set aside as possible blasphemies. In the most influential of these accounts, Geoffrey Robertson's *Crimes against Humanity*, history is a storehouse of missed opportunities and

---

99. For the 'turning point' idea (no longer would war criminals be 'protected' by state sovereignty), see Antonio Cassese, *International Criminal Law* 2nd ed. (Oxford University Press, 2008) 27–31; for the sense in which international criminal law (this 'great business') might have its own momentum, somehow detached from history, see Geoffrey Robertson, 'Ending Impunity: How International Criminal Law Can Put Tyrants on Trial', 38 *Cornell International Law Journal* (2005) 649–671, at 670. The early historical accounts of the development of international criminal law that fail to stick with this script have been more or less, themselves, written out of history (see chapter iv).
100. See chapter iv.

mistakes. The Moscow Show Trials are read as a vulgar politicisation—to be contrasted with the rise of human rights or the establishment of an international criminal law—rather than a possible unfortunate but symptomatic precedent for the Nuremberg and Tokyo War Crimes Trials.[101]

There were maverick accounts, of course: the journalism of Rebecca West, the *New Yorker* essays of Hannah Arendt, the political theory of Judith Shklar and the dissenting judgement of Justice Pal in post-war Tokyo. But it is striking that these writings adopted a much more sardonic mode in their style and tone. For a long time, this jarred with the existing conventions of solemnity. Pal's history, for example (one that, in recounting the story of international criminal law and empire, applied irony and tragedy rather than romance) was not published by the International Military Tribunal for the Far East (IMTFE) following the trial. It was too early for such things. Arendt encountered a different set of problems with her *New Yorker* essays on Eichmann. The tone was occasionally flip, and the method was loose and journalistic (this was, decidedly, not *The Origins of Totalitarianism*), and this left Arendt open to accusations that she had failed to understand the predicament of the Jewish leadership or had been cavalier with legal principle or had adopted an ironic sensibility when nothing but moral propriety was acceptable.

Wherever one stands on such matters, Arendt at least opens up the possibility of speaking about crimes against humanity in a style that rejects the hubris and moral self-satisfaction of the dominant conventions of international criminal law (from Robert Jackson 'staying the hand of vengeance' a few weeks after Hiroshima and Nagasaki, to Richard Goldstone entitling his autobiography, 'For Humanity'). Indeed, one of the reasons I keep coming back to Rebecca West and her description of the Nuremberg Trial as a 'citadel of boredom' is because of the way in which she decentres the Nuremberg Trial in the vernacular of irony while applying the journalistic equivalent of a micro-historical method. The tone is humorous, but the method is deadly serious.

West, Arendt and a handful of others were the exception to prevailing accounts. Now, however, we find ourselves in an 'after method' moment in the field (or at least a moment when its methods have become more varied

---

101. Geoffrey Robertson (n 10) 23–25.

and irresolute, and its histories more iconoclastic).[102] Mostly, this involves the retrieval of alternative sites of criminalisation (forgotten local, hybrid, internationalised trials), new origins (the Moscow Show Trials, the 19th-century's anti-slavery agitations) or an 'international criminal law' that is not retributive at all. It is possible, also, to hear a tonal difference in some of the new work in the field (it needs to be said that this new scholarship remains a minority enterprise). Histories of international criminal law now come in a variety of styles: pastoral, tragic, satirical, zen.[103]

iv. at Tate Britain

The phrase 'after method', in this chapter, is intended to convey two different meanings. In developing the first meaning, I have described an encounter between the historical disciplines and international law that seems full of promise. The methodological inheritance I have sketched can clearly offer international lawyers a fresh way into their own histories. The dilemmas of presentism or context seems much more alive to us now but we might want to understand 'method', less as a tranche of prohibitions or list of dispensations, and more as an invitation to think about, defend and elaborate a distinctive method of one's own. I have insisted, too, that method does not fully capture what we find appealing or resonant about the work we read and respond to. So, in the second case, 'after method' refers to the extra-methodic virtues of compelling and resonant history.

I will finish this chapter by offering a brief epilogue (perhaps more of a prolegomenon) on what I want to call literary virtue after method. And the reason we might want to think of this as literary is because it resembles the best fiction. What is it to be Shostakovich in the 1930s? One answer is found

---

102. Earlier work in this vein includes: Ed Morgan, 'Retributory Theater', 3(1) *American University Journal of International Law and Policy* (1988) 1–64; Shoshana Felman, 'Theaters of Justice: Arendt in Jerusalem, the Eichmann Trial, and the Redefinition of Legal Meaning in the Wake of the Holocaust', 27(2) *Theoretical Inquiries in Law* (2000) 465–507; Immi Tallgren, 'The Sensibility and Sense of International Criminal Law', 13(3) *European Journal of International Law* (2002) 561–595.
103. See e.g. tragic: Tor Krever, 'Dispensing Global Justice', 85 *New Left Review* (2014) 67–97; pastoral: Gerry Simpson, 'One Hundred Years of Turpitude', 33 *Australian Yearbook of International Law* (2015) 1–14; zen: Barry Hill, *Peacemongers* (University of Queensland Press, 2015); satirical: Immi Tallgren, 'Who Are "We" in International Criminal Law?', in Christine Schwöbel (ed.), *Critical Approaches to International Criminal Law: An Introduction* (Routledge, 2014) 71–95.

in Julian Barnes' novel, *The Noise of Time*, which I happened to be reading as I wrote this. The quality that emerges from the exchange between writer (Barnes) and writee (Shostakovich) is sympathetic engagement with predicament.[104] Similarly, and this hews close to some familiar and proximate methodological credos, a tonally convincing history might at least start with the predicament of a treatise writer in 1884 or a publicist in 1589 or an institution-builder in 1919 or indeed, the predicament of those who had been in the habit of receiving international law rather than making it. When we feel the predicament of writer and subject as we do in literature from Kafka to Jean Rhys, this history produced seems both indirect and more plausible. In theories of laughter, there is a Bergsonian comedy of correction, which doesn't sound very funny. And here I suppose I am concerned about corrective histories, or histories that are merely corrective or hubristically corrective. Bloch, again, calls this 'the mania for making judgments'.[105] Some of the wisest historiographers seem highly attuned to this. Indeed, in the case of someone like David Scott, it becomes the subject matter itself: a mood of tranquility and regret, or rumination that some historians have demanded as a substitute for strident revision.[106] There is a history that consists in a tirade against the past or, at least, the people who lived there and the terrible mistakes they made. Then, there is the historiographical equivalent, which most of us are susceptible to, of condemning all previous historians who failed to properly understand or describe that past. There is little point in writing history unless one thinks one can amend it in some way (the omnibus history, which simply collects everything previously written and synthesises it into a bestseller is an obvious exception). But, attention to predicament requires a certain amount of sensitivity to the past.

An associated literary virtue requires sensitivity to the present and future as well. A lot of conventional history in these fields holds the present in a certain position as it moves into the past. So, the present is understood to be, say, obviously, the era of globalisation or technique or market or, to go back to earlier 'presents', the clash of universalist ideologies or the culmination of this or that progress or anti-progress narrative. This is not quite a methodology—though certain methodologies will enact it—but more of

---

104. Julian Barnes, *The Noise of Time* (Cape, 2016).
105. Bloch (n 9) 23.
106. Scott (n 33).

a predisposition or what Hartog calls 'a regime'.[107] In Hartog's case it is not so much that only the present exists but that the present exists only as a present.[108] Thus we have the idea of 'a history of the present'—one that unnerves and reveals the conditions of possibility that define the present.[109] Or, to put it less abstractly, historians are enjoined to vigilantly watch over the present (Charles Péguy).[110]

The question that might dog us (or inspire us) here is the question of what we want from history or what history demands from us. What conceptions of the present force us into a certain way of thinking about the past.[111] What attitude to the present or demand made by an imagined present threatens to obliterate those strange or alien aspects of the past histories and past thinkers that might be suggestive of a different politics? If every political arrangement is understood as 'sovereignty' or even anti-sovereignty then we might deny ourselves the resources to think about alternative political futures. I am not even sure if this is a literary style or an aesthetic or a matter of craft.[112] It may be more and less than 'method'.[113] Sometimes it might even be 'a mood'. Lukács wrote his *Theory of the Novel* in a mood of 'permanent despair over the state of the world'.[114] It is likely that such a mood will inform if not determine certain methodological predispositions.

★ ★ ★

A few years ago, the Tate Britain curated an exhibition called *Artist and Empire*. Apart from giving the impression that Empire had been a series of glorious defeats or, at least, 'Last Stands' (Gordon, Wolfe), there was a surprisingly large number of paintings depicting treaty-making and negotiation. So, one story offered (though I am mutilating the exhibition here), as one moved from Room 2 to Room 3 of the gallery, was of imperial expansion

---

107. Hartog (n 6).
108. As he argues *passim*, capitalism has neither a past nor a future.
109. See e.g. Akbar Rasulov, 'New Approaches to International Law: Images of a Genealogy', in José Maria Beneyto and David Kennedy (eds.), *New Approaches to International Law: The European and the American Experiences* (TMC Asser Press, 2012) 151–191.
110. As quoted in Hartog (n 6) xvii.
111. Upendra Baxi, 'New Approaches to the History of International Law', 19 *Leiden Journal of International Law* (2007) 555–566. Baxi invokes Benjamin's 'redemptive history': one filled by 'the presence of the now'.
112. Christopher N. Warren, *Literature and the Law of Nations, 1580–1680* (Oxford University Press, 2015).
113. See Bloch's defence of the poetic: (n 9) 8.
114. Georg Lukács, *The Theory of the Novel*, trans. Anna Bostock (MIT Press, 1971 [1920]) 12.

as a period of treaty-formation followed by a catalogue of British military disasters: as if the British had somehow been hoodwinked by international law into a bunch of unequal treaties. Of course, things tended to work the other way. But the paintings themselves are actually quite ambiguous. This was not just international law being brought to some extra-European world. There was, at the same time, a degree of mutuality (though one wouldn't want to overstate this). The most striking thing about one of the paintings (dating from 1773), Agostino Brunias' *Sir William Young Conducting a Treaty with the Black Caribs on the Island of St. Vincent*, is the representation of the Black Carib chief, Chatoyer, who assesses his interlocutors with a look of wry appraisal: as if the historical context of empire had stepped out of the painting to comment directly upon it. Suddenly, this subaltern gaze at the treaty-makers suggests treaties as instruments of anachronism: not quite fit for purpose or out of step with the times, or fictions to be treated with amusement or disdain.

'After method', then, we might look at history anew. Yes, with sympathy for the choices and milieux of our protagonists and a greater sensitivity to the detail of their social, cultural and political lives and their worlds of struggle (Scott), yes, with a refusal of the easy traditions of linearity and expansion and unity (history as a history of 'dead effects'—Benjamin) in favour of a setting down of complexity in its fullness. But most of all with the intuition that after method, we might be able to see history in all its strangeness.

For us, as lawyers, history, for sure, is an itinerary (and generator) of norms or precedents—sometimes wrenched from their context—but also a place where we might go to feel estranged from the current world so that we might revisit it as strangers *and* habitués, and experience both its abject familiarity and closedness and inevitability as well as, and at the same time, its sheer unlikeliness and mutability.

vi
a declaration on friendly relations

i. elegiac friendship	148
ii. four unfriendly characters	151
enemies	153
criminals	156
pirates	158
neutrals	159
iii. thin friendship	161
iv. thick friendship	169
duellists	169
merchants	171
summiteers	172
v. lawful friendship	174
Nixon in China	179
Nehru in Belgrade	181
Khrushchev in Havana	183

Beautiful lofty things: O'Leary's noble head;
My father upon the Abbey stage, before him a raging crowd: ...
Maud Gonne at Howth station waiting a train,
Pallas Athene in that straight back and arrogant head:
All the Olympians; a thing never known again.

W. B. Yeats, 'Beautiful, Lofty Things', *New Poems* (1938)

He wrote me beautiful letters ... and we fell in love.

Donald Trump on Kim Jong-un (2018)

> Will not therefore an agreement about friendship, which makes nations friends, furnish something greater?
>
> Alberico Gentili, *de jure belli libri tres I* (1933 [1598])

i. elegiac friendship

In this book, I have been trying to think of international law as a cultural project, with a language, set of symbols and micro-politics, part of whose task is to patrol its own boundaries and the boundaries of the sayable and unsayable—international law as a deeply embedded way of seeing and thinking. In order to bring this into relief, I have put the discipline into conversation with subjects that might be thought of as 'literary'. In the previous chapter, I wrote about methods that aren't methods—styles of thought, conventions, instincts, tastes—in order to enliven or make an indirect approach on the disagreements about how to conduct international legal history. Earlier chapters considered the bathetic and the comic as international legal styles. In the next and final chapter, I approach international law's utopian aspect through the practices and intellectual apparatus of gardening. In this penultimate chapter, I turn to the topic of friendship—something often, though not of course exclusively, thought of as 'literary'—and bring it to bear on the field of international legal diplomacy. In it, I ask: can international legal relations be addressed in terms of friendship? What are 'friendly relations' in international law? Is there a politics of friendship in international law? Is there a law of friendship or, better, a lawful friendship that would animate a politics of international law?

Friendship and international law have a chequered relationship. What I propose to do here, then, is to reconstruct thin (e.g. amity, laws of friendly relations) and thick (drawing on Schmitt, Rawls, Reagan–Gorbachev) laws of friendship out of the existing material of international legal practice and doctrine as a prelude to constructing, afresh as it were, a concept of lawful friendship that might be useful in invigorating—might even have a bracing effect on—the study and practice of interstate diplomacy.

I want to go about this in the following way. I begin by setting 'the friend' among four other, more familiar, characters found in inter-sovereign relations: the enemy, the criminal, the pirate and the neutral. Each of these figures generates its own field of law (the law of force and war, the law of war crimes, the international law of terrorism/piracy and the law of neutrality;

there is no equivalent law of friendship—the law of peace is too expansive *and* too modest to do this job), and I want to show how each is dependent on, even if only as a matter of contrast, some incipient idea of what a friendly relationship might be. I then track friendship back to Greco-Roman and liberal political philosophy and consider why they disappeared from among the core preoccupations of political theory. Following from this, I think around friendship's many appearances and reappearances in international law and diplomacy in order to reconstruct a provisional law of friendship from these limited principles and practices that do exist (this might take the form of an imagined table of contents in an international law textbook).[1] Three thicker, but suspect, conceptions of friendship (the Schmittian *Jus Publicum Europaeum*, the liberal-institutional family of nations and the idea of meaningful interpersonal friendship among statespersons) are then sketched out.

I finish by elaborating a politics of international legal friendship and make a plea for a tentative, careful friendliness suggested by the lawful friendships found in Montaigne, Nietzsche and Derrida and through a reading of three moments of friendship set in the Cold War: one literary (the depiction of friendship in John Adams' opera, *Nixon in China*), one an unlikely performance of anti-imperial friendly relations (a return to the origins of the Bandung Conference in the friendship between Nehru and Tito, begun in Belgrade, at what Vijay Prashad has called the 'NAM Yalta' (Non-Aligned Movement Yalta), and one epistolary (a letter sent by Nikita Khrushchev to Fidel Castro in the aftermath of the Cuban Missile Crisis). Each represents in its rudimentary way a 'lawful friendship', a declaration on friendly relations.

Put in more brute terms, this chapter reconstructs, in a descriptive and aspirational mode, lawful friendship through an encounter between the literary figure of 'the friend' and an international law of friendly and unfriendly relations. My preliminary remarks are incited by two declarations of friendship: one a poetic gesture of elusiveness and out-of-reachness, the other a claim to instant friendship.

Yeats composed 'Beautiful, Lofty Things' late in life. The poem was published at the beginning of a year when Hitler was to annex the Sudetenland and enter Vienna. A world was about to come to an end (Yeats himself died in the opening month of 1939). These verses elegise a private

---

1. And in the world of international lawyers, what is friendship? Are theoretical schools just assemblies of friends? Are they cultural, or conceptual affairs? Something more, something less?

world that was also a public world—a father on the stage, a love affair famous around the world—and offer glimpses of Olympian friendships never known again, indeed only fully understood as friendships in the moment of their passing.[2] Yeats is describing here a Ciceroan ideal of friendship: friends who become friends in the moment of their death, when the friendship is transformed into a unilateral, unencumbered expression of poetic love.[3] From Aristotle *via* Derrida and Montaigne, comes the vocative: 'O friends, there are no friends'.[4] In Yeats, there is friendship, but it is always already over or perhaps fully consummated only in death—exemplary friendships experienced by a very rare (for Cicero, an aristocratic) few. Corporeal friendship lasts for three score years or more, or less, but the exemplary friendship is eternal, a model of non-reciprocal relations between humans. So, in some versions of Aristotle, to be a friend is to love without thought of reciprocity (in the example of the grieving friend, loving her lost comrade in death).[5] To be loving, without thought of reciprocity, even knowledge, on the part of the beloved is the highest form of friendship. And yet there are 'no friends'. To experience friendship is to already enter an experience of eulogising grief ('a thing never known again').[6]

An international legal world built on a series of utilitarian calculations or reciprocal obligations does not seem very hospitable to such sublime friendships. Almost everyone who writes on the subject begins by noting that the public worlds of politics and law make uneasy bedfellows with the intimacies of friendship.[7] Something is lost in translation. Friendship has its sociological (Robert Putnam's *Bowling Alone*) and anthropological (James Clifford's 'Anthropology as/and Travel') dimensions, and it has, at the very least, its literary-artistic biographical aspects (e.g. the friendships between Woolf and Sackville-West, Braque and Picasso, Davis and Morrison, or McCarthy and Arendt), but in international diplomacy, friendship itself

---

2. In Montaigne this is reversed. The friend is known before the friendship commences: 'We sought one another long before we met'. The meeting itself is 'some secret appointment of heaven', Michel de Montaigne, *Of Friendship*, transl. Charles Cotton (Penguin, 2004 [1580]).
3. See also Peter Goodrich, 'Laws of Friendship', 15(1) *Law and Literature* (2003) 23–52, at 30.
4. Jacques Derrida, *The Politics of Friendship* (Verso, 1997) 1.
5. On variations of friendship in Aristotle, see A.W. Price's philosophically exacting study, *Law and Friendship in Plato and Aristotle* (Oxford University Press, 1990) esp. 134–143.
6. This is the eulogising friendship that Derrida is searching for in *Politics of Friendship* (n 4) 271: 'a world is drawing to a close, fatally, at a moment when ... things have only just begun: only a few brief millennia, and it was only yesterday that "we were friends" already'.
7. But see Peter Goodrich's remark that while 'lawyers define friendship as external to law ... it is nonetheless lawyers who have most often written on friendship': Goodrich (n 3) 23.

seems just, ungraspably, out of reach. 'O friends, France has no friends only interests', to paraphrase de Gaulle. Friendships are declared, amity is invoked, but 'O friends, don't be deceived', these declarations seem to declare, 'there are no friends'.[8]

Yet, as I embarked on this chapter, I had the uncomfortable experience of finding myself part of a zeitgeist, with a burgeoning literature on the international politics of friendship (there is, it turns out, even a journal called *Amity*, dedicated to theorising around questions of friendship).[9] Then, some time before I began writing, President Trump made his remark about Kim Jong-un ('He wrote me beautiful letters . . . and we fell in love').[10] This was generally regarded as one more example of Trump's caprice. But, taken seriously, what are we to make of this? 'O friend, you are no friend (but instead a mortal enemy)'? Or, perhaps, 'O enemy, you are, secretly, a loved friend, if only we can make a deal'? It is probably the case that the former president's statement was delivered with a cynical wink to his then-permanently installed campaign trail audience. But I want to read this remark, I hope not implausibly, a bit differently. What if we stage Trump's speech as a plea for a diplomacy of love and friendship, a desire divorced, or at least separable, from the icky self-regard and callousness of many of Trump's intuitions (and policies)? A friendship between states or a friendship of diplomatic persons? A friendship of states as persons?

ii. four unfriendly characters

Friendship is not a regular stop on the international legal curriculum. I have read around 500 essays on statehood or neutrality and war but very few on friendship, comradeship, fraternity or love.[11] This could be, of course,

---

8. De Gaulle was not entirely consistent on this point. See the French–German Élysée Treaty (1963) with its formal and substantive commitments to Franco–German friendship.
9. Though Horst Hutter made a similar point about friendship as the 'spirit of the times' in 1978. See Horst Hutter, *Politics as* Friendship (Wilfred Laurier University Press, 1978) 3.
10. Ben Jacobs, 'Trump Professes Love for Kim', *The Guardian*, 30 September 2018, at https://www.theguardian.com/us-news/2018/sep/30/trump-love-kim-nasty-democrat-kavanaugh-west-virginia. Even the president himself suggested that 'they' might find this 'unpresidential'.
11. This is no longer the case in political theory, where friendship is undergoing a mini-revival. See e.g. P. E. Digeser, 'Friendship between States', 39 *British Journal of Political Science* (2008) 323; Charles A. Kupchan, *How Enemies Become Friends: The Sources of Stable Peace* (Princeton University Press, 2010); Felix Berenskoetter, 'Friends, There Are No Friends? An Intimate

because friendship, like the offside rule or micro-conducting, really is not related in any meaningful way to public international law. International law is what international lawyers do, and we don't *do* friendship. Instead, we think of ourselves as being engaged, mostly, in the study of sovereigns in the abstract: sovereigns as opaque, featureless equals—every state a 'most-favoured nation', international law as a field of sovereigns *qua* sovereign. The international legal order is dedicated to screening out the peculiar vices or virtues of individual sovereigns (at the outer limits of this practice of sovereign equality, diplomats from Denmark found themselves sitting next to the representative from the Khmer Rouge—Cambodia now styling itself as 'Democratic Kampuchea'—at the UN in 1978).

When we do give the state an identity or character, it tends to be a formal, usually provisional, identity (a 'like-minded state' at the Rome Statute negotiations in Rome, for example), worlds away from the timeless friendships of Yeats, Cicero and Aristotle. There are, though, qualifications to this general principle of sovereign abstraction. So, let me describe four more substantive characters who inhabit the international legal space: four characters in search of a legal order, or in search of a place in (or outside) the legal order, or established as figures to be ordered or disordered through law.[12] And, as in Pirandello, these characters are both constitutive and disruptive.[13] Each of these characters (enemies, criminals, pirates and neutrals) has activated or provoked, or been brought to life by, a legal infrastructure, a 'law of . . .', and yet each of them undercuts or threatens the existence of another character, that of the characterless international legal subject, or 'sovereign without qualities'. I want to take each of them in turn and not just as a way of 'situating' friendship but because each of these characters needs to be brought into relations with the friend in order to make sense of this character and in order to think through the laws associated with these figures as laws of friendly relations to come.[14]

Reframing of the International', 35(3) *Millennium: Journal of International Studies* (2007) 647, 652–653.

12. Of course, it is possible to think of other legal persons (corporations, self-determination movements, NGOs) that are not included in this list of characters. But this is a list of sovereign persons not legal persons and, in a sense, it operates on a spectrum of affection rather than personhood.
13. Pirandello, *Six Characters in Search of an Author* (1921). I thank Charlie Peevers for alerting me to Pirandello.
14. The laws of enmity (Geneva, The Hague), crime (Rome, Nuremberg, Tokyo, Kampala), piracy/terror (New York, Washington) and neutrality (Nyon, Vienna).

enemies

There is an international legal pessimism that grounds all of international law in a kind of law of enmity.[15] Or, as the old German saying goes, with its tangy, Brexity flavourings, *feind—Todfeind—partifreund* (enemy—deadly enemy—fellow party member).[16] This law of enmity (a law of force and a law of war) lies at the heart of what international law thinks of itself as being about: organising relations among enemies and would-be enemies, i.e. trying to prevent, or juridify, combat and encouraging the return of a post-enmity state of amicable relations or, at least, suspended enmity.

One of international law's self-narrated success stories was to control enmity or bring law to bear on certain aspects of it.[17] Enemies would be encouraged to become friends or neutrals and those that failed to become friends, or were deprived of even proto-friendship, were converted into criminals (their lawful adversaries became prosecutors and judges or, more boldly, representatives of humanity, latterly 'the international community').

The *ius ad bellum* defines when it is lawful to make war on an enemy. The right to use force in self-defence requires the existence of an armed attack by what we might describe as an enemy state (a state that has made, or is imminently on the cusp of making, the initial attack; a violently disposed enemy). The law tells us too when another state is entitled to befriend the victim state (collective self-defence) and the point at which such friendship must give way to the larger claims of the international community.[18]

The collective security provisions of the UN Charter, meanwhile, do not declare the existence of an enemy but instead the existence of a threat to the peace, breach of the peace or act of aggression for which a state will sometimes be, in a loose sense, liable. In certain circumstances, the application of this power also creates another disruptive character (the pirate, of which

---

15. The enemy has been the subject of large doctrinal (the *ius ad bellum*, the *ius in bello*) and conceptual (Carl Schmitt alone has induced a whole sub-field of 'enemy' scholarship) studies. For a general account, see Robert Howse, 'Schmitt, Schmitteanism and Contemporary Legal Theory', in Anne Orford and Florian Hoffman, *The Oxford Handbook of the Theory of International Law* (Oxford University Press, 2016) Chapter 11.
16. Graham Smith, *Friendship and the Political* (Imprint, 2011).
17. This is the story told in Oona Hathaway and Scott Shapiro, *The Internationalists: And Their Plan to Outlaw War* (Allen Lane, 2017).
18. See *Case concerning Military and Paramilitary Activities in and against Nicaragua (Merits)* 1986 I.C.J. 14 (finding that the US had failed to establish a right to engage with El Salvador and Honduras in collective self-defence).

more later.) On the whole, though, when it comes to collective security, the Security Council has often been more concerned with circumstances of unfriendliness or threat rather than the identification of specific malefactors or enemies.[19] Indeed, in most respects the Security Council does not think of itself as having 'enemies'; instead, it responds to, or remains seized of, 'situations'.

There is an exception to this. The Charter contains an explicit, but largely forgotten, reference to 'enemy states' in Articles 53 and 107:

1. ... no enforcement action shall be taken under regional arrangements or by regional agencies without the authorization of the Security Council, with the exception of measures against any enemy state ...
2. The term enemy state as used in paragraph 1 of the Article applies to any state which during the Second World War has been an enemy of any signatory of the present Charter.

These enemies exist outside the inherently universalising framework of the UN and are, as well, an exception to the general rule that regional (or indeed, any other) enforcement action must be taken under the authority of the Security Council. These provisions posit a United Nations of friends with two principal enemies, Germany and Japan.[20] This makes sense because the United Nations begins, after all, as a coalition of willing friends at the war's end (the 'united nations' referred to in the International Military Tribunal Charter at Nuremberg, for example).

The provision has never been invoked, but nor have proposals for its deletion (in the High Level Panel Report in 2004 and at the World Summit in 2005) resulted in its removal.[21] So, for example, in discussions at the 49th session of the UN General Assembly, many states called for the deletion of the term 'enemy states' on the basis that some of these so-called enemies—Japan was the most commonly invoked example—were in fact friends of the UN's. North Korea objected to the deletion of Japan on the basis that

---

19. There are exceptions: Iraq's 'flagrant violations' made it an enemy of the Council. See e.g. Security Council Resolution 678 (1991).
20. The other enemy states were Romania, Bulgaria, Italy, Hungary and Finland.
21. See *Repertory of Practice of United Nations, Suppl. 3, Vol. II* (1979–1984); Article 55, *Repertory Suppl. 6 Volume III* (1979–1984); The UN Secretary General's High-Level Panel on Threats, *A More Secure World*, A/59/565 (2004), Article 298.

it had not settled its historical obligations to other states nor undertaken in good faith an obligation 'not to repeat such acts'.[22]

To put this in slightly opaque terms: Japan, often referred to as a friend of the UN remains (textually at least) an enemy of the UN because it is an enemy of North Korea, itself now thought of, in many quarters, as a universal enemy.[23]

Article 107, meanwhile, is even more definitive:[24]

> Nothing in the present Charter shall invalidate or preclude action, in relation to any state which during the Second World War has been an enemy of any signatory to the present Charter, taken or authorized as a result of that war by the Governments having responsibility for such action.[25]

There were serious debates about these clauses in the late 1940s and early 1950s, with some states taking the view that all problems concerned with 'the liquidation of the consequences of the Second World War and with situations resulting directly from the war were beyond the competence of the United Nations'.[26] This is heady stuff and broadly interpreted might mean that the UN had very little competence over anything because almost everything *was* related to the post-war peace (this was not the usual understanding at this time).

The UN, then, at its origins, can be thought of as a coalition of friends with a smattering of official enemies (who themselves, in a very material sense, became close friends of the UN by providing it with disproportionate funding support). But as we shall see, this new coalition of allies (the *United Nations*) was also engaged in an effort to abolish enmity altogether and replace it with policing. The UN was to become an organisation that made friendship compulsory.

---

22. See G A (28), 1st Com., 1957th mtg., Democratic People's Republic of Korea, para. 48 at Article 107, *Repertory of Practice of United Nations, Suppl. 83, Vol. VI*.
23. Japan is now the third largest contributor to the UN's budget (for a long time it was second only to the United States).
24. For references to Article 107 in connection with the question of deletion or amendment of the Article, see Article 107, *UN Repertory, Suppl. 5, Vol. V* (1970–1978) (e.g. G A (25), Plen., 1841st mtg: Brazil, para. 6; 1842nd mtg: Japan, para. 80; 1847th mtg: Ecuador, paras. 103 ff; 1875th mtg; Kenya, para. 7; Nicaragua, para. 20; 1376th mtg).
25. See too Article 77, which applies trusteeship arrangements to 'territories which may be detached from enemy states'.
26. See 'UN Repertory of Practice' at http://legal.un.org/docs/?path=../repertory/art107/english/rep_orig_vol5_art107.pdf&lang=EFS

Meanwhile, the *ius in bello* organises relations among enemies when these enemies are already in conflict, regardless of whether there has been a declaration of unfriendly relations (i.e. war). The Geneva and Hague rules are configured around the idea of an adversary to be vanquished humanely. The laws of war, if they do anything, also, at the very least immunise millions of killers from legal proceedings. Soldiers cannot, normally, be prosecuted for the killing of other soldiers unless those others are fighting alongside them (the interpersonal friendship produced by the laws of war (by war itself) is, of course, a form of camaraderie or *esprit de corps*). But, in some respects, like the friendship stimulated by a Security Council resolution and establishing a coalition of allies, this camaraderie can be short-lived, exclusive, a product of the moment.[27] Friendship does not always survive the peace.

The law of war is more conventionally understood as the law of the injured enemy, or the civilian enemy: the enemy whose incapacitation (because she is *hors de combat*) or innocence (because she is a civilian child) renders her protected from annihilation.[28] And just as the law of force limits the kinetic violence deployable against the enemy (e.g. the rules of proportionality and necessity), so, too, the laws of war place limits on what can be done to enemy soldiers (no unnecessary suffering, no wanton mass slaughter, another appeal to proportionality). In this moment, the enemy becomes a potential friend to be treated with a certain amount of respect and care, and one of the achievements of law is to make as smooth as possible the transition, after the war, from enmity to friendship.[29]

criminals

But, over the past few decades, at least, pressure has been placed on this idea of enmity as a form of suspended friendship. As far as the Great Powers are

---

27. See Maurice Blanchot, *Friendship* (Stanford University Press, 1997) 31. It is not that old comrades do not build lifetime friendships, but rather that these friendships are founded not on the passage of time but instead on a 'coup de foudre', the moment of comradeship forged in war. See Simon Critchley, 'The Other's Decision in Me', 1(2) *European Journal of Social Theory* (1998) 259–279. For a fictionalised account of this idea, see Kate Atkinson's *A God in Ruins* (Black Swan, 2016), in which a pilot from Bomber Command visits a former crew-member in Canada but finds the visit an anticlimax. Their friendship, forged in the confines of a Lancaster bomber in raid after raid across Germany, does not reignite.
28. See Rebecca Sutton, *'The Humanitarian'*, doctoral thesis, LSE (2018).
29. In this sense, it resembles Derrida's thought that Schmitt's friend–enemy distinction is always, already, unstable.

concerned, the idea of enmity itself has fallen into disrepair, if not disuse, as the protections afforded the enemy have withered.[30] Enemies have become pests or criminals.[31] To unfriend is to criminalise or to declare radically other. To criminalise or demonise is to unfriend. There is only friendship, and outside it the zone of lawless detention and killing. 'O my enemy, there are no enemies, only criminals and friends'.

This is the opposite of Joan of Arc's answer to her interrogators at her trial when she is asked whether God hated the English: 'I do not know whether God loves or hates the English; I only know that they must be driven out of France'.[32] In 1919, Kaiser Wilhelm was (eventually) driven out of France, but this was no longer enough. There was to be no polite revival of a suspended amity here, as there had been in Vienna in 1815, at the end of the Napoleonic Wars. It had to be demonstrated, too, that God hated the Germans. This was to be done through international law.[33] Wilhelm II was indicted at Versailles for a variety of acts that no one had previously thought of as illegal far less criminal.[34] Here was a man who had gone to war as, at worst, an enemy (in fact a cousin of the British King George) and had ended it as a fugitive from an unprecedented criminal justice.[35] Now, enemies had become criminals. There was little prospect of a resumption of friendly relations in these circumstances. Instead, a language of punishment (arraignment, arch-criminality, war guilt) was adopted as the model for diplomatic affairs. Germany was no longer to be treated as an enemy state (subject to the classical rules of rehabilitation, concordat, resumption) but was regarded as an outlaw, a state incapable of re-entering the realm of diplomatic equals.[36]

Robert Ley, the German Labour Secretary indicted at Nuremberg two decades later, was a former friend who could not conceive of himself as a

---

30. Around these themes, see Gerry Simpson, *Law, War and Crime* (Polity Press, 2007).
31. This is not the moment to revisit Schmitt. Suffice to say, we can think of the *ius publicum europaeum* as a law of friendship or, at least, a law between cold hearted monsters who, in a moment of civility, have agreed to spare each other annihilation. See Carl Schmitt, *The Nomos of the Earth* (Telos, 2006).
32. Carl Schmitt, *Theory of the Partisan* (Telos, 2007) 92.
33. On the historical relations between theological and secular concepts, see various works by Hans Blumenberg, e.g. *The Legibility of the World* (1979).
34. For an alternative view, see Hendrik Simon, 'The Myth of *Liberum ius ad bellum*', 29(1) European Journal of International Law (2018) 113–136.
35. The story is told in William Schabas, *The Trial of the Kaiser* (Oxford University Press, 2018).
36. This is something I have taken up in *Great Powers and Outlaw States* (2004).

criminal. In a transcript of his interview with interrogators, he says at one point: 'Put us up against a wall by all means and shoot us but don't call us c ... c ... c ... c ...criminals'.³⁷ Ley, then, is neither the defeated enemy nor the suspended friend but rather a criminal-enemy who must be hanged (after (im)proper legal procedure). In my work, I have long argued that international criminal law is the law applied to enemies of mankind: the terminal cessation of friendship.

But if the enemy is now a criminal, what becomes of the friend? After Versailles, we have a new kind of friendship, a universal friendship, a friendship becoming 'humanity' or 'civilisation'.³⁸ Those who were not criminals were no longer in relations of enmity with those who were (the friend-enemy had been replaced by the prosecutor-felon relation), and they were in a different sort of friendship with each other as well—no longer an alliance of war-makers but a condominium of righteous prosecutors or judges: a new form of friendly relations, absolute enmity producing unconditional friendship.³⁹

pirates

But even the object of international criminal law is not entirely friendless. The accused war criminal or torturer has friends in court (a judge will guide an accused through the accusations, or a lawyer will enable the defence; sometimes an *amicus* is appointed to give aid to the court and the defendant). Indeed, one can think of the court itself as a friend. Not all 'criminals', though, are treated as potential subjects of the criminal law. As Carl Schmitt put it—to his friend Sombert—towards the end of the war and with Nazi Germany facing imminent defeat:

> From an Anglo-Saxon perspective, we are the pirate—the enemy of humanity. Pirate—that means not the individual, but the ship and its entire crew ... everyone will be hanged: captured together, hanged together ... pardon will not be given.⁴⁰

---

37. See Michael Marrus, *The Nuremberg War Crimes Trials* (Palgrave Macmillan, 1997). See also Richard Overy, *Interrogations* (Penguin, 2002) 498.
38. See discussion in chapter iv.
39. See Gabriella Slomp, 'Carl Schmitt on Friendship: Polemics and Diagnostics', 10(2) *Critical Review of International Social and Political Philosophy* (2007) 199–213, at 203. Schmitt (n 31) 147.
40. Gopal Balakrishnan, *The Enemy: An Intellectual Portrait of Carl Schmitt* (Verso, 2000) 240

After the war, the Nazi elites were treated as criminals rather than pirates, of course. Historically, though, pirates have been refused the protections of the criminal law. They were given the protection of neither the law of enmity (the laws of war) nor the enmity of law (the criminal law). This pirate figure is understood to possess an attitude of universal hostility towards 'mankind', and 'mankind' in return adopts the same posture in relation to the pirate. So, for example, in *Republic of Bolivia*, an insurance case that turned on whether the insured shipping company was indemnified against attacks by pirates or insurgents, an English court was asked to determine whether the El Acre rebels were at war with one state (Brazil) and were therefore insurgents, or were at war with all states (or capable of plundering shipping in general) and were therefore pirates.[41] For the court, what marked out the pirate was his lack of discernment; he will loot anything (it is doubtful that many actual pirates had any hostility at all; they plunder but were motivated by avarice or daring, not anything that could be described as hostility). The victims of piracy (e.g. the great Atlantic powers in the 18th century) did, though, constitute a kind of humanity, a loose friendship defined by its mutual and shared contempt for the pirate. But, paradoxically, this 'humanity' has not always felt itself to be bound by the laws of humanity (either the humanitarian laws of war, the due process rights in the criminal law or the 'laws of humanity' emerging in the early 19th century). The pirate is radically other and radically friendless.[42]

neutrals

The re-emergence and reproduction of the terrorist-pirate figure and the criminal state/individual put further stress on the neutral, the final figure in our character study. Neutrality is what Lorimer calls an abnormal relation, the causes of which are found in humankind's lack of rectitude. As he puts it, neutrality, like enmity and the various forms of criminality he

---

41. Republic of Bolivia v. Indemnity Marine Insurance Co. Ltd [1909] 1 KB 785.
42. The pirate is often regarded as stateless and friendless and can be killed with impunity. This Agambenesque quality can be seen in the treatment of Abu Bakr al-Baghdadi, the former ISIS leader. Indeed, when the then-leader of the opposition in the UK, Jeremy Corbyn, suggested that Baghdadi should be tried he (Corbyn, that is) was branded a 'terrorist sympathiser' in the British press. For a lengthier disquisition on piracy, see my *Law, War and Crime* (n 30). See for a description of friendship among pirates, Marcus Rediker, *Villains of All Nations: Atlantic Pirates in the Golden Age* (Verso, 2004)

seems to enjoy cataloguing, is an 'aberration from the natural life of man', a life in which there would be only normal relations or an international law in which all relations would be relations of 'peace and amity' (punctuated by the odd squabble).[43] Neutrality can be understood as a domain poised between friendship and enmity, but it has moved back and forth between these two conditions, sometimes in the same period or treatise. In Grotius, we have the strict requirements of neutrality (impartiality, free passage, furnishing supplies to both sides) only in 'doubtful' cases (i.e. cases where it is unclear which side is the just protagonist). In circumstances where one side is obviously 'wicked', then friendship is due to the just warrior.[44] The history of the US Republic can be traced through its isolationist and internationalist phases, of course, but there has also been at the same time a slow movement over the decades from friendly neutrality to a more robust mix of compulsory alliance and criminality. In 1801, Thomas Jefferson, giving his First Inaugural Address, depicted the US as a friendly neutral seeking: 'Peace, commerce and honest friendship with all nations—entangling alliances with none'. Two centuries later, a different kind of approach to neutrality was in evidence in George W. Bush's address to the nation after the 9/11 attacks: 'Every nation, in every region, now has a decision to make. Either you are with us, or you are with the terrorists'.[45] There were only war-making pacts and terrorists: no space, now, for the standoffish impartiality of neutrality's classic age where the idea was to maintain 'friendship' though non-entanglement.

★ ★ ★

To sum up so far, then, the interplay of these four characters might provide us with some resources for a deeper form of lawful friendship. The law of enmity contains the seeds of an international law of friendship, a friendship

---

43. James Lorimer, *Institutes* (Blackwood, 1883, reprinted Elibron) 7.
44. Hugo Grotius, 'On Those Who Are of Neither Side of War', in Stephen Neff (ed. and annotation), *On the Law of War and Peace* (Cambridge, 2012) 410–412.
45. The story is, of course, much more complicated than this. It may be that the Second World War and the move from the US 1939 Neutrality Act to Lend-Lease marked the end of US neutrality or, alternatively, that the creation of international organisations like the League of Nations made it unlawful for states to maintain a neutral posture or that neutrality waxes and wanes according to the nature of the wars being fought (e.g. the distinction between duel wars and major, multi-state, Great Power wars). See e.g. Georg Schwarzenberger, *International Law and Totalitarian Lawlessness* (Cape, 1943) 30–31. For a comprehensive history, see Stephen Neff, *The Rights and Duties of Neutrals* (Manchester University Press, 2000).

that survives even the most potently adverse, warlike, circumstances: a friendship despite, not a friendship because. This is especially true of the laws of war. Could these be redeemed from their associations with legitimation, with punishment, with hubris?[46] Perhaps, instead, there might be a law of hospitality, care, kindness, a 'banality of the good', a law materialised on the Western Front on Christmas Day 1915, when German and Allied soldiers exchanged presents and played football together in No-Man's-Land.[47] The law of criminality, too, might be liberated from its associations with unilateral punitiveness by a commitment to listening to the stories of wartime adversaries, by offering care and (legal) aid to the 'enemies of humanity'. A law of piracy might take up the solidarity of pirate society as a form of friendship serving as an antidote to the strictures of imperial or sovereigntist friendly relations. And finally, might there not be a neutrality beyond neutrality, a Bandungian neutrality of communitarian experimentalism rather than one of moral indifference or self-interested non-belligerence?

iii. thin friendship

Before building on some of this, I want to put international law in relation to friendship in a more general sense in order to prepare the way for a vision of 'lawful friendship' in the fifth and final section of the chapter. First, though, I want to ask what became of political friendship? Ideas of political friendship, after all, seem less visible in political theory and philosophy than, say, questions of political justice, or equality.[48]

Here we might compare two traditions of thinking about friendship: liberal and Greco-Roman. Mostly, contemporary liberal political philosophers think of friendship as an extra-political condition integral to neither, say, Dworkin's respect-giving, freestanding, rights-bearing citizenry, nor Rawls' friendless inhabitants of the original position. In the latter case, the veil of ignorance returns us to a pre-intimacy, atomistic state—the circumstance in which we are best equipped to make decisions about the distribution of political goods. This is because friendship and fraternity engage, what Rawls

---

46. Chris af Jochnik and Roger Normand, 'The Legitimation of Violence', 35(1) *Harvard International Law Journal* (1994) 49–96.
47. I borrow this term from Mark Osiel.
48. Smith (n 16) 3–4.

called, 'ties of sentiment and feeling' rather than *mores* extendable to communities larger than families or friendship groups.⁴⁹ (Of the revolutionary triumvirate of equality, liberty and fraternity, only the first named pair had become concerns of political theory, and the arrangement of the first two principles is the primary task of *A Theory of Justice*.)⁵⁰ Fraternity, for Rawls, was limited as a political concept because it could not harden into democratic rights or realisable distributive policies.

It is easy to see why liberal political and legal theory might take this position. Keeping politics and friendship separate makes a certain amount of sense, after all. Is a political friend, a friend? If politics is the realm of calculation and self-interest, do we want a politics of friendship? Why would we want friends who endlessly make cost-benefit decisions about how and whether to pursue friendship? We have all experienced the metric friendship: 'She missed my birthday two years in a row, and I ended the friendship'. Obversely, friendship *in* politics can sail very close to nepotism (in its broadest sense). Liberal politics is ideally the realm of the loveless calculus (the politician, regulator, bureaucrat acts—ought to act—in the name of the whole, exchanging the particularism of the companion for the generalism of the citizen).

And yet, these liberal assumptions about friendship and politics have not always held. Even Rawls, in an Aristotelian move, concedes that while fraternity is not a political concept, it 'conveys instead certain attitudes of mind and forms of conduct without which we would lose sight of the values expressed by these rights [to equality and liberty]'.⁵¹ He associates amity with 'civic friendship' and 'social solidarity'. Indeed, his difference principle, with its concern to ensure that social and economic arrangements in a polity do not disadvantage the least advantaged, is itself as close as liberal theory gets to a formal standard of fraternity. In this sense, society resembles that most obviously fraternal of social arrangements: the family unit.⁵²

But in Aristotle, friendship is not just necessary to the functioning of a well-ordered city, it is also the highest end of the political regime. What he called 'concord' was more important than various distributive or corrective

---

49. John Rawls, *A Theory of Justice* (Oxford University Press, 1973) 105.
50. Ibid.
51. Paul Schollmeier, *Other Selves* (State University of New York, 1994) 4 (arguing that the Greeks had a broader public conception of friendship than our largely privatised understandings).
52. Rawls (n 49) 105.

forms of justice because friendly concord between citizens held the community together and gave it a meaningful life.⁵³ Famously, he compared three *genera* of friendship: a friendship of utility, a friendship of pleasure and perfect friendship.⁵⁴ The friendship of utility is reciprocal and self-interested, a pact of mutuality and expedience as much as one of affection. According to Aristotle, it is too instrumental—too capable of being directed at unfriendly anterior ends—to count as real friendship. The friendship of pleasure, meanwhile, is light, transient, breezy but also precarious and decadent. Who said friendship was supposed to be fun?

In *Politics*, Aristotle set a high bar for political friendship: 'the political friendship must be regarded as being for the sake of noble acts not for the sake of living together'.⁵⁵ Perfect friendship is the friendship we direct towards 'another self' in whom we will the good. In Cicero, it is a form of love and not calculation.⁵⁶ Aristotle's perfect friendship (*philia*), though, is also a form of self-love; the friend is the other self (rather like love's 'twin' figure), a self whose otherness must disappear in the moment of being loved.

The first response to this tradition might be to suggest that there is not, indeed cannot be, any international law of friendship, certainly not a friendship of virtue. It may be that relations of friendship, then, are structurally impossible. To paraphrase a classical realist dictum: 'friendship' is just preparation for enmity. From this perspective, states find themselves in a violent and lawless state of nature in which alliances are shifting and mutable. Violent combat lurks as a perennial possibility. Especially mordant, bio-deterministic types like E. O. Wilson thought of states as giant sea slugs on the ocean floor.⁵⁷ When one giant sea slug meets another, the larger of the two simply ingests the smaller one.⁵⁸ The project is one of relentless gurgitation. This image coalesced nicely around Hobbesian ideas of the *bellum omnium contra omnes* and then onto Machiavelli's friendless manoeuvrings, Darwin's evolutionary fatalism and Freud's discontented drives to violence and, even, death. It isn't

---

53. Aristotle, *Nicomachean Ethics*, Books 8 and 9.
54. Ann Ward, 'Friendship and Politics in Aristotle's *Nicomachean Ethics*', 10(4) *European Journal of Political Theory* (2011) 443–462; Schollmeier (n 51) 38.
55. Aristotle, *Politics* 1280b, 36–40.
56. Cicero, *On Friendship* VIII.
57. But states are not like sea slugs and, in any case, are not easily ingested or digested. Invading is one thing. Digesting is another. This is at least one of the lessons of the Iraq War in 2003.
58. Michael Walzer, *Just and Unjust Wars* (Basic, 1992).

easy for friendship to get much purchase in the face of this kind of pessimistic, necessitarian logic.

If there is a legal order, according to this view, it is grounded in a law of non-friendship: at best, a law of acquaintanceship or at worst, a series of declarations of unfriendly relations. Only unfriendly or coldly disassociated legal persons need law. States, then, have entered into agreements to organise or mask these unfriendly relations and to temporarily suspend enmity. That might be why the most credible legal suborders are those with the most modest ambitions—for example, the agreement not to kill one another's ambassadors or shoot down passenger airliners that stray into one's airspace.

Patricia Williams, in her book *The Alchemy of Race and Rights*, describes an incident where she and her law school colleague, Peter Gabel, are searching for housing as they prepare to take up their new academic posts teaching contracts together.[59] When they meet to discuss their new rental properties, it turns out that Williams has entered into a typical contractual arrangement with her landlord (someone already known to her but someone she wanted to reassure through an arms-length arrangement) while Gabel has become friends with his landlord (their agreement is concluded, not with a contract but with a handshake). For Gabel, friendship with a stranger is an escape from a set of alienated legal relations. For Williams, it is the law that offers protection from the vicissitudes of friendship and enmity, a place of agreement and futurity. The world of tenant–landlord substitute friendship is denied to her, and it is in friendless lawful relations that she finds some sort of remedy or refuge. As Peter Goodrich argues: 'friendship . . . is also defined as the antonym or obverse of the relationships that legal practice enacts'.[60]

If this law of non-friendship seems too unpalatable a depiction of international law, maybe we can think of the international law of friendship as an interim state, an a-legal or sub-legal form of interstate relations. States often describe the lawful but injurious or belligerent acts of other states as 'unfriendly'. So, unfriendliness occupies a position somewhere above illegality, and below lawfulness, permitting a certain gradation of response. A state that imposes protectionist measures on another state's agricultural goods or engages in elaborate military manoeuvres close to an international border or refuses to reveal details of criminal behaviour within an embassy abroad, is generally characterised as having engaged in 'unfriendly acts'. In 2018, the

---

59. Patricia Williams, *The Alchemy of Race and Rights* (Harvard University Press, 1991) 146–148.
60. See also Goodrich (n 3) 28.

French Foreign Minister, Florence Parly, describing Russian satellite activities, said: 'Trying to listen to your neighbours is not only unfriendly. It's an act of espionage'.[61] Angela Merkel adopting the same theme said: 'Spying among friends—that simply isn't done'.[62] This sub-legal language seems to be a valuable enough usage. It is not always appropriate to sue someone for forgetting to send you a birthday card, however unfriendly the original gesture.

A final possibility though is that breaches of international law are unfriendly acts undertaken in the midst of a general system of friendly relations under law created through forms of bilateral and multilateral treaty-making with other states. In other words, international law is *already* a law of friendship albeit a thin friendship of merely living together—from the Westphalian substitution of virtue with sovereignty to the Cold War law of coexistence. In *The Ethics*, Aristotle suggests that 'love is a passion and . . . friendship is a habit'.[63] International law is certainly a law of habit, repetition, practice and acquiescence, and the syntax and language of friendship are not, after all, entirely absent from the texts of international law (even if the references to friendship or amity seem ritualistic or phony or insubstantial in some way, as if nothing much lies behind the declaration of friendship—or, at least, nothing resembling friendship).[64]

This thin form of friendship—a living together that resembles an Aristotlean friendship of utility—is largely founded on the idea of international legal relations as equal contractual relations.[65] These sorts of friendly relations are present in treaties of amity that have long populated the world of international trade and navigation.[66] So, for example, the earliest Treaty

---

61. https://www.thelocal.fr/20180908/france-says-russia-tried-to-spy-on-satellite. Note that the unlawfulness of espionage itself is questionable. See Emily Haslam, 'Information Warfare: Technological Changes and International Law', 5(2) *Journal of Conflict & Security Law* (2000) 157–175.
62. 'German Intelligence Also Snooped on White House', *Der Spiegel*, 22 January 2017.
63. *Ethics* 8.5 1157b, 28–29.
64. See Evgeny Roshchin, 'The Concept of Friendship: From Princes to States', 12(4) *European Journal of International Relations* (2006) 599, 611; Jacques Derrida, 'Politics of Friendship', 50(3) *American Imago* (1993) 353–391; I do not mean to diminish the role of ritual in international law. See Thomas Franck, *The Power of Legitimacy among Nations* (Oxford University Press, 1990).
65. See Ward (n 54).
66. For a book-length dissection of these themes and a genealogy of ethical and contractual conceptions of international friendship, see Evgeny Roshchin, *Friendship among Nations: History of a Concept* (Manchester University Press, 2017)

of Amity entered into by the US, *The Treaty of Amity and Commerce between the French King and the thirteen United States of North America* (signed by Benjamin Franklin), states: 'There shall be a firm, inviolable and universal Peace, and a true and sincere Friendship between the most Christian King, his Heirs and Successors, and the United States of America'.[67] A Treaty of Alliance signed on the same day is much more hard-hitting and founds friendship on a shared antipathy (towards the British Crown). This is the first 'Most-Favoured Nation' treaty. Friendship here is a minimal concordat: no state shall be treated more favourably by the other side than its treaty partner. Trade, openness, guarantees against discrimination, access to courts, and equality are the bases for such friendship treaties, which were also used as a way of opening up markets in the extra-European world during the early era of commercial empire,[68] or binding sovereigns in exclusive amity to various European imperial powers,[69] or were transacted with radically weakened indigenous partners.[70] Often, these treaties of amity contained an implicit threat of violence: offering friendship or annihilation.[71] The price to be paid for a betrayal of friendship was often very high indeed (such betrayals were largely understood in unilateral terms; the indigenous group was bound to maintain relations even in the most adverse of circumstances).[72] Later, these treaties of amity tended to include provisions regulating expropriation of foreign assets (they have fallen out of favour and been replaced by bilateral investment treaties). This law of friendship, then, was also a law permitting friends to invest but preventing friends

---

67. 6 February 1778, at http://avalon.law.yale.edu/18th_century/fr1788-1.asp.
68. See e.g. the English agreement with the King of Sumatra in 1601 insisting that the exploitation of resources by the British Crown was ordained by God and organised around friendship: *Calendar of State Papers* (1864) 120–121.
69. E.g. the British Agreement with the rulers of Malwa and Sirhind in India 1809, where 'friendship requires that the Chiefs join the British Army with their forces and ... act under obedience and authority': 23 *British Foreign State Papers* 1081. Quote in Roshchin (n 66) 214.
70. See e.g. the 1677 Treaty between Charles II and the First Nations groups in Virginia, announcing 'Mutual League and Amity' in exchange for 'due obedience and subjection'. Quoted in Roshchin (n 66) 190–191.
71. Ibid.
72. While most of these friendships lacked the free contracting, bilateral quality of even the most basic notions of friendship and were preludes to further acts of predatory violence and expansion, some treaties of amity were expressions of equal relations and sometimes the superiority of the non-European host state. For discussion, see Gerry Simpson, 'The Globalisation of International Law', in Chris Reus-Smit and Tim Dunne, *The Globalisation of International Society* (2016) 265–284. See also examples in Charles Alexandrowicz, *An Introduction to the History of the Law of Nations in the East Indies* (Oxford University Press, 1967).

from expropriating.[73] In addition, such agreements have provided the basis for assertions of jurisdiction before the International Court of Justice (ICJ) (in these cases, treaties of amity often order deeply unfriendly relations, e.g. *Nicaragua v. United States; Iran v. United States*).[74] The ICJ has tended to interpret preambular friendship clauses to refer only to commercial, financial and consular relations and not to any generalisable promise to comply with international law.[75] Though treaties of amity still exist, many of them have been rendered redundant by the General Agreement on Tariffs and Trade (GATT) and the World Trade Organization (WTO), each in its own way dedicated to universalising, or at least generalising, a law of friendly relations among economic actors.

Inevitably, there are references to friendship, too, scattered through the classical corpus of international law. Grotius writes of sovereign friendship in *De iure ac belli pacis* (but his interests were directed towards the analogy to familial, hierarchical relations).[76] Sometimes, these references to friendship take on a retrospectively ironic cast. In *De indis*, Vitoria insists on natives giving the Spaniards 'a friendly hearing'.[77] Very often, the language of friendship is there to beef up the ethical underpinnings of empire or provide a kind of rubric to more concrete commercial relations or acts as a synonym for a whole sequence of relationships associated with the ties between sovereign equals.

The 1970 *Declaration on Principles of International Law*, of course, purports to be more explicit about these relationships of friendliness but the Declaration is a rather disappointing set of prescriptions based on the existing law of nations (albeit lightly refurbished and in the shadow of greater contestation) and on sovereign equality.[78] The harm envisaged by the Declaration seems

---

73. Andreas Paulus, *Treaties of Friendship, Commerce and Navigation* (Oxford Public International Law, 2018) at http://opil.ouplaw.com/view/10.1093/law:epil/9780199231690/law-9780199231690-e1482.
74. Though the US argued in the *Oil Platforms* litigation that a treaty of friendship does not deal with warlike unfriendliness: 'There is simply no relationship between these wholly commercial and consular provisions of the Treaty and Iran's Application and Memorial, which focus exclusively on allegations of unlawful uses of armed force' (para. 18, *Oil Platforms*, at http://opil.ouplaw.com/view/10.1093/law:icgj/73icj96.case.1/law-icgj-73icj96. See *Nicaragua* (n 18) para. 273).
75. Paulus (n 73).
76. Stephen Neff, *Grotius on the Law of War and Peace* (Cambridge University Press, 2012) Book I, Chapter I, # 3.2.
77. *De indis* (Carnegie, 1917) 156.
78. *The Declaration on Principles of International Law concerning Friendly Relations and Co-operation among States in accordance with the Charter of the United Nations*, GA Resn. 2625 (XXV) (1970).

to lie in a system in which friends are chosen on the basis of 'their political, economic and social systems or the levels of their development'.[79] The UN Charter, itself, in its preamble, does not mention friends but does contain a reference to neighbourliness (or 'living together as good neighbours'). One of the purposes of the UN is to develop friendly relations based on equal rights and self-determination, but these two ideas have been a source of enormous tension between states. The principle of self-determination has provoked unfriendliness on countless occasions (in relation to East Timor, Bangladesh and Biafra, for example). Meanwhile, Article 55 of the UN Charter reveals much more about what a system based on friendly relations might look like: that is, one in which there are very higher standards of living, universal respect for human rights, full employment and the amelioration of cultural, social and economic problems. This is either eccentrically utopian or creepily totalitarian, depending on one's tastes.

This, then, is the thin version of friendship. But international law, in its standard mode, has long been poised between two quasi-Aristotelian concepts of friendship: the friendship of utility and the friendship of *philia*, or between thin and thick versions of friendship. And this maps onto the distinction between classical international law and progressive international law. In the writing of Hans Morgenthau, for example, classical international law (real law) was a utilitarian law of diplomacy or trade, a set of legal relations in which levels of compliance were relatively high.[80] Progressive international law, on the other hand, was a newer ensemble of not-quite-legal relations that were largely aspirational, humanitarian, worthy—*desiderata* rather than law. Morgenthau looked with disfavour on the latter; for him, compliance and engagement were the tests of friendship. The everyday acts of cooperation and respect constituted a realm of friendly relations or at least the basis for such relations. The thicker aspirational norms are messages in a bottle, a field of disputation, a manoeuvring for position by groups of

---

79. But see J. E. U. Vinuales (ed.), *The 1970 Declaration at Fifty* (Cambridge University Press, 2020), which promises to revise our views on the Declaration, if not friendship itself. In the one chapter I have seen, Sam Moyn and Umut Ozsu revisit the background negotiations to the Declaration (organised through a familiar dialectic between sovereignty and self-determination) and resituate those in the clash between First, Second and Third World constellations of international ordering (see 'The Historical Origins and Setting of the Friendly Relations Declaration').
80. Hans Morgenthau, 'Positivism, Functionalism and International Law', 34(2) *American Journal of International Law* (1940) 260–284; Gerry Simpson, 'Duelling Agendas', 1(1) *Journal of International Law and Relations* (2005) 61–74.

states seeking advancement for their values: not friendship but alliance or ideology.

iv. thick friendship

Alongside these thinner modes of friendly relations, there is a whole world of feeling and sentiment determining the way sovereigns relate to each other. One thinks of the kinship foundations of European diplomacy or the manner in which European states, during the 19th century, conceived of themselves as a 'Family of Nations' (to be distinguished from the political communities who were merely legal persons or states). Meanwhile, we have declarations of 'eternal friendship', and special relationships (the UK–US friendship is conceived of in these terms, at least in Whitehall).[81] The British Commonwealth, too, styles itself as an organisation of friends (a group of friends with a shared history of having been colonised by one of their number). But there are, at least, three thicker accounts of friendship found in international legal work and practice that I want to sketch as a prelude to issuing my own declaration on friendly relations.

duellists

Carl Schmitt celebrates the 19th-century *ius publicum europaeum* as a world of friendly relations among European sovereigns.[82] In this imagined world, states at war are like duellists. Their aims are limited, the rules of combat intensely ritualised. One of the standard filmic gestures of friendship is that of the duellist who, having shot his rival in the shoulder, rushes forward to cradle him in his arms while pleading with him not to die. In Schmitt's depiction of intra-European relations, states very much did *not* want other states to die. There were wars, but these were, to use Schmitt's language, 'bracketed' and in two different ways. The aims of war were bracketed, or subject to a set of discrete political limits, and law was bracketed off from war in the sense that the decisions to go to war were sovereign decisions not subject to some supervening legal code (of justness or rightness).

---

81. The British are always referring to the 'special relationship' with the US, yet it is rare to meet an American who has heard of it.
82. Schmitt (n 31).

But what sort of friendship is represented in the idea of the duel and in Schmitt's idea of the duel? In Chekhov's *The Duel*, Laevsky challenges von Koren to combat. On the evening prior to the encounter, von Koren discusses with Samoylenko what might happen during the duel. Von Koren assures Samoylenko that Laevsky will fire into the air and that he, von Koren, will probably 'not fire at all'. As is typical in duels, there is a great deal by way of 'formalities': where, how, using which pistols, at what distance, under which conditions (though one of the 'seconds' panics and, unaware of the formalities, proposes a reconciliation).

A shoot-out takes place. Laevsky fires into the air, von Koren fires a shot.[83] The moment is ambiguous. Indeed, in the film version, it is unclear whether Laevsky has been killed or not. Some time later, the film ends with the pair shaking hands as von Koren leaves on a boat. There is a return to civilisation with the duel's formalities smoothing the transition from enemy to friend. It is a way of making friendship through war and enacts and represents the fluidity of enmity and friendship.[84]

This image of a 19th-century *liberum ius ad bellum* has not gone unchallenged, but it represents a potent image of friendly violence under international law and is a masterpiece of formalism/anti-formalism.[85] The conditions leading to the duel and the outcome of the duel are taken to be rule-less, a matter of choice for the protagonists. The justness of the cause is screened out of the 19th-century cabinet war: war as a sovereign prerogative. But the duel itself is subject to a highly formalised structure of gentlemanly rules (seconds, paces, weapons and timing are all subject to administration). Like all formalism/anti-formalisms, this is subject to reversal.[86] Perhaps the anterior causes (a particular dispute over defamation, or money, or women) and the proximate causes (a slap on the face) are formalised, while the conduct of the duel is subject to all sorts of ad hoc improvisations (shots are fired into the air or on the ground, or against a tree behind the rival duellist). But however this is played out, the end of the duel then signals either the resumption of friendship, and/or noble, redemptive death or injury. In each case, the duel represents a form of friendship: a refusal to annihilate. Annihilation was an activity confined to wars beyond the Amity Line, the

---

83. *The Duel* (dir. Dover Koshashvili, Music Box Films, 2009).
84. Not all duels have happy endings of course. The musical, *Hamilton*, ends with a duel between Aaron Burr and Alexander Hamilton, which results in the latter's death.
85. Walter Benjamin, *Critique of Violence* (1920–1921).
86. Duncan Kennedy, *A Critique of Adjudication* (Harvard University Press, 1998).

colonial wars that Schmitt so feared would become a model for European war in general.[87]

merchants

As international law was universalised and as war became both juridified and annihilistic, Schmitt worried about the demise of the special European international law he celebrated. He was right in certain respects (international law did become a universal project, wars did become either humanitarian and collective or aggressive and illegal). But it could be argued that the European and North Atlantic states have extended the idea of the *ius publicum europaeum* into the late 20th and early 21st centuries by adopting a thicker, if not quite Aristotlean, liberal-internationalist conception of friendship. It is a feature of a certain kind of liberal-legal internationalism, after all, that it depends on an inside/outside structure of international legal politics: an 'inside' with its thick skein of institutions, alliances and liberal commitments (a sphere of 'friendly' relations), and an 'outside' encompassing diverse ideologies, preferences and values (a sphere of thinly cooperative 'diplomatic' relations).[88] This, of course, mirrors work which distinguished a friendly, liberal, anti-pluralist zone of harmonious, thickening, judicialised collaboration with a pluralistic sphere of much looser cooperation and far fewer shared values, a mere getting on, or rubbing along reluctantly.[89] Kant is the great describer of these friendly relations: free-trading, republican states would become so enmeshed that war and enmity would end.[90] The European Union seemed at one point to manifest this form of friendly relations. But these friends continued to exercise their violent appetites elsewhere. Beyond the Amity Line, there was a reversion to pseudo-imperial counter-insurgency (in Iraq, in Afghanistan, in Yemen) but this time in the

---

87. See Sven Lindqvist, *A History of Bombing* (Granta, 2001).
88. See G. John Ikenberry, 'The End of the Liberal International Order?', 94(1) *International Affairs* (2018) 7–32, at 10.
89. Gerry Simpson, 'Two Liberalisms', 12(3) *European Journal of International Law* (2001) 537–572; John Gray, *Two Faces of Liberalism* (Polity, 2000).
90. For classic statements, see Anne-Marie Slaughter, 'International Law in a World of Liberal States', 6(3) *European Journal of International Law* (1995) 503–538; Anne-Marie Slaughter, 'The Liberal Agenda for Peace: International Relations Theory and the Future of the United Nations', 4 *Transnational Law and Contemporary Problems* (1994) 377–419; Fernando Tesón, 'The Kantian Theory of International Law', 92(1) *Columbia Law Review* (1992) 53–102.

guise of 'humanity', or the international community. A warrior friendship now casting itself as apolitical, a friendship of vengeful militarised judges.

summiteers

A third form of potentially thicker friendship took fresh resonance with President Trump's highly personal—frankly emotional—diplomacy. Of course, individual persons can certainly have an attitude of friendliness towards particular states. I feel friendly towards Vietnam, less friendly towards North Korea: 'Good Hamlet, look on Denmark as a friend'.[91] In Trump, though, we had a president—by no means the first but certainly the most—who wanted to, or claimed to want to, form intimate and instantaneous bonds with political leaders, especially adversaries. Indeed, Trump reversed the usual assumptions about diplomatic friendship. He made friends with sworn enemies (the 'Little Rocket Man') and made enemies out of long-term friends (the Europeans, the Canadians). But this was more than a change of direction or an affection for authoritarian leaders; it was a rejection of a form of diplomatic intercourse forged over decades, sometimes centuries, in favour of a series of unstable playground alliances. Of course, personality matters in international diplomacy (think of Margaret Thatcher, after years of ironladyness, saying of Mikhail Gorbachev: 'I can work with this man'), but Trumpite diplomacy was an adolescent rampage through the conventions of interstate relations. One can never be quite sure when the playground bully will turn nasty—suave, young, sophisticates were at particular risk (Macron, Trudeau), something prompted perhaps by envy, while there was a failure of comprehension around powerful women (May, Merkel).

President Trump, then, is not the most promising example, but a recent body of scholarship in international relations has developed a theory of political friendship, though it is striking that the word is rarely used

---

91. And international lawyers are friends with each other of course: As writers, we write and think in relative solitude and yet friendship is important to the construction of international law. A comradeship between different thinkers has, in a way, been a defining mark of a particular way of co-habiting theoretical space in the field (Chinkin and Charlesworth, Weston and Falk, McDougal and Laswell). See also David Kennedy's hymn to Tom Franck ('Tom Franck and the Manhattan School', 35 *New York University Journal of International Law and Politics* (2003) 397–436). For a lawful friendship, see Peter Gabel and Duncan Kennedy, 'Roll Over Beethoven', 36(1) *Stanford Law Review* (1984) 1–55.

(perhaps Lord Palmerston's famous dictum about there being no permanent friends or enemies only permanent interests has spooked political scientists). Recent writing has drawn and developed earlier studies by political scientists on the role of trust in international relations.[92] In such writing, friendship really matters as a form of interpersonal trust, especially among enemies.[93] Friendly encounters take place (Gorbachev and Reagan at Reykjavik; Vajpayee and Sharif) in which a personal chemistry is formed that then seems to lead to some warming of relations between states or, at least, a humanisation of the rival and, most of all, an empathy for the position of the adversary (Lawrence Freedman has said that this is essence of friendship—a shared acknowledgement of the other person not as a human but as a fellow politician in a kind of tragic circumstance).[94] Trust suspends the usual postures of anticipatory violence and insecurity. The assumption, though, is that it is possible, just by spending time with someone, to intuit whether the person is trustworthy or not; 'enemy images' will then be dislodged. This is an attractive idea, but it seems to require a lot of our politicians and statespersons.

And, in the end, perhaps if the thin utilitarian international law of amity corresponding to Aristotle's first image seems weak and unsatisfying, there is also a dark side to these three thicker forms of friendly relations sketched above. Sometimes summits go badly wrong (Trump–Trudeau), or the personal warmth and charisma of a leader hides a murderous domestic and foreign policy (Stalin as 'Uncle Joe'), or the summit goes well but the results are disappointing (instead of general disarmament, Reagan went for Star Wars; instead of 'Peace in Our Time', Hitler chose world domination and mass slaughter). And friendship can sour. Meanwhile, liberal internationalism either replays the centre–periphery fantasies of the imperial caste or leads to obviously illiberal, warlike and deeply unfriendly forms of behaviour, and Schmitt's public law of Europe has the qualities of a violent, mythic origin or nostalgic casting back in the name of darker, political projects of the present.[95]

---

92. See e.g. work by Yarhi-Milo, Trager, Horowitz.
93. Nicholas Wheeler, *Trusting Enemies: Interpersonal Relationships in International Conflict* (Oxford University Press, 2018)
94. Lawrence Freedman, 'Trusting Enemies' 94(6) *International Affairs* (2018) 1440–1441.
95. José Alvarez, 'Do Liberal States Behave Better? A Critique of Slaughter's Liberal Theory', 12(2) *European Journal of International Law* (2001) 183–246.

v. lawful friendship

Article I of that US–Iran Treaty of Friendship provides that: 'There shall be firm and enduring peace and sincere friendship between the United States . . . and Iran'. In its submissions to the ICJ in the preliminary phase, Iran contended that this provision:

> does not merely formulate a recommendation or desire . . . but imposes actual obligations on the Contracting Parties, obliging them to maintain long-lasting peaceful and friendly relations. (Para. 25)

The US rejected this expansive definition of friendship, preferring a more confined, contractual understanding in which amity imposed a series of discrete and formalised legal obligations and little else besides.

The Iranians appeared to be arguing for a friendship not just of contract and obligation but of familiarity, maybe even intimacy. Michael Oakeshott describes these deeper covenants in the following terms:

> [In the case of friendship] attachment springs from an intimation of familiarity and subsists in a mutual sharing of personalities . . . To discard friends because they do not behave as we expected and refuse to be educated to our requirements is the conduct of a man who has altogether mistaken the character of friendship. *The relationship of friend to friend is dramatic, not utilitarian; the tie is one of familiarity, not usefulness.*[96]

Is this perhaps what a diplomatic politics of lawful friendship look like? In *De iure belli libri tres*, Alberico Gentili offered the most detailed treatment of friendship in the literature of international law.[97] In a chapter entitled 'de amicita & societate', he talks about the prospect of friendship 'furnish[ing] something greater?' Presumably, he means something greater than the thin conception of friendship that assimilates it to already existing international law or to shared commercial and navigational interests or to the provision of aid during a belligerency. This 'something greater' is parasitic on a bold understanding of neutrality; Gentili is trying to work out how a state is to behave when two of its friends are at war with one another. Here friendship becomes an assertive and unapologetic neutrality, a way of being friends to

---

96. Quoted in Fred Dallmyr, 'Derrida and Friendship', 2(4) *Critical Review of International Social and Political Philosophy* (1999) 105–130 (emphasis added).
97. A. Gentili, *De iure belli libri tres* [1589] (edition: Carnegie, 1933)

those who are, vis-à-vis each other, enemies.[98] In James Lorimer's vocabulary, this is neutrality as mutual friendship, a jural relation not a posture of indifference.[99]

Like Oakeshott, Aristotle would have rejected the thin forms of friendship described in the first half of the essay as too democratic, too utilitarian and too sybaritic ('neither recommendation nor desire') to sustain anything meaningful and durable.[100] The true friend, for Aristotle, was the twin or mirror-twin, a person with whom one could strive together in the pursuit of virtue. Or, as Suarez writes: 'For a friend is a second self'.[101] Thus the perfectible friendship, without temporal limits, is a friendship with the self, or, at least, a friendship with the perfectible self, the imagined self, the other as self.

These perfectible Greco-Roman friendships, though, adopt what Derrida describes as a 'fraternalist–familial–narcissistic' form.[102] They are aristocratic, masculine, and self-regarding. So, for example, in Nietzsche, women are incapable of friendship (they know love but do not have the temperament for friendship).[103] And, as Valeria Ruiz-Perez, one of my former LLM students at LSE, wrote in an essay: 'When the friend is another self, others may be recognised only as enemies', or, perhaps unrecognisably, other.[104]

Derrida's search for a redemptive friendship is directed against the fratricidal–fraternal lineaments of the philosophy of friendship, and against what he calls 'the double exclusion of the feminine'.[105] Maybe we can find something sustaining, then, instead in Montaigne's famous definition of friendship: 'If a man should importune me to give a reason why I loved him, I find it could no otherwise be expressed, than by making answer: because it was he, because it was I'.[106] In such a friendship, the autonomy of both

---

98. For a useful discussion, see Roshchin (n 66) 93–96.
99. Lorimer (n 43) 7, 235.
100. Only equals could be friends; indeed, only aristocratic equals could be friends since friendship required an understanding and orientation towards the good that only the highly educated could master. See also Schollmeier (n 51) 771 (elaborating on the need for shared tastes or what he calls 'unanimity').
101. S. J. Suarez, *The Classics of International Law: Selections from Three Works of Suarez* (Clarendon Press, 1944) 804.
102. See also Goodrich (n 3) 26.
103. Friedrich Nietzsche, *Thus Spake Zarathustra* (Penguin, 1969) 83–84. This excludes of course, not just friendships among women but the friendship that can occur between a man and a woman.
104. Valeria Ruiz-Perez, 'Friendship and Enmity in International Law', LLM essay, LSE (2019).
105. Derrida (n 4) 279–290, esp. 281.
106. Montaigne (n 2).

parties is protected—indeed, more than protected—it is this autonomy, this life-world, that is the *subject* of the friendship ('because it was he', because it was she, we could add).

Might not this combination of a mediated Aristolean *philia* (a love for the other as a mirrored twin), the Montaignesque encounter (the friend as particular, unique) and a Derridean hesitancy around familial-fraternal models offer a more promising form of friendship for international law? To begin rather modestly, and in light of this, a declaration on friendly relations would involve, at least, a recognition of the sovereign as another self. There is, after all, a very limited number of them in the world. In their best versions, they are all engaged in the unusual tasks of trying to govern or administer a territory and people and engaging with other sovereigns on the terrain of international law, politics and diplomacy (these are not activities in which NGOs or corporations or international institutions or oil companies are involved to anything like the same extent). This presence of the 'friendly other' might also prevent conversations between the two selves of the international sovereign (people/government; conservative/labour; republican/democrat) from descending into something hermetic or violent. Indeed, in Nietzsche's parable of the hermit, in dialogue with himself, the 'I and Me are always too earnestly in conversation with one another: how could it be endured, if there were not a friend?'[107]

Here, Aristotelian philosophy offers the resources to think of sovereignty as a sympathetic engagement with the other self neither as utilitarian calculus nor vain extroversion but rather as shared predicament. It is this intuition, surely, that prompted states to make their best efforts, in the *ius in bello* and the *ius ad bellum*, to 'emnify' their deadly rivals by converting them into protected enemies—immortal enemies, we might say. So, to return to something I said earlier, the displacement of the enemy and the criminal (two different sorts of protected species) by the outlaw-terrorist, represents a failure to experience the sovereign as self and other at the same time. The 'enemy' character at the heart of, say, the Geneva Conventions, is slowly disappearing in the solvent of post-imperial humanitarianism, a humanitarianism that belongs to the worst aspects of Derrida's 'fraternizing humanisation'.[108] In response to this, those in exile from the 'the international community' (the Iranians, the North Koreans, the Taliban, latterly ISIL), if

---

107. Nietzsche, *Thus Spake* (n 103) 82.
108. Derrida (n 4) 273.

they could speak, might speak like Zarathustra: 'At least be my enemy!' For Nietzsche, to be a friend, you must be capable of being an enemy as well and in your friend you possess your best enemy.[109] The friend then, is always the other self, in this regard. The other self is always potentially the enemy. Montaigne, again: 'Love him so as if you were one day to hate him; and hate him so as you were one day to love him'. Or better still, imagine relations with your earth enemy as a star friendship, something transcendent, perhaps even a beautiful lofty thing. In *The Gay Science*, Nietzsche thinks of all friendships as reversible in this way. All friendship ends in estrangement, and this estrangement is 'the law above us'. For our purposes, the law above us—international law—organises and administers this estrangement (this may be a thin version of the friendships I spoke of earlier in the chapter) but with an eye to the revival of the star friendship.[110]

The sovereign then is another self, but it is also another 'other' ('because it was he, because I was I'). The lawful friendship would be organised through an encounter with the other sovereign as the same but different: a sovereign equally entitled to respect and consideration but also a sovereign as sometimes unrecognisably other—a sovereign with her own laws and cultures, sometimes alien and inscrutable (involving 'difficult knowledge and abstruse discovery') but capable of being befriended on her own terms ('because it was she').[111] A friendship that refuses to deny the 'absolute singularity of the other'.[112] This is not a fraternal friendship—a friendship of blood and bone, with its implications of brotherhood, sacrifice, class and with the originary spectre of fratricide hovering above it—but a friendship of 'manners, parts and inclinations' (Montaigne): a form of amity extendable beyond fraternity (with its liberal cores, like-minded states), beyond family and the family of nations (with its hierarchies and disparities and its roots in European cultural exclusivities) and beyond utility and pleasure.[113]

All of this may seem to set a very high standard for friendship among sovereigns. Isn't it enough just to avoid war? Clearly, what I have sketched is a highly aspirational and tentative, diplomatic friendship. But how might we aspire?

109. Nietzsche, *Thus Spake* (n 103) 82–83. See Werner Herzog's account of his friendship with Klaus Kinski, in *My Best Fiend* (dir. Herzog, 1999).
110. Nietzsche, *The Gay Science* (Cambridge University Press, 2001) Book 4, para. 279.
111. Montaigne (n 2) (discussing the love between Achilles and Patroclus).
112. Derrida (n 4) 276.
113. 'Why is it necessary that the correspondence of manners, parts and inclinations, which begets the true and perfect friendships, should always meet in these relations?': Montaigne (n 2).

A *leitmotif* of writing on friendship emphasises the presence of communication and habit, friendly relations 'refined by practice' (Montaigne) and a sense that friendship can be willed and struggled for. In *The Politics of Friendship*, Derrida points to precisely this slow accretion of friendliness when he discusses Kant and the requirement of sometimes untruthful 'courtly gallantry' and 'warm verbal assurance of friendship' gradually leading to a 'genuine disposition of the soul'.[114] If we read Derrida a certain way, we might posit the law as the third friend beyond the 'face-to-face of singularities' of the friendships I have described so far.[115] This 'uprising of the third friend' (found in Kant, in Nietzsche, and in Eliot's 'third' who walks beside you), then, contains the seeds of at least one model of friendship enacted through a law that 'commands me to recognise the transcendent alterity of the other who can never be anything but heterogeneous and singular'.[116] The true sovereign friend is recognised as a sovereign equal, an enemy to come, a singular political creature and a bearer of its own laws and its own international laws. In short, international law must recognise that which will be resistant to its own generality and universality. The third friend (international law) becomes as heterogeneous as the sovereign itself.[117]

This portrait of international legal friendship may seem excessive, theoretical or idealistic. But it should be read not as a prescription for friendship but as a declaration of friendly relations and at the same time—and in the spirit of the canonical performances of friendship I have tracked here (Cicero, Montaigne, Kant, Yeats, Derrida)—an elegiac meditation on the friendship that is, to repurpose Janet Malcolm, not only impossible but difficult: a friendship that refuses the 'reciprocalist, mutualist schema', a loving preferred over a belovedness, a lofty thing.[118]

I want to finish with three brief representations of diplomatic friendship in which there are traces of friendly relations and the phantom presence of lawful friendship. In the first, I emphasise a friendship of gesture, precision and 'abstruse discovery'. In the second, I think of friendship in Lorimer's

---

114. Derrida (n 4) 274.
115. Ibid. 276.
116. Ibid. 277.
117. For Bodin, lawful communities depend on and are distinguished by ties of friendship. This allows him to contrast states with pirate bands (though his pirate band is described in attractive terms as a group who 'liue in neuer so much amitie and friendship together, and with great equalite to divide the spoile'), quoted in Roshchin (n 66) 59.
118. Derrida (n 4) 10. This connects to the idea of maternal joy (the joy in loving a baby incapable yet of returning that love). See Robin West, 'Jurisprudence and Gender', 55(1) *University of Chicago Law Review* (1988) 1–72. See also Derrida (n 4) 11–12.

lexicon of mutual friendship combined with Derrida's insistence on the singularity and particularity of the friend. The third example is a description of a performative friendship of elegiac pastoralism, an attempt to revive a friendship that has become estranged, a friendship that perhaps was never—in the first place—fully alive and a friendship that came close to ending life on earth: a star friendship of earth enemies.

★ ★ ★

Nixon in China

In 1967, then Republican presidential candidate, Richard Nixon, published an essay in the US foreign policy establishment's house journal *Foreign Affairs* calling for a détente with China and articulating this in classic familial-fraternalist terms: 'We simply cannot afford to leave China forever outside the family of nations'.[119] Chinese–US relations were, at this time, largely defined by the presence of the third, i.e. the Soviet Union. The 1969 border skirmishes between the Chinese and the Soviet Union (threatening to topple into a general war) opened up the possibility of rapprochement between the US and China (a relationship defined, at that point, by the Vietnam War). Both Nixon and Mao had to move with great care, with neither wishing to alienate the Soviets (Nixon was committed to détente; for Mao, there was the persistence of socialist brotherhood). Most of the early negotiations were conducted through proxies (the Pakistanis, the Romanians) and the initial, preparatory visit to the People's Republic of China was made by Henry Kissinger who flew from Islamabad—a trip given the code name 'Polo'—in the dead of night, after pretending to take ill at a banquet in Pakistan's capital. Kissinger arrived in Beijing several hours later promising 'co-existence, equality and friendship'.[120] (Amid all of this the US table tennis team, competing in Tokyo in the World Championships, received an unexpected invitation to play several exhibition matches in China—this became famous as 'Ping-Pong Diplomacy'.)

On 18 February 1972, Nixon descended the steps of Airforce One and became the first US president to set foot in China. Richard Nixon might seem an unusual choice for a central figure in a story of redemptive

---

119. Richard Nixon, 'Asia after Viet Nam', 46(1) *Foreign Affairs* (1967) 113–125.
120. O. A. Westad, *The Cold War* (Allen Lane, 2017) 408.

friendship (one thinks of the 'secret' bombing of Cambodia, Watergate, his oleaginous self-evasions, the impeachment process, his resignation). Yet, the 'opening of China' is regarded as one of the masterstrokes of 20th-century diplomatic relations.[121] In John Adams' modern opera *Nixon in China*, we have the performance of a friendship between Chou En-lai and Richard Nixon (or a performance of a performance of friendship): a friendship in which the strangeness of the two sides is respected, a diplomacy of small, ritualistic gestures, a slow accretion of trust through performance. In her dialogues, Adams' librettist, Alice Goodman, used much of what was actually said at the meeting or verbatim reports of Chinese statements in and around the meeting.[122] She emphasises the deliberate pace of friendly relations and the fierce individuality of Chinese sovereignty.[123] Meanwhile, the neo-Wagnerian arrival music (Nixon's plane landing in Beijing) representing US confidence and bombast is juxtaposed with the singular otherness of the Red Army Choir chanting a proletarian anthem on the runway ('The People are the Heroes Now'). This encounter of two life-worlds then gives way, in this intricately scored exchange, to the sort of conversation we all have when we emerge from a long plane ride:

CHOU EN-LAI: 'Your flight was smooth I hope'.
NIXON: 'Oh yes, smoother than usual, I guess . . . the Prime Minister knows about that. He is such a traveller'.
CHOU EN-LAI: 'No, not I; But as a traveller come home for good to China'.

The conversation continues as a kind of highly finessed diplomatic small-talk that prefigures the high politics to come. After Nixon's paranoid aria, 'News Has a Kind of Mystery' (in which he imagines the effect of his visit around the world, wonders about the rats eating at his reputation and his standing at home, and asks: 'Who are our friends?'), there is a sequence of very indirect,

---

121. It may have contributed to the end of the Vietnam War, it certainly prompted Brezhnev to move towards a more rapid conclusion to the Strategic Arms Limitation Talks and it was the beginning of China's re-entry into the international system. Of course, there were losers (Japan was nervous, and Lin Bao, Mao's anointed successor but now on the wrong side of history, died in a plane crash on the Mongolian border during an attempted defection to Moscow) and even the gains could be viewed as ambiguous.
122. Having said that, Nixon spoke out against friendship at several moments during the conversations in China: 'I know that friendship . . . cannot be the basis upon which an established relationship must rest' (R. Nixon, *Memoirs* (Arrow Books, 1979) 566).
123. At one point, during Polo II, Kissinger had received a (counter) draft joint statement from Chou. He responded by saying: 'We can't have an American President sign a document which says . . . "the people's revolutionary struggles are just"!' See Nixon (n 122) 555.

subtle evasions and pauses: a meeting with Mao that is all philosophy and no diplomacy, a banquet ending in a series of cheers ('comrades and friends!'), a theatrical performance of 'The Red Detachment of Women' (with its revolutionary violence) and a solo from Madame Mao in which, like Auden's tyrant weeping while children die in the street, she punningly sings:

> When I appear
> The People hang
> upon my words.

The hybrid singularity of China is maintained throughout. There is cultural revolution kitsch and anthemic socialism; there are scenes that prefigure its economic rise (Pat Nixon's visit to the factories). Then finally, there are the characters. Nixon's leaden-footedness, Mao's enigmatic manoeuvrings, Kissinger's bumbling Cold War dinosaurism—still engaging in espionage or name-calling or missile counting and missing the qualities needed to contribute to the slow intimations of familiarity going on all around him—and, in the end, Chou, establishing a deep love for country in the midst of these exchanges, subtly signalling, too, China's nervousness about its own geostrategic ambitions and an awareness of her imperfections:

> How much of what we did was good?
> Everything seemed to move beyond
> Our remedy.[124]

Nehru in Belgrade

Over a decade before Nixon shifted the tectonic plates, an equally unlikely friendship was being forged between East and West. It culminated at Bandung where a new diplomacy was imagined and enacted through the performance of friendship in culturally rich settings.[125] In the final communiqué at Bandung, there is a greater emphasis on forms of cultural exchange and a sense of a shared colonial past, a plea that 'confidence and goodwill' become the grounds for the development of interstate relations in Africa and Asia, and a nuanced combination of anti-colonial self-assertion and a tactful (maybe tactical) willingness to receive support from former colonial states. But this goodwill and openness became vital elements in the staging

---

124. According to Nixon, this was what Chou was like. See Nixon (n 122) 571.
125. The Bandung Conference (1955) (Final Communique), in 11(1) *Interventions* (2009) 94–102.

of the Conference on the streets of Bandung, where leaders mingled freely with the people.[126] This is a world away from the staged contrivances of recent European summits (Tony Blair winning a cycling race) and the frozen securitisations of today's international gatherings, where the proceedings are vacuum-sealed and friendless. But this Bandung friendship contains an episode that is less well celebrated, one that led to the NAM Yalta: the friendship between India and Yugoslavia and between Tito and Nehru. Here were two countries and statesmen trying to protect or achieve some alterity removed from the bipolarities of the Cold War (indeed, Nehru wanted to defeat the Cold War itself).[127]

In 1954, Tito arrived in Delhi and was described as 'the first great European statesman who came to Asia not as a representative of the colonisers, but as a great friend of Asian nations'.[128] His visit was an enormous success and led to the Tri-Continental meeting at Brioni between Nasser, Nehru and Tito where the three leaders forged a friendship outside the confines of the Cold War and its twin trajectories of European modernity, a friendship in which another self was encountered (a Third World, non-aligned self) but another sovereign too, in all its particularity and singularity (a multi-ethnic, independently socialist, European state, an anti-colonial Arab state at one point willing to absorb itself into another Pan-Arab state during the Syria–Egypt one-state experiment and an Asian state carving out its own development path and refusing to be 'an improved edition' of other countries).[129] This commitment to 'un-commitment' was costly for the Yugoslavs, who were under tremendous pressure from the Soviets at this point (Khrushchev had launched a scathing attack on Tito at the 1958 Bulgarian Party Congress, and the Yugoslavs were being derided as imperialist lackeys, their pose of neutrality 'carrying the distinct odour of the American monopolies').[130] By the time Tito embarked on the second of his Third World tours, he had some ground to make up; there were difficulties with Nasser over Iraq, and

---

126. See also Sundhya Pahuja, *Letters from Bandung: Encounters with Another Inter-National Law* (2017, on file with author).
127. Westad (n 120) 433.
128. Jovan Cavoski, 'Between Great Powers and Third World Neutrality: Yugoslavia and the Belgrade Conference of the Non-Aligned Movement, 1961', in Natasa Miscovic (ed.), *The Non-Aligned Movement and the Cold War* (Routledge, 2014) 187–210.
129. Indira Gandhi, *Speech in Delhi*, 1 April 1980.
130. For a useful description, see Svetozar Rajak, 'From Passive Neutralism to Active Un-Commitment: The Critical Role of Yugoslavia', in Sandra Bott, Jussi Hanhimaki, Janick Schaufelbuehl and Marco Wyss (eds.), *Neutrality and Neutralism in the Global Cold War* (Routledge, 2016) 72–89, 79.

Nehru had become obsessed with Pakistan and Kashmir. But at the end of the meeting with Nehru, the friendship seemed to have been rekindled and it was decided that the two leaders would 'exchange letters, as often as possible'.[131]

Initially, this fierce independence even encompassed a refusal to establish a permanent institution around the NAM. Nehru was very wary of creating a Third Bloc (which he feared would precisely mimic the problem of the two blocs he wanted to work against). But, ultimately in the absence of this, perhaps *because* of the absence of this, in Bandung and in Belgrade, there was a practice of invigorating friendship and an effort to rethink the whole shape of international society through these friendships.[132]

Khrushchev in Havana

The Cubans joined the NAM in 1961 when they sent representatives to Belgrade (though Castro and Tito never managed to forge any sort of friendship within the confines of the NAM). But it was hard to take this non-alignment entirely seriously when within a year, Cuba had almost become the *casus belli* for the end of planetary life itself. Indeed, the whole idea of a South or East with shared values and interests became harder to sustain after Mao's invasion of India in 1962. In the aftermath of the October crisis, though, the Soviets and Khrushchev in particular began to redevelop, consolidate and reimagine a socialist internationalism of deeply congenial relations. I want to sketch this pastoral international diplomacy of Khrushchev's (anticipating the concerns of the next chapter of the book) through a reading of his letters to Castro at the end of the Cuban Missile Crisis (this is a sketch; I continue the reading at the end of the final chapter). These exercises in Kant's 'courtly gallantry' are poignant efforts to rekindle a broken friendship and to read these letters is to be transported back to a different diplomacy, a contrast to the crudeness and bombast of Trumpean low style (where a vicious human rights record is recorded as 'rough and tough') or the Obama-era condescensions of US–Russian relations or the

---

131. ibid. 77.
132. Eventually, and rather like the Cold War itself, this all petered out. The unravelling was partly down to India's relations to Pakistan (especially at the time of the Kashmir War and the intervention in East Pakistan). These wars pitted India against Chinese and US interests (in the latter case, just as Nixon was arriving in Beijing) and drove India away from her non-aligned position and into the embrace of the Soviets.

apocalyptic jokiness of Reagan's evil empire period. But it also represents a departure from the frozen, mathematical ultra-masculinities of Kissinger-era nuclear diplomacy and the cool disassociations of international law's thin friendships.

The letter is sent a short time after Castro had urged Khrushchev to defend Cuban sovereignty, if necessary with nuclear arms.[133] The opening paragraph of the letter—a *paean* to an interrupted friendship—is devoted to the idea of temporality (how long Khrushchev has been thinking about writing to Castro, where he began writing the letter, the passage of time as the letter is written). Khrushchev situates his writing of the letter in a series of tenses: 'I have been thinking of writing this letter to you'; 'And now I am writing this letter to you'. When Khrushchev is not talking about time, he is invoking the beauty and fragility of the Russian countryside (see chapter vii) and his hope that Castro will one day see it for himself. The letter is, in a sense, a sequence of deferrals, and these deferrals are really the point, because the letter is designed to produce warmer Soviet–Cuban relations (Castro had wanted a more muscular approach from the Soviets during the crisis—perhaps even a nuclear attack) and also to configure a kind of poetic–diplomatic friendship. Khrushchev is placing the interests of time and landscape ahead of those of 'sovereignty' or personal self-assertion at a moment when Cuba, the Soviet Union and the US came 'close to war'. In these bucolic musings, Khrushchev is developing an international diplomacy of friendship as a counterpoint to international legal and political nuclearism: a pastoral internationalism, as we are about to see in the next chapter, but also a complex series of friendship gestures.

---

133. See Nikita Khrushchev, *Khrushchev Remembers* (Little Brown, 1970). From the US side, see Robert Kennedy, *Thirteen Days* (W.W. Norton, 1969).

vii
gardening, instead, or, of pastoral international law

i. luxury items   185
ii. utopian experiments   188
ii. gardening, instead   198
    Candide's farm   198
    Woolf's irises   204
    West's cyclamens   205
    Khrushchev's letter   207

'Rank and titles' said Pangloss, 'are often dangerous, as all the philosophers agree: witness Eglon, King of the Moabites, who was assassinated by Ehud; Absalom was hanged by his hair . . . And you will recall in what manner death came for Croesus, Astyages . . . Mary Stuart and Charles I . . . And you must also know . . . '
—'All I know', said Candide, 'is that we must cultivate our garden'

Voltaire, Candide (2005 [1759]): chapter 30, 93

i. luxury items

Everything that is unqualified is pathology.

Nietzsche, Beyond Good and Evil (1886)

At various points over the past few years—in Lexington, Virginia; at Osgoode Hall; in Greenwich Village; at a Writers Festival in Adelaide; in Amsterdam—I have been delivering a paper on gardening. Sometimes this talk has been called 'A Hundred Years of Turpitude: Some Thoughts on War

Crimes Trials and Gardening'. At other times, the gardening gets slipped in without notice in a paper that is advertised as being about 'modes of liability in international courts' or 'the crime of aggression at the ICC', or 'the future of international law'.

The gardening conceit arose out of a number of different experiences I had been having. Mostly, I was trying to figure out a way of responding to the routine question asked of those of us who are unhappy about the present distributions or the institution at hand: namely 'what would you do instead?' or, in its Leninist variant, 'What is to be done?' This is a complicated question, a question often asked of the international legal sceptic but a question with broader significance.

Because I have seen people struggle with variations on this question in seminars and public lectures, I began to try out a few different answers to it. One answer was not to give an answer. This refusal to answer is an important gesture in the repertoire of a certain type of international lawyer.[1] So often we find ourselves trapped in the wrong kind of questions: the 'when did you stop beating your dog?' question. We are asked whether we support intervention in some place or other (often coupled with a demand from the interlocutor that we not prevaricate or over-intellectualise, 'people are dying after all'). 'Do you support intervention in Syria?' I was once asked, and I immediately drifted into a long disquisition about the origins of the modern Syrian state in French colonialism, its status as a mandate, the politics—an ahistorical politics—behind the term 'intervention'. From the back of the room, the questioner shouted out, 'Just answer the question! Yes or No, it's not that hard'. But it is hard, terribly hard. Not answering questions is so much harder than answering them. And it is a recipe for losing an audience already weaned on the idea that the worst sort of intellectuals are fence-sitters or people who cannot take their own side in an argument, and that the best sort are the talking heads and great simplifiers who pronounce authoritatively and concisely on every question. By the time they have been proved wrong, these untouchables (and the public) have moved on to a new arrangement of certainties.[2]

---

1. The fatal consequences of making a plea for a new institution are discussed in Martti Koskenniemi, 'Epilogue', in From Apology to Utopia (Cambridge University Press, 2005) 562–617.
2. 'To cultivate the garden, then, is not simply to mind one's own business . . . it is to decide not to seek answers to questions that can have none; to remember the concrete "buts" that lie in wait of every grand abstraction'. See Michael Wood, 'Introduction', in François Voltaire, *Candide* (Penguin, 2005) xxiii.

Not answering is of course possible: I have seen it done well; I have done it myself. But there is a risk that the speaker will come across as a bit pompous, or worse, as someone who doesn't know the answer. Answering has its risks too. Occasionally, when I talk to friends and they ask me about my position on human rights, I can see their utter bafflement when I say I am not altogether in favour.[3] Sometimes this becomes a kind of anger ('so, you propose leaving X languishing in prison?' or 'Do you support Pol Pot?'). At other times eyes begin to glaze over.

Giving a paper is not a popularity contest, of course, but still, these experiences made me wonder if I didn't need a more upbeat story, a retort to the ringing simplifications that seemed, so often, to carry the day. Of course, this demand for reconstruction has long been a bugbear of a certain kind of oppositional or, at least, doubtful, international lawyering. Protesting is one thing, reconstituting society is quite another. The thrill of dissent or opposition is just so much more appealing than the hard yards of political reconstruction. Shared opposition is relatively easy, a shared programme not so easy. One of the complaints made about critical international lawyers is that they are corrosive or cynical or naïve, possessing a Menshevik mentality, always likely to be outflanked by nastier forces to the left and right, unable to find common ground with reformist allies, liable to capture by the forces of reaction.

My experience, in fact, has been quite the opposite. The reason many of us became attracted to this sort of work was precisely because it seemed so hopeful compared to the old routines around customary international law or the latest treaty on international humanitarian law with its qualifiers, its evasions, its legitimators. And yet, the thought persists—indeed becomes more pressing as this inconclusive book itself winds to a conclusion—what, indeed, is to be done?

On the fifteenth anniversary of the Iraq War, I spoke on a panel in which I quoted from Sloan Wilson's novel, *The Man in the Grey Flannel Coat*, to the effect that it was possible to be sick of justice, sick of giving it and sick of receiving it. Maybe it is a luxury to say that one is sick of justice. And I am now sensitive to this idea of luxury itself. After my talk (during which I had called for an end to panels on the Iraq War), I was accused of being rude to my hosts and of 'luxuriating in my position'. A week later I was in a bar with a friend of mine, the Dean of an aspirational law school, who

---

3. For reasons, see chapter ii.

said that everyone in his faculty was hardworking and that he could not afford 'luxury items like you'. International Law itself may be a luxury item; I think it is taught more frequently in elite law schools. International legal theory, then, must be super-luxurious: a kind of Louis Vuitton sub-subject in the law school curriculum. How luxurious, then, is an essay on gardening in international law?

ii. utopian experiments

One way into this is to think of gardening as utopian experiment, or enclave. In particular, I want to propose gardening as a sentimental—and not entirely allegorical—response to the badgering calls for normativity or reform. But I get to gardening in a roundabout way *via* a more general plea for an international legal imagination.

Someone once told me, jokingly, that the American Society of International Law's (ASIL) Annual Prize for 'a creative contribution to international law scholarship' was the award the society gave to scholars who 'made it up themselves'. There were other prizes for those who examined, synthesised or brilliantly analysed the actual law. The implication was that a certain sort of international law was more akin to fiction than it was to law. This international law tried to summon up worlds that did not yet exist or offered interpretations of legal texts that went well beyond what the text could reasonably permit. The most brute description of the distinction between 'actual law' and 'making it up' is found in James Shand Watson's speech at an ASIL Annual Conference where he warned lawyers against being importuned by utopian fantasies about what might be, and cautioned them instead to concentrate on really existing law or *lex lata*.[4] Thirty-five years later, in Naples, Andrea Bianchi made a plea, and in an entirely different vein, for a different approach—a way of being, maybe—when he warned against 'the fatal attraction of unimaginative thinking'.

This duality is, by now, familiar enough.[5] International law, we are told, has always possessed its material or sublunary form, derived from activities

---

4. James Watson, 'State Consent and the Sources of International Obligation', 86 *American Society of International Law Proceedings* (1992) 108. Others have pursued similar themes from Prosper Weil through to the current crop of positivists: see Prosper Weil, 'Towards Relative Normativity in International Law?', 77(3) *American Journal of International Law* (1983) 413–442.
5. See e.g. E. H. Carr, *The Twenty Years' Crisis, 1919–1939: An Introduction to the Study of International Relations* (Macmillan, 1966).

or practices embedded in something we might call social reality (maybe the 'practice' of states or the 'consent' of sovereigns). The lawyer's necessarily etiolated task involves a combination of interpretation, decision and description (something will turn on the particular office being occupied or role being played). Here, imagination is reduced to Hobbes' 'decaying sense'. The prejudices (a term of approbation for Edmund Burke), derived from a study of the already-existing social world, serve to tame this decaying sense and the excesses and dangers of the programmatic thought it tends to favour.

On the other hand, there is the law of possibility: either a law containing its own immanent prescriptions for a good or better life or, in a different version, a law to be used instrumentally in the advancement of certain anterior ends. From this perspective, the constant reversion to experience or practice over-embeds legal thought. Or, as Kant argued: 'it is to the highest degree reprehensible to limit or deduce the laws which dictate what I ought to do, from what is done'.[6] The lawyer's task here is to work out what the ends of a legal order might be or, to put this in vaguely JFK-ish terms, to discover not what the law might require of us but what we might require of the law.

It is worth noticing here that even the first relatively thin version of lawyering requires a capacity to somehow project a world in advance (for example, a world in which a particular interpretation of a legal text will be regarded as acceptable or a world in which a decision will be followed and deemed plausible, or even, compelling). As James Boyd White said: 'the lawyer is at heart, a writer, one who lives by the power of his imagination'.[7]

In the more aspirational version of international lawyering, though, it seems even more obvious that the imagination will be strongly in play. Indeed, the critique of this way of being a lawyer will tend to suggest that there is *nothing but* imagination at work (this is 'imagination' as a close cousin of the imagined or imaginary). Either way though, law, like community, is an imagined activity. But what does it mean to 'live by the power of imagination' and how would we recognise it when it happened? These seem to me to be under-explored questions of our legal work.

---

6. Immanuel Kant, *Critique of Pure Reason* (Dent, 1986) 180.
7. James Boyd White, *Legal Imagination* (University of Chicago Press, 1985) 208 (in a gesture of anti-imagination, one reviewer of this book said it was well worth 'skimming').

But before I say something about this, I want to say something about the relationship between imagination and international law more broadly. 'Imagination' is, of course, not a concept of international law at all in the sense that sovereignty or war or jurisdiction are concepts. Imagination does not provide intelligibility or widespread understanding or popularity. Sometimes the effect is the opposite; think of Beckett's *Murphy* (seven copies sold in the year after its publication) or *Finnegan's Wake* (I do not understand it, and I wrote an undergraduate dissertation on the 'Aeolus' episode in *Ulysses*) or Alasdair Gray's *Lanark*). Nor is imagination 'fundamental' to how we understand international law.[8] As with 'reason', imagination might be deployed in the construction of a concept; like 'faith' it might help us live amid (either passively or creatively), maintain the existence of, and provide openings for the dissolution of, such concepts. Epistemically, then, imagination can be thought of as one way in which international legal concepts get made, refined and radically refurbished.

As a politics, it might be possible to think of imagination as the opposite of complicity or acceptance. It involves at the outset a capacity, or at least willingness, to stand at a distance from the current orthodoxies, necessary, perhaps, in the totalising world in which we live now. But standing outside is not simply a matter of political will or personal inclination. The sheer intensity and pervasiveness of a certain, highly economistic way of thought means that we either imagine or succumb. And so, to misquote Trotsky, you might not be interested in imagination but imagination (or lack of imagination) is interested in you. Or, in David Bromwich's formulation, 'the absence of imagination . . . allows us to construct the sort of world we live in'.[9] The description of things as they are is merely the adoption of some other's act of imagination as one's own. As Raymond Geuss put it: 'There are overpowering imaginative constructs of such seductive power and attraction that they prevail for centuries against all resistance'.[10] And so, one of the earliest acts of imagination in our field is that of Hugo Grotius, who creates, through a 'reflexive imagination', a new way of embarking upon political philosophy.[11] Yet, to glance at a contemporary textbook is to realise not how much has changed since Grotius wrote but rather how

---

8. These terms, and parts of this chapter, are drawn from my chapter on "Imagination" in Jean D'Aspremont and Sahib Singh, *The Concepts of International Law* (Elgar, 2019).
9. David Bromwich, *Moral Imagination* (Princeton University Press, 2014) 23.
10. Raymond Geuss, *Politics and the Imagination* (Princeton University Press, 2010) 67.
11. Ibid. 68.

perennial our preoccupations appear to be. It is worth considering whether we think of the Syrian air-strikes as a form of self-defence because of an act of imagination of a Dutch diplomat over three and half centuries ago, or because they essentially or necessarily *are* acts of self-defence.

Imagined worlds are powerful, then, but how much should we reimagine? Or what are the limits on imaginative legal politics? Is there a requirement that we imagine but not too much? The dangers of unmoored ethical absolutes and imagined politics are apparent. To paraphrase Auden: 'when the tyrant cries, the children die in the street'.[12] The totalitarian dream-state can appear as a thinly mediated projection of the Dear Leader's unconscious, or a consciously willed version of a childlike fantasy. The constraints of existing material conditions or ordinary human expectations and frailties are swept aside in the urge to translate imagination into life. Totalitarian and late-capitalist architecture, for example, serves the fantastic mind and not the material context. Think of the innumerable monstrosities constructed under Stalin or of Ceausescu's 'systemisation' programme, which resulted in the destruction of seven kilometres of Bucharest's old city to make way for a parliament building unlikely ever to be rehabilitated merely through the passage of time.[13]

But these over-imagined absolutisms are not just a function of 20th-century totalitarianism. Indeed, they may lie at the centre of a distinctively liberal western tradition of thought: a neo-Kantianism in which a priori norms radically transcend and reorder the messy life of institutions and political history, bypassing what one scholar calls 'institutional inheritance' but at the same time oriented towards an idealised but never existent past.[14]

This combination of a projection onto an inevitable future and fetishisation of an idealised past is very much a mark of today's political imaginaries. When we think of the avatars of late capitalism—Margaret Thatcher and Ronald Reagan—we see how this Janus-like looking back and forwards

---

12. But why paraphrase Auden? 'Perfection of a kind, was what he was after, And the poetry he invented was easy to understand...When he laughed, respectable senators burst with laughter. And when he cried the little children died in the street': W. H. Auden, 'Epitaph on a Tyrant' (1939).
13. For some partial rehabilitations, see Owen Hatherley, *Landscapes of Communism: A History Through Buildings* (Penguin, 2015). This is not, of course, an architectural hubris restricted to the command economies. Melbourne, the city in which I wrote some of this, is being reimagined in an under-regulated skyscraper boom that is transforming its Victorian centre into an anonymous space for global capital.
14. Andrew Russ, *The Illusion of History* (Catholic University of America Press, 2013) 10–11, 13.

adopts potent political forms. Thatcher, for example, remembered an England that was forever smallholding: a Poujadist fantasy Little England in which grocers supplied goods in a flourishing market while keeping their finances in good order. This unstable amalgam of austerity, prudence and local market was a feature of her ruleship. Yet, Thatcherism led to a future of globalised markets, de-professionalised services and mass private ownership (one that ended up destroying many of the remnants of the first fantasy).

When it comes to projected futures and imagined pasts, Marx and Rousseau are two of our interlocutors. Marx (and Engels especially) offer detailed descriptions of the workings of the contemporary late-Victorian system of capital and the immiserations it imposed, but their thoughts are perpetually turned to an end of history in which class antagonism withers as surely as the state itself and in which men and women enjoy the collective fruits of unalienated labour. This imagined future is not so different, in some respects, from the fantasies of the current neo-liberal intellectual classes (with some people enjoying the benefits of unfettered consumption instead, labour of course becoming more and more intensely alienated).

Rousseau, on the other hand, looks back to a past in which men and women occupied a pre-political state of civil association. It is this past—a past before property and before politics—that provides the grounds for Rousseau's critique of contemporary circumstances.[15] Marx's future and Rousseau's past might be thought of as the work of utopia (though neither would have been happy with the term). There was certainly something destabilising and radical about these visions, far removed from the existing state of affairs. Utopia, though, is now everywhere but nowhere. The completeness of post-industrial globalised capitalism means that virtually all genuinely oppositional thought is marked as utopian and a certain sort of transformative utopian thought has been relentlessly exiled to the margins of permissible political debate. To oppose is to engage in critique at a distance from the conditions of global capital. Yet to take that distance is to be condemned as excessively utopian. And to be condemned as excessively utopian is not simply to be dismissed as a crank or fool but to find this foolishness linked to the excesses of 20th-century experiments in social

---

15. This is most obvious in *Discourse on the Moral Effects of the Arts and Sciences* (1750) and in his celebration of the state of nature in *Discourse on the Origin and Foundation of Inequality among Men* (1775). Even *The Social Contract* (1762), ultimately a defence of civil society, famously begins: 'Man is born free; and everywhere is in chains'.

VII. GARDENING, INSTEAD, OR, OF PASTORAL INTERNATIONAL LAW 193

and political reconditioning.[16] How does one enact a cultural revolution that is not the Cultural Revolution? A utopia that is not terror? In this sense, reimagining political and legal life seems both necessary and impossible (this is what Mark Fisher has called 'capitalist realism'): a good moment, then, for international law to attempt the leap into utopian reimagination.[17]

Of course, utopian thought has always had purchase on the field of international law. Indeed, in some respects, to do international law is to make an imaginative leap, or place some sort of utopian bet, on the future of global life. When I speak to students at the beginning of the university term, it is remarkable how many of them continue to make this bet (even if the numbers are declining as students begin to either pre-absorb the pragmatism of the modern profession or simply no longer believe in the future at all). International law here is understood as a field of imagination hitched, almost accidentally, to an unconvincing idea of itself as a legal order. Students might feel less aggrieved at its apparent lack of legal grounding if a course on international law was simply advertised as, say, 'a history of political imagination'.

The imaginative projects of certain writers certainly form at least one conceptual infrastructure for the discipline to be set alongside the proponents of consolidation. For every Grotius, a Suarez; for every Vattel, a Pufendorf; for every Brownlie, an Allott. These utopian projects are rarely imaginative efforts to be released from law but rather represent attempts to redeem or renew legal reasoning and institution building. This is law at the service of imagination. Martin Wight described thinkers in this vein as

---

16. I wrote this a few years ago as Jeremy Corbyn was being elected leader of the British Labour Party. In the reaction to Corbyn, we had the panoply of responses to anything even marginally outside the mainstream (Corbyn's policies seemed at the time to be a series of very modest variants on Labour party policy from the mid-1940s: a return to a dismantled utopia with a small amount of distribution, a secure safety net, a protected National Health Service). Even this is now impermissible. As Peter Mandelson suggested, ten days after Corbyn's election, 'it's too early to force [him] out'. Capitalism moves at a blisteringly fast anti-utopian pace. See Patrick Wintour and Nicholas Watt, 'Mandelson: It's Too Early to Force Corbyn Out', *The Guardian* (online, 25 September 2015).
17. Mark Fisher, *Capitalist Realism: Is There No Alternative?* (Zero Books, 2008). Fisher's book makes a similar argument to the one made by Jameson and Zizek about the difficulty—in some versions impossibility—of imagining alternatives to late-capitalism. The alternatives, according to Fisher, have already been absorbed into capitalist realism. Resistance is commodified, 'alternative' music is a just one more Spotify genre, art becomes 'pastiche and revivalism' (6–7). This 'exhaustion of the future' is not just a problem for the future but also a problem for the present and the past which have no 'new' against which to develop and renew (this is the argument of T. S. Eliot, 'Traditional and Individual Talent', in The Sacred Wood, 1920)).

'revolutionists'. When revolutionists look around them they see a deeply unjust world and imagine the prospect of a perfectible future world. Wight divided this tradition into two distinct strands. The first he called a catastrophic revolutionism, inspired by a violent impatience with the existing system and a desire and will to overturn and transform this system, often through force of might and arms. This was the revolutionism of (early) Lenin, (mid-period) Mao, (first-term) Reagan, (mid-to-late period) Hitler, the Jacobins and, according to Wight, Philip II of Spain.[18] The other form of revolutionism, Wight called 'evolutionary revolutionism' (the terms are unfortunate): a philosophy of international order and a practice of international diplomacy that emphasised the need for programmatic change but sought to achieve this through incremental improvement or non-violent reform or generalised piety. The various 'World Government' and cosmopolitan routines of international legal thought represent the most familiar examples of this tradition. Kant is a central figure here because of his *Articles on Perpetual Peace* and his commitment to an international order based on trade (the spirit of commerce) and republicanism (the spirit of enlightenment): an order in which states traded their way out of existence or democratised away their warlike impulses (the European Union used to be idealised in these terms).

The first tradition is often thought to offer little as an imaginative space of international law except as warning. It is now common ground among the Right, the Centre, as well as the social democratic and anti-Marxist Left that a certain sort of utopianism ends in the gulag or the camps (and on the Marxist Left itself, utopian thought was, in any case, often associated with the depoliticised pastorals of some anarchists or bourgeois fantasists).[19] And so, politics today could be understood as deliberately unimaginative: a retreat to the mundane and anti-programmatic. Meanwhile, the softer second (cosmopolitan) tradition has kept alive an idealist vision of internationalism grounded in concrete conditions. There is some of this in the League of Nations, less in the UN Charter and more in the various philosophical

---

18. 'Late Hitler' because, as Wight pointed out, Hitler was, at first, Machiavellian, focusing on 'incremental exactions' rather than grand plans for world domination. See also David S. Yost, 'Introduction: Martin Wight Philosophers of War and Peace', in Martin Wight, *Four Seminal Thinkers in International Theory: Machiavelli, Grotius, Kant, and Mazzini* (Oxford University Press, 2004) xvii–lxiii.
19. Fredric Jameson, *Archaeologies of the Future: The Desire Called Utopia and Other Science Fictions* (Verso, 2005)xi.

cosmopolitanisms of the late 20th century. In philosophy, this tradition is represented by John Rawls with his realistic utopia (more realistic than utopian, it in fact strongly, and disappointingly, resembled the principles already found in contemporary international law); in international law, a version was present on the fringes of the Yale School and in the Carnegie-sponsored World Order Model Project (Burns Weston, Richard Falk, Saul Mendlovitz), and in political theory more generally, it was found in the cosmopolitanisms of people like David Held and Mary Kaldor at the LSE.[20] These projects are not without critical bite, but the tendency has been to model existing institutions: a more effective or gender-sensitive UN, a more democratic EU, better peacekeeping.

Adopting a different tack, Fredric Jameson's *Archaeologies of the Future* retrieves utopian thought through what he calls 'anti-anti-utopianism'.[21] The most promising acts of imagination are those that 'fail the most comprehensively'.[22] The implicitly Beckettian thought is that such failures are necessary to replenish a field. Here, Jameson contrasts utopia as programme and utopia as impulse. The programmatic utopias will tend to yoke themselves to inverted forms of centralised power ('the dictatorship of the proletariat') or mimic existing institutional arrangements (a 'UN Parliament'). His call, then, is for utopian speculation at the margins of the existing discursive and institutional range, in places he describes as 'enclaves'.

Is a certain sort of international law precisely enclaval? According to Jameson, enclaves—not yet fully enclosed or captured spaces—in the past have included monasteries and courts, while enclaval thinking has encompassed everything from the 18th-century hobby of constitution-drafting to periodic defections from the money economy. No one these days could assert with a straight face that the teaching and practice of international law occupies a monastic space or is anyone's idea of a hobby. And indeed a mark of late capitalism is precisely the relentless closing off of such spaces; hobbies become marketable self-improvement businesses or professionalised sport; enclaves are monetised and administered. Very little strangeness is permitted in this sort of society. So, for example, the teaching of international law (subject to market and government disciplines like any other educational 'sector') has become increasingly technical and differentiated

---

20. E.g. David Held, *Democracy and the Global Order* (Polity, 1995).
21. Jameson (n 19).
22. Ibid. xii.

as it is encouraged to service the economy (arbitration, trade), the war on terror (international criminal law) or security (humanitarian intervention) rather than be a site for flights of imaginative fancy or rebellious thinking, or, even, humanist pedagogy and liberal education.

Yet, might not a course in public international law function as 'the last of the humanities'—the final resting place of a non-vocational study of the world for its own sake? If so, we need to consider what could provide the content of our work.

Projects of this type abound from Ayça Çubukçu's anthropological jurisprudence to the rediscovery of non-alignment at Bandung as a possible past-future for international lawyering, to Kate Miles' art-law combinations, to Maddy Chiam's plebeian legalisms, to Jay Winter's 'Minor Utopias'.

Winter's project, which I want to talk about shortly, works within a dialectic noted by Jameson when he remarked: 'the more surely a given Utopia asserts its radical difference from what currently is, to that very degree it becomes, not merely unrealisable, but what is worse, unimaginable'.[23] In this sense, then, maybe it is those utopias that can barely be imagined that ought to act as an inspiration for the sort of work we do as international lawyers.

Dismay at our collective failure to even bother trying to imagine a different arrangement is at the heart of the work of one of international law's most powerful works of imagination, Philip Allott's *Eunomia*. His is not a fantastic creature of science fiction or an out-of-this-world parallel global order but a piece of moral imagination in which a transformed mental world opens up a change in the way the world self-constitutes. This is an imaginative book about imaginative possibility. In a sense, there is very little of what we might call utopian speculation in the book. It is not as if Allott proposes or anticipates a world of material plenty or pastoral bliss or technological transcendence. What is on offer here, if we have the means and will to grasp it, is a reimagined language and politics. And for Allott, the imagination itself is central to this remaking of the world: it is, in a sense, a constitutive force in international law—more fundamental than sovereignty or peace or security, because these concepts are themselves the products of mental transformations. Of course, they are, like much of international law, the creation of certain arrangements of words. As Allott puts it:

23. Ibid. xv.

Social history is thus as much a history of words as it is a history of deeds. The history of words has as much explanatory power as any history of politics or diplomacy or political life . . . we are what we have said, we will be what we are now able to say.[24]

If international law is a linguistic-imaginative enterprise, the imaginative possibilities appear boundless and Allott and others are right to de-emphasise or denaturalise the taken-for-granted political world. 'We made it, we can transform it' might be a eunomic slogan, reduced to t-shirt proportions. This is an important insight in the midst of a set of disciplines in which the material is very often given priority or in which reality is posted as something extra-linguistic or even extra-social, a reality in which anarchy or sovereignty or capital, for example, are simply *there*.[25] It recognises the ideational foundations of social order and the priority to be given to language constructs in transforming these foundations into institutions and practices. This idea—and the idea that imagination lies at the heart of our capacity to transform our political or social situation—is a familiar one, from Plato's caves to the widespread belief that the recent financial crises are a product of changes in thought (or 'numbers') rather than plagues of locusts or the invasion by foreign armies.[26]

But though it may be the case that we can do anything with words, there are only a very small number of words that we can do anything with. This is the way in which a vocabulary might limit and constrain possibility. These vocabularies can be understood as 'formative contexts', and the work of social and political revision has to take place within these contexts. But these contexts themselves were once imagined and then institutionalised. And so acts of political imagination encourage us to think, propose and act in ways that 'allow us to escape a striking consequence of current views of social reality which is to equate the realism of a proposal for reconstruction with its proximity to current arrangements'.[27]

In the end, the resources of the imagination might be best directed towards forms of incrementalism, localism and situated utopia that are nevertheless

---

24. Philip Allott, *Eunomia* (Oxford University Press, 2001) 9.
25. For a response to this, see Alexander Wendt, 'Anarchy is What States Make of It: The Social Construction of Power Politics', 46(2) *International Organization* (1992) 391–425.
26. See e.g. Paul Auster and J. M. Coetzee, *Here and Now: Letters 2008–2011* (Faber & Faber 2013) 18–19.
27. Roberto Mangabeira Unger, *Politics: The Central Texts,* ed. Zhiyuan Cui (Verso, 1997)3, 80.

aimed at broader not-yet-fully-realisable ends. Reform without utopia is likely to simply humanise (and then legitimise) existing deformations in the social and economic order; utopia without situatedness runs the risk of a dictatorship of virtue or authoritarian fantasy. My interlocutors in this chapter offer ways into political imagination that seek to resist these tendencies.

Given the power of pre-constituted experience, imagination, then, can be thought of not as a set of programmatic ideals towards a better world or the creation of already-existing utopias against which current realities must inevitably fall short, but rather as an adoption of 'the exterior glance' combined with a relentless process of resistance, questioning and estrangement—a literary project as much as a political one—in relation to this pre-constituted experience and the institutional and political arrangements that concretise it.[28]

iii. gardening, instead

Candide's farm

How might one, then, enliven this exterior glance? In this work on sentimentality, what I thought was about language has sometimes turned out to be about 'excruciation', or about uncomfortable social and intellectual situations, about the sense I have (to go back to the opening of this chapter) that I am perpetually providing the wrong answer to the wrong questions. Take my experience of giving the Michael Kirby Annual Lecture in Australia where I ended by saying:

> International criminal justice—the great institutional machine engineered by talented and humane diplomats, kept in motion by lawyers who have sacrificed material reward for a life in pursuit of humanitarian ends, directed at putting defeated enemies and human rights violators in jail, and celebrated every week in a public lecture advertising its virtues—might now be one of the less auspicious ways to do good in the world.[29]

---

28. See John Rajchman, *Michel Foucault: The Freedom of Philosophy* (Columbia University Press, 1985). The 'exterior glance' is from Paul Ricoeur via Jay Winter, *Dreams of Peace and Freedom: Utopian Movements in the Twentieth Century* (Yale University Press, 2006).
29. My 'Human Rights with a Vengeance: One Hundred Years of Retributive Humanitarianism', 33 *Australian Yearbook of International Law* (2016) 1–14.

That went down badly with Michael Kirby, a well-known former Australian High Court judge, who asked me how I would respond to a Korean mother he had interviewed whose son had been tortured to death by the North Korean regime. What would I say to her demand for justice?[30]

In the spirit of responding to all of this, then, let me be quite concrete and offer some examples where gardening was chosen instead, where a different international law-diplomacy was configured or played out, where some sort of exterior glance was made possible. I make these suggestions in the knowledge that a call to pastoralism will be deemed eccentric. I have now been at several conferences where I have been parodied as the person who called on everyone 'to go and do some gardening' (instead of, say, solving the problem of global misery or ending violent empire—projects where public international law has hardly met with great success).[31] In a European capital recently, I was accused of calling for the abolition of the International Criminal Court (ICC) and the burning of its books (I had not in fact called for either of these things) and was asked to suggest an alternative to the ICC. There are only three possible retorts to this. The first is to refuse the invitation to elucidate a reformist policy or come up with a new institutional design—for example, a Truth Commission or a hybrid court or better complementarity provisions (this refusal, though, invites the counter-retort that one is engaging in mere Ivory Tower 'cynicism'). The second is to accept the invitation to suggest reforms to the ICC itself (this is to die a little). A third is to make a bold prescription for social and political change (which I did by calling on everyone who worked on international criminal law to work instead to alleviate poverty in Bangladesh or to make war on the war on drugs in order to challenge the rise of the narco-state). But these headline calls for change are generally dismissed as cranky or 'unworkable', or 'political' (Jacqueline Rose once told the story of some leftish New Yorkers who noticed that to even *comment on the existence* of homeless people was to be deemed a communist. Thus is the available latitude for proposed change subject to very rapid shrinkage).

30. I had cause to think about this when I read Han Kang's frankly upsetting novel, *Human Acts* (Granta, 2018), where the careful treatments of loss, torture, memory and trauma are a model for the sorts of things both Kirby and I were trying and failing to do and say at the lecture.
31. See China Mieville, *Between Equal Rights: A Marxist Theory of International Law* (Brill, 2005) esp. 319. For the view that the international legal order is in many respects culpable of facilitating the conditions of mass poverty and unhappiness, see John Linneralli, Margot Salomon and Muthucumaraswamy Sornarajah, *The Misery of International Law* (Oxford University Press, 2018).

Earlier in the chapter, I referred to Jay Winter's minor utopias. Some of these, from the Universal Declaration of Human Rights through to the ICC, appeared at first to offer international law a post-statist energy and dynamism but have often ended up as insufferably bureaucratic, self-referential or punitive. But the first of Winter's minor utopias is created by Albert Kahn, a man who devoted himself to documenting the world through photographing it (in his 'Archives of the Planet'). His legacy is a formal 'international garden' in Boulogne-Billancourt on the outskirts of Paris. Modern international law, in a way, begins, not far from Boulogne-Billancourt in the gardens at Versailles, but my gardens, like Kahn's, are more indirect examples of pastoral international law, gardens perhaps not even recognisable as utopian moments at all. These gardens offer an indirect approach to the problem of the enclave or the alternative space.

In the first issue of the 2015 volume of *The London Review of International Law* there is, on the cover, a photograph by Simon Norfolk from his series *A Place of Refuge: The First Safe Place*. The setting is a refugee camp on the border of Chechnya and Ingushetia. Many of the people living there have been in the camp since 1999. It's a bleak spot, but at the centre of the photograph is an image of Malika Hussienova and her family standing outside their military green tent. Surrounding the tent is a formal vegetable garden: a mini-Versailles and a small gesture of imaginative defiance and hopefulness after atrocity. The study of such places, I argue, might provide a new imaginative ground for international law.

Throughout history, gardens, have, of course, been idealised as places of nostalgic loss—think of Virgil's small-holders ('when shall I see my native land again? . . . see the turf-dressed roof of my simple cottage' (*Ecologues*) or utopian promise or romantic love (Boccaccio) or pre-lapsarian paradise (*Genesis*).

In one of the most painfully nostalgic passages in philosophy, Rousseau regrets the moment when human beings 'civilise' themselves through law:

> The first man who, having enclosed a piece of ground, bethought himself of saying, 'This is mine', and found people simple enough to believe him, was the real founder of civil society.[32]

---

32. Jean-Jacques Rousseau, *The Social Contract and Discourses* (Dent, 1938) 207.

The time immediately prior to this was, for Rousseau, a moment of simplicity, like a landscape 'adorned only by the hands of nature'. For Rousseau, it was all about getting back to the garden, a garden of pre-industrialised wilderness, a place before politics, a garden of Eden.

Gardening though has a double plot, so to speak: at once both Edenic, wild and anarchic but also suburban, aristocratic, manicured and stately.[33] The First Man (in some respects also a forerunner of the Nietzschean Last Man) *leaves* the garden in order to inhabit and delimit another garden, this time the garden as an enclosed space and, as Zygmunt Bauman has pointed out, an authoritarian space where a lot of (social) weeding might be done.[34] Meanwhile the garden, and especially a certain kind of organic horticulture, had its nativist, even fascist, overtones and undertones. Hitler's vegetarianism is notorious, of course (trotted out every so often as a conversational debating point by meat eaters), but less well remembered was the Nazi commitment to various blood and soil forms of gardening (thus biodynamic herb plantations at Dachau, a model garden at Theresienstadt, Himmler's affection for homeopathic cures, Speerean ideas about Nazi garden cities to be planted in Poland (expelled of all weeds of course), the institution of the Reich Small Garden Day every July).[35] The British Far Right, too, has its pastoral fantasies about a land free of foreign elements.

We ought not, then, to adopt a starry-eyed view of the 'pastoral' or what has been called an 'unpolitical ecologism or ruralism'.[36] The garden also has dark and banalising effects. Indeed, the idea of enclosure itself was a prelude to the capitalist remaking of common land and common life and the privatisation of British spatial existence. Even the unkempt commons, one of the last redoubts of pastoralism, are held out for consumption as 'wilderness parks' or 'experiences'. Meanwhile, the idea of the garden as a private, bourgeois space is one with multiple associations. This is the place from which to escape the rigours of contemporary industrialised or post-Fordist life into a little sanctuary replete with 'tanks of pesticide and industrial-strength

---

33. On the idea of the 'double plot' in theatre and poetry, see William Empson, *Some Versions of the Pastoral* (1935).
34. See Zygmunt Bauman's *Modernity and the Holocaust* (Polity, 2000) on the similarities between the gardener and the dictator (each a compulsive weeder). 'Certain gardens are described as retreats when they are really attacks' (Ian Hamilton Findlay, *Ian Hamilton Findlay and His Work*, at littlesparta.org.uk).
35. See e.g. George McKay, *Radical Gardening* (Frances Lincoln, 2011) 60–65; David Crouch and Colin Ward, *The Allotment: Its Landscape and Culture* (Five Leaves, 1997) 136–137.
36. Raymond Williams, *Politics and Letters* (Verso, 2015) 323.

mowing machines'.³⁷ The white picket fence enclosing the front garden is an Australian trope for a kind of small-minded conservative, individualistic voter (with a 'whipper snipper' ready to cut down any offending dandelion, and grass blower perpetually at hand in order to blow grass into someone-else's garden or into a communal space).³⁸ I write this very close to Hampstead Garden Suburb, a London postcode that seems, in its three constituent words, to suggest an archetypal, petit-bourgeois existence.³⁹

Conversely, as the garden is returned to nature, there is a return to something pure and un-ruined. In W. G. Sebald's *The Emigrants*, the author visits a garden in East Anglia to find it inhabited by a Dr Selwyn Lloyd (who is quick to say that he is not the owner). The garden, once a substantial enclosed space capable of feeding a large household, is overgrown but still provides Lloyd with fruit and vegetables that had reseeded. Sebald eats a fairy-tale apple 'which really did taste better than any I have eaten since'.⁴⁰ I live on Hampstead Heath, one of the world's great urban parks. But there, too, we have clash between the garden as enclosure and the garden as wild, free common.⁴¹

And at various times, gardening has been understood as exploitative, fascist or imperial. Raymond Williams does many complicated things with the pastoral in *The Country and the City*, but the book is always engaged in alerting us to the material conditions that produce gardens: the labourers who grow the fruit trees waiting to have their bounty plucked by passing aristocrats, the extraction of surplus capital that permits such gardens to be constructed, the class relations that are obscured in the pastoral poetry of rustic life.⁴²

---

37. Simon Schama, *Landscape and Memory* (Knopf, 1995), 16. See also Rachel Carson, *Silent Spring* (Houghton-Mifflin, 1962).
38. On the destruction of the larger garden of citrus groves and rivers in the name of the private dwelling with garden, see Mike Davis, 'How Eden Lost Its Garden', in *City of Quartz: Excavating the Future in Los Angeles* (Verso, 1990) 60–91 (the scandals are endless: a thousand citrus trees burned every week in the 1950s (p. 79), three billion tonnes of concrete poured over urban LA in the name of driving (p. 80), the substitution of real-life pastoral utopias with their suburban simulants, but topping them all is the decision to *pave* the Los Angeles River).
39. For a description of the early socialist roots of the garden city movement and its various incarnations in Gretna, New Lanark and Letchworth Garden City, see McKay (n 35) 26–41.
40. W. G. Sebald, *The Emigrants* (Vintage, 2002). 8–9
41. See Schama (n 37) 517–526.
42. Raymond Williams, *The Country and the City* (Oxford University Press, 1975) 28–30. This motif is very much present in the work of someone like Mike Davis, too. In a eulogy to the last unspoilt Southern Californian citrus groves, he reminds the reader that the 'picturesque landscape ... masks the long history of paternalistic exploitation, social segregation, and labor

Meanwhile, modern international law, as I say, begins in a garden: the magnificent gardens at Versailles, where the great post-war order of 1919 is constructed and where new forms of empire are invented.[43] But the Garden itself—in all its formal beauty—is a monument to human mastery over nature (and to the Sun King and his glory). The inspiration for the gardens at Versailles comes from a visit Louis XIV made on 17 August 1661, to a party in the newly built gardens of his then finance Minister Nicolas Fouquet at Vaux-Le-Vicomte. *Le Roi Soleil* was so outraged by the impertinence of Fouquet in constructing such a garden that he had Fouquet confined in a dungeon for the rest of his life and hired Fouquet's team of landscape gardeners and architects to build the great gardens at Versailles.[44] Fouquet was in the garden at 6pm on the 17th and in the dungeon by 2am on the 18th.[45]

The garden, then, has its dark history. Against all of this, though, I think we can still reclaim it as a space in which to work against the grain, a space, both literal and figurative, in which projects can be pursued at a distance from the governing orthodoxies. At its best, international law might become a form of gardening, a tending to the world through artisanal labour in collective self-realisation or contemplative solitude. This enclaval international law might resemble, at its best, say, the monasteries of the Middle Ages or, what Rachel Cusk has called, the 'untenanted wastes where ... creativity was quietly nurtured'.[46] Here, gardens are put to work to produce critical histories (Nietzsche) or reparative readings (Sedgwick).

In *Candide*, the eponymous hero adventures from Westphalia (where he is expelled from a garden of Eden for kissing the Baron's daughter, Cunegonde) to Northern Europe where he is tortured by Bulgars and to an Abar village raised to the ground 'in accordance with international law', and on to Lisbon (an earthquake, an *auto-da-fé*, a hanging) then Cadiz, Suriname,

---

violence'. See Davis (n 38) 60. At the beginning of the coronavirus epidemic, Hampstead Heath (with its high liberal, bohemian, elite patronage) stayed open while Victoria Park, a few miles east and more heavily policed, was closed because of 'anti-social behaviour').

43. For a more upbeat assessment of the mandates system established at Versailles, see Susan Pederson, *The Guardians* (Oxford University Press, 2017).
44. Robert Pogue Harrison, Gardens: An Essay on the Human Condition (Chicago University Press, 2008), 111–112.
45. Not quite. I am paraphrasing Voltaire here, who said that Fouquet was the King of France in the evening and a nobody by the morning. In fact Fouquet ended up in prison after a lengthy trial but the dye had been cast as the King returned to Versailles in his carriage.
46. Rachel Cusk, 'Aftermath', 115 *Granta* (2011) 11.

Eldorado and Buenos Aires where his misadventures are legendary. He dines with kings, he slays noblemen, he engages in politics. At the end of the book and his journeys, his teacher Dr. Pangloss, by now fully recovered from his hanging in Portugal, begins to recite the causes and effects of this journey and the fate of biblical and European kings. In the final line of the book, Candide responds to all of this by saying, 'we must cultivate our garden'. This is not an empty abstraction. The group forms a little society and succeeds in providing for itself through labour and a form of communal living.[47] How long could it last for? Who knows? But perhaps this does not matter so much. Failure might be our inspiration.[48] It is these failed projects of internationalism that might be retrieved as we search for the resources to resist.[49] Mike Davis begins *City of Quartz* with a Jamesonian story of failure at Llano del Rio in Southern California where a group of young socialists established a utopian community in 1914. There was a newspaper, a night school, a film company, communal kitchens, May Day celebrations, and, long before the United Nations had been established, a General Assembly. But, most of all, there were gardens—orchards, alfalfa fields, vegetable plots, and an irrigation system 'supplying the colony with 90% of its own food (and fresh flowers as well)'.[50] By 1918, the water had been turned off after a lawsuit and the community relocated. Ranchers entered the next day and destroyed everything except the 'twin fireplaces' of the General Assembly Hall.[51]

Woolf's irises

A year later, the Great Powers met near the gardens at Versailles where they engineered one of the most transformative reforms in international

---

47. Voltaire himself was no great fan of Rousseau's simple life: 'Those who are unhappy with London just have to go off to the Orkneys; there they will eat oat bread, and cut each other's throats for sun-dried fish and a straw hut. Those who recommend it should set the example': David Williams (ed.), *Voltaire's Political Writings* (Cambridge University Press, 1994) 131.
48. These projects are not always 'failures', of course. Think of the mass turn to organic urban farming in Cuba after access to Soviet fertilisers and pesticides was denied.
49. See Deval Desai, Adil Khan and Christopher Gevers, 'Sifting through the 'Successful Failures' and 'Failed Successes' of International Law: Introducing Two Essays on Law and Failure', 7(2) *London Review of International Law* (2019) 143–148.
50. Davis (n 38) 9.
51. Ibid. 11. See also the destruction by developers of the community 'Garden of Eden' in New York City in 1986, or the proposed demolition of the community garden on Elizabeth St. in Little Italy.

legal history when war, for the first time in history, became crime, when colony became mandate and when fragmented international society became League of Nations. These engineering works of the interwar era, of course, unravelled. Different kinds of European territorial empire were, by then, envisioned.[52] The crime of aggression became international policy (in Spain, in Manchuria, in Abyssinia and then, in Czechoslovakia and Poland). Meanwhile, a monumental city of Germania was being designed by Albert Speer for his Führer. This was to have banks of epic buildings, grand boulevards and manicured gardens, built by slave labourers from Russia, from Yugoslavia; by Jews and by political prisoners. Jay Winter has asked us to set these flights of totalitarian–utopian imagination against his 'minor utopias'. For every ground-clearing horticultural project, a modest pastoral one; for every Versailles, a provincial *jardin publique*; for every Speerian grand design, a small girl growing cyclamens in a greenhouse; for every large internationalist project, a smaller, local success story.[53]

Twenty years after the Versailles Peace Treaty, Leonard Woolf, working outside his greenhouse in Sussex, was interrupted in his gardening by a call from his wife Virginia. 'Hitler is on the radio giving a speech', she shouts. Leonard calls back: 'I shan't come. I am planting iris, and they will be flowering long after he is dead'. *Iris reticulata* is a violet-coloured iris. In the final sentence of Leonard Woolf's biography, *Downhill All the Way*, these irises are still blooming twenty-one years after Hitler's suicide.[54]

West's cyclamens

Nine months after Hitler's suicide, the Nuremberg War Crimes Trial began. In *A Train of Powder*, Rebecca West remembers being asked what was the most remarkable thing she had witnessed at Nuremberg.

> Often people said, 'You must have seen some very interesting sights when you went to the Nuremberg Trial'. Yes, indeed. There had been a man with one leg and a child of twelve, growing enormous cyclamens in a greenhouse.[55]

---

52. Mark Mazower, *Hitler's Empire* (2008).
53. Pogue Harrison (n 44) 109.
54. Victoria Glendinning, *Leonard Woolf: A Life* (Simon and Schuster, 2006) 344
55. Rebecca West, *A Train of Powder* (Virago, 1984) 127.

The bathos in this makes us laugh or, as a famous song goes, smile, in the face of mankind. In the citadel, after all, mankind was busy inventing itself or setting down some juridical markers ('crimes against humanity', the 'conscience of mankind' and so on). Outside, though, there is the everyday business—a kind of anticlimax—of growing flowers and getting around on one leg. These cyclamens (like nightingales, brass bands, and influenza) suggest sentimentality.[56] But they are also a quiet pastoral rebuke to those who would over-sentimentalise the victims of war and a rejoinder to the idea of politics as a series of transformative events; instead, they represent a decentring of the trial, of the grand political moment. So, alongside a wry bathos (Goering, von Ribbentrop, the cyclamens), there is in this reference a reversion to the everyday: a familiar that war had rendered unfamiliar.

Of course, this is sentimental but not in the way that lurid descriptions of the effects of bombing, or monumental histories of the Trial might be.[57] In these latter cases, a demand is being made that we weep over the victims, that we abhor or condemn, that our legal rituals determine and define, and provide a definitive pronouncement on the nature of evil or the course of history. In West's case, it is not quite clear how we should respond: we are being asked to think about something else altogether. The child is a victim of the war but she is neither passive nor just a victim (in the way we demand victims be just victims in criminal trials). The passage engenders a sense of responsibility for her as a cylamen grower. We want her horticulture to succeed. She wants our engaged sentiments but not pitying tears. Here she is, growing her cyclamens only a few months after Bomber Command's final gratuitous assault on the civilian population of Nuremberg on the night of 16–17 March when 277 Lancasters pulverised, for the second time, the remnants of the city's historic centre.[58]

'Nuremberg' refers to the trial, of course, but also now, for me at least, the bombing and the greenhouse. These cyclamens decentre the trial with its effusive self-congratulations. Transitional justice is about trial and conviction,

---

56. One story is that life continues outside the courtroom. The hidden history is that perhaps what matters is how the flowers grow after the trial is over. This, indeed, has been a major question asked of international war crimes trials. Are they integrated properly into the existing or future local criminal justice machinery? What effects are they intended to produce or do they produce on the rebuilt state or the transitional democracy or the traumatised population?
57. On monumental history, see Nietzsche, 'On the Uses and Disadvantages of History for Life' (1874).
58. A. C. Grayling, *Among the Dead Cities: Was the Allied Bombing of Civilians in WWII a Necessity or a Crime?* (Bloomsbury, 2006) 12–13.

but it is also a law and redemption of small spaces in small circumstances. It is a thousand acts of growing and nurturing that will make a society decent again and not, perhaps, the great trial followed by the botched judicial execution. And the girl with the cyclamens reminds us that the victors have to offer remedy for their violence wrought over several miserable nights in Nuremberg. West sounds as if she is a little disaffected by the justice on offer at Nuremberg. And this mirrors the mood of Hannah Arendt when she goes to Jerusalem in search of justice and discovers instead spectacle: a proceeding from which she expected majesty and reckoning but one that left her feeling 'stinknormal'. Sometimes, it is permissible to be sick of justice: sick of receiving it, sick of giving it, sick of its imperfect instantiations in an imperfect world.[59]

Khrushchev's letter

If Rebecca West is speaking back to the mass destruction of human populations from the air, how should we speak of those weapons designed to remove a people from the face of the earth, devices that Philip Allott called a 'permanent insult to humanity'.[60] Do we have, or can we create, a language capable of breaking out of or undercutting the conventions of legal diplomacy and the routines of international legal nuclearism? I have written elsewhere about the prospects for an alternative lawful language of objects, of monuments and of sentiments.[61]

Here, and at the conclusion of a chapter that has traced the possibility of gardening or thinking about gardens as an alternative to the performances of international legalism, I want to return to the letter I ended the last chapter with and gesture towards a different sort of performance, a pastoral international law—and a law of friendship—for the end of times.

---

59. Here gardening seems like a leap of faith, an act of imagination and a necessary luxury all at the same time. Sometimes of course, gardening instead, truly is a luxury. On 20 June 1942, a young Jewish girl in hiding wrote in her diary: 'Jews must be indoors by eight o'clock and cannot even sit in their own or their friends' gardens after that hour'.
60. Philip Allott, 'The Emergence of a Universal Legal System', 3(1) *International Law Forum* (2001) 12–17. The phrase is from Hannah Arendt's *Eichmann in Jerusalem* where she describes Eichmann's unwillingness to share the earth with the Jewish people. See Hannah Arendt, *Eichmann in Jerusalem: A Report on the Banality of Evil* (Penguin, 1994 [1963]).
61. See e.g. my 'OS Grid Ref. NM 68226 84912 & OS Grid Ref.TQ 30052 80597', in Dan Joyce and Jesse Hohmann (eds.), The Objects of International Law (Oxford University Press, 2018).

On 31 January 1963, two months before I was born and a few months after the Cuban Missile Crisis had ended, Khrushchev sent his famous letter to Fidel Castro.[62] It is important to place this letter in two different contexts. First, it took place in the aftermath of what was not just a fearful episode in superpower relations but a moment of serious discord in Cuban–Soviet friendship: a threat to the whole idea of a socialist brotherhood of nations joined at the hip and in common cause against the capitalist states.[63] In the letter, Khrushchev is trying to repair the damage ('the trace, albeit hardly perceptible') done to their relationship (Castro had felt betrayed by the US–Soviet rapprochement following the crisis, by Khrushchev's agreement to remove missiles from Cuba and by his refusal to countenance starting a nuclear war to defend Cuban sovereignty).[64]

The second context, though, is Khrushchev's own experience of having stared into two abysses: one actual, the other imagined (the 20 million Soviet dead in the Great Patriotic War and the near-inevitability of nuclear war over Cuba). He recoils from them in a gentle, meandering poetic style that is at the same time full of potency. Khrushchev's letter is, in a way, a gesture to a world in which time and space have suddenly become precarious in the aftermath of a moment in history when nuclear war threatened an end to time and an end to inhabitable space on earth. The opening paragraph of the letter is all about the passage of time at a moment when a certain kind of time very nearly passed forever. There is then a childlike wonder at the consummation of the task. Khrushchev goes on to describe a particular passage of time through the cycles of the seasons: 'every season . . . spring, summer, autumn and winter—has its own delights'. But he wants to invoke too, the possibility of endless time to set alongside the near-miss of the October crisis. So, there are references to 'a long time' and Cuba's 'eternal summer'. Many people in the world, after all, thought 1962 would be the last summer on earth. 'We are looking to the future', as Khrushchev puts it later in the letter.

Khrushchev describes the Russian landscape: 'the earth covered with snow . . . the forests covered with frost; I wish you could see it now'. The letter continues in this, frankly romantic, vein for some time before Khrushchev

---

62. For the definitive work on the legal aspects of the Cuban Missile Crisis: A. Chayes, *The Cuban Missile Crisis: International Crises and the Role of Law* (Oxford University Press, 1974).
63. The general literature is vast, but see esp. Graham Allison, *Essence of Decision* (Little Brown, 1971).
64. See Nikita Khrushchev, *Khrushchev Remembers* (Little Brown, 1970). From the American side: Robert Kennedy, *Thirteen Days* (1969).

puts a stop to what he calls 'these ramblings about nature'. But the ramblings are really the point because the letter is designed to restore Soviet–Cuban relations (Castro had wanted a more muscular approach from the Soviets during the crisis—perhaps even a nuclear attack) but also to restate in a kind of poetic-diplomacy why Castro's hot-headedness was so misguided. Khrushchev is placing the interests of time and landscape ahead of those of 'sovereignty', or personal self-assertion at a time when Cuba and the Soviet Union came 'close to war'. In these bucolic musings, Khrushchev is developing a kind of pastoral international diplomacy as a counterpoint to international legal and political nuclearism (or what he calls 'a verbal-abuse' contest). The Russian forests, the earth and time itself are the very things threatened with extinction at this point in history. Khrushchev is asking us to care for time and land: a pastoral internationalism in both senses.

★ ★ ★

It is easy to think of a call to gardening as a withdrawal or a seclusion, maybe even a form of complacency. This is, of course, a danger, but I have offered here some vignettes that illustrate the possibilities of a pastoral international law of defiant, world-weary worldliness (Voltaire); of ironic, hopeful disengagement (Woolf); of indignant, recuperative, sentimental, celebratory engagement (West); and of meandering, subtle legal diplomacy (Khrushchev). To go back to the questions I asked at the beginning of the book in chapter i, these might be examples of ways of speaking international law with hesitation not conviction (there may be reasons why 'the best lack conviction'), with a sardonic lightness and nuance, not with an oppressive solemnity, without risking bathos or absurdity or the dead hand of relevance, while keeping at bay the cynicism that sometimes threatens to engulf our best selves. It might be possible then to make international law, again, a compelling language for our times.

Let me end on a perhaps melodramatically upbeat note. There is an Aboriginal community called Utopia in the Australian Northern Territory. In an old-fashionedly cynical gesture, the place was named 'Utopia' by some earlier European settlers who regarded it as a benighted and inhospitable place. Now it has been reclaimed as an artistic community for Aboriginal artists. It is not, apparently, and by any means, a perfect place. Problems persist. And yet the reclamation of an imperfect, everyday utopia from cynicism seems, for my purposes, emblematic. In August 2019, while I was drinking coffee at an old General Store on the Mornington Peninsula, just south of Melbourne, I saw a sign for 'Utopia and Beyond', an exhibition of Aboriginal Art. I turned to my companion, Laura, and said that I would like to go there. 'You're already here', she replied. And sure enough, we were; I'd been drinking coffee outside a tiny exhibition space full of Utopian art, bathed in sunshine and displaying artists (e.g. Gwen and Jeannie Petyarre) who in their art—an art of landscapes, flowers, earth—had reconstructed worlds, dreams, practices, gardens.[65]

Michael Wood has spoken about the idea of the garden as a world of writing itself,

> a recurring assemblage of words that remind us what the world is like and invite us to think about which pieces of it we can change. Satires don't correct anyone but some readers may find their mingled horror and laughter suggest work for them to do. That would be their garden.[66]

I began writing this book in one garden (in North Fitzroy) and ended it in another (in North London). At one point, I cultivated a third garden—an English meadow (Queen Anne's Lace, Blue Cornflower, nasturtiums)—in a nature strip at the front of the house in which I was living. It became popular with children passing on their way to the local primary school; they would gather round it and pick the odd Californian or Shirley poppy. I was writing an essay one morning on diplomatic history and international law's complicity with projects of imperial ordering when I heard a threshing machine moving across the public areas at the front of the house. I ran out to find the meadow had disappeared, raised to the ground by a council worker wearing a facemask and wielding a petrol-powered Flymo grass-trimmer. I gave up trying to cultivate the pastoral at that point. But the following spring, the meadow had returned: a minor miracle of natural growth; a riot of little blue starbursts, dusty red velvet petals and white lace.

---

65. Merricks House Art Gallery, 'Art from Utopia', 8 February to 1 March 2020.
66. Wood (n 2) xxvi.

postlude: last thoughts on sentimentality

In his essay on 'The Uncanny', Freud quotes Schelling who defines the uncanny as 'something that should have remained hidden but has come into the open'.[1] A few years ago, a long, thin aquatic creature emerged from the ocean in California. No one had seen anything like it before. It was killed almost immediately. There was a newspaper cutting of several 'grinning people on a Californian beach' proudly displaying the dead mammal.[2]

International law has been killed off a thousand times. It has been interred, disinterred and 'critiqued' to within an inch of its life. It is no longer clear whether it is dead or alive. Is it, to refer back to Freud, an animate object that has really expired or an apparently lifeless object that might perhaps be animate?[3] It certainly continues to fascinate and mobilise people. In this book, I have tried to do less of the interring and disinterring, and instead engaged in acts of defamiliarisation as a way of establishing the lifelessness of some of international law's familiar routines and the liveliness of its unfamiliar subterranean existence.

---

1. Sigmund Freud, *The Uncanny* (Penguin, 2003 [1919]) 148.
2. Joy Williams, 'The Art of Fiction No 223', 209 *Paris Review* (2014) 32–55.
3. Freud (n 1) 135.

select bibliography

Adorno, T. (2007) *Negative Dialectics*. Continuum.
Ahern, S. (2007) *Affected Sensibilities: Romantic Excess and the Genealogy of the Novel 1680–1810*. AMS Press.
Ahmed, S. (2019) *What's the Use? On the Uses of Use*. Duke University Press.
Alexandrowicz, C. (1967) *An Introduction to the History of the Law of Nations in the East Indies*. Oxford University Press.
Alexievich, S. (2013) *Second-Hand Time*. Fitzcarraldo Editions.
Allott, P. (1971) 'Language, Method, and the Nature of International Law', in 45 *British Yearbook of International Law*. Oxford University Press, pp. 79–136.
Allott, P. (1988) 'State Responsibility and the Unmaking of International Law', *Harvard International Law Journal*, 29(1), pp. 1–26.
Allott, P. (1993) 'Self-Determination: Absolute Right or Social Poetry?', in Tomuschat, C. (ed.) *Modern Law and Self-Determination*. Martinus Nijhoff, pp. 77–210.
Allott, P. (2001) *Eunomia: New Order for a New World*. Oxford University Press.
Alston, P. (2019) *Report of the Special Rapporteur on Extreme Poverty and Human Rights on His Visit to the United Kingdom of Great Britain and Northern Ireland*.
Alvarez, J. E. (1998) 'Rush to Closure: Lessons of the Tadić Judgment', *Michigan Law Review*, 96(7), pp. 2031–2112.
Amis, K. (1954) *Lucky Jim*. Victor Gollancz.
Arendt, H. (1958) *The Human Condition*. University of Chicago Press.
Arendt, H. (1994 [1963]) *Eichmann in Jerusalem: A Report on the Banality of Evil*. Penguin.
Arendt, H. (2018) *Thinking without a Banister*. Schocken.
Aristodemou, M. (2014) *Law, Psychoanalysis, Society: Taking the Unconscious Seriously*. Routledge.
Auden, W. H. (1940) *'In Memory of W. B. Yeats': Collected Poems*. Faber & Faber.
Auden, W. H. (1956) *Making, Knowing, and Judging*. Oxford University Press.
Auster P. and J. M. Coetzee (2013) *Here and Now: Letters 2008–2011*. Faber & Faber.
Baasner, F. (1986) 'The Changing Meaning of "Sensibilité", 1654 till 1704', in 15 *Studies in 18th Century Culture*, pp. 77–96.
Bakhtin, M. (1965) *Rabelais and His World*. Indiana University Press.
Bakhtin, M. (1981) *The Dialogic Imagination*. University of Texas Press.
Balakrishnan, G. (2000) *The Enemy: An Intellectual Portrait of Carl Schmitt*. Verso.

Bauman, Z. (2000) *Modernity and the Holocaust*. Polity.
Beckett, S. (1951) *Malone Dies*. Les Éditions de Minuit.
Begicevic, A. (2018) *'Money as Justice'*. Melbourne University, unpublished dissertation.
Belgion, M. (2017) *Victors' Justice: A Letter Intended to Have Been Sent to a Friend Recently in Germany*. lulu.com.
Benton, L. (2019) 'Beyond Anachronism: Histories of International Law and Global Politics', *Journal of the History of International Law*, 21(1), pp. 7–40.
Berger, J. (2009) *About Looking*. Vintage International.
Berlant, L. (2011) *Cruel Optimism*. Duke University Press.
Berman, N. (1993) '"But the Alternative Is Despair": European Nationalism and the Modernist Renewal of International Law', *Harvard Law Review*, 106(8), pp. 1792–1903.
Bianchi, A. (2016) *International Law Theories: An Inquiry into Different Ways of Thinking*. Oxford University Press.
Birch, D. and Drabble, M. (eds.) (2009) *The Oxford Companion to English Literature*. Oxford University Press.
Blair, T. (2010) *A Journey*. Cornerstone.
Blanchot, M. (1997) *Friendship*. Stanford University Press.
Bloom, H. (1973) *The Anxiety of Influence*. Oxford University Press.
Boer, L. (2019) 'Narratives of Force: The Presence of the Writer in International Legal Scholarship', *Netherlands International Law Review* 66(1), pp. 1–20.
Bourdieu, P. (1990) *Homo Academicus*. Polity Press.
Bourdieu, P. (1991) *Language and Symbolic Power*. Polity Press.
Brassett, J. and Bulley, D. (2007) 'Ethics in World Politics: Cosmopolitanism and Beyond?', *International Politics*, 44(1), pp. 1–18.
Bromwich, D. (2014) *Moral Imagination*. Princeton University Press.
Brooks, P. (2001) *Troubling Confessions: Speaking Guilt in Law and Literature*. University of Chicago Press.
Buchan, J. (2012) *Capital of the Mind: How Edinburgh Changed the World*. Birlinn.
Bull, M. (2004) 'State of Exception', *London Review of Books*, 26(24), pp. 3–6.
Butler, J. (2006) *Precarious Life: The Powers of Mourning and Violence*. Verso.
Cass, D. Z. (1996) 'Navigating the New Stream', *Nordic Journal of International Law*, 65(3–4), pp. 341–383.
Cesarani, D. (2005) *Eichmann: His Life and Crimes*. Random House.
Charlesworth, H. (2002) 'Discipline of Crisis', *Modern Law Review*, 65(3), pp. 377–392.
Chiam, M. (2021) *International Law in Public Debate*. Cambridge University Press.
Clark, I. (2013) *The Vulnerable in International Society*. Oxford University Press.
Coetzee, J. M. (1999) *Elizabeth Costello*. Knopf.
Cohen, S. (1995) 'State Crimes of Previous Regimes: Knowledge, Accountability, and the Policing of the Past', *Law & Social Inquiry*, 20(1), pp. 7–50.
Collier, R. (2009) *Men, Law and Gender*. Routledge.

Collini, S. (2007) *Absent Minds, Intellectuals in Britain*. Oxford University Press.
Connolly, C. (1938) *Enemies of Promise*. Routledge.
Constable, M. (2104) *Our Word is Our Bond: How Legal Speech Acts*. Stanford University Press.
Courtenay, T. (2005) *Pretending to Be Me*. Hachette Audio.
Cover, R. (1983) 'Foreword: Narrative and Nomos', *Harvard Law Review*, 97(4), pp. 4–68.
Crangle, S. (2010) *Prosaic Desires: Modernist Knowledge, Boredom, Laughter, and Anticipation*. Edinburgh University Press.
Crangle, S. and Nicholls, P. (eds.) (2010) *On Bathos*. Bloomsbury Academic.
Craven, M. (2009) *The Decolonization of International Law*. Oxford University Press.
Critchley, S. (1998) 'The Other's Decision in Me', *European Journal of Social Theory*, 1(2), pp. 259–279.
Çubukçu, A. (2015) 'On the Exception of Hannah Arendt', *Law, Culture and the Humanities*, 15(3), pp. 684–704.
Cusk, R. (2011) 'Aftermath', *Granta*, 115, pp. 7–29.
Daigle, M. (2016) 'Writing the Lives of Others: Storytelling and International Politics', *Millennium*, 45(1), pp. 25–42.
Dallmyr, F. (1999) 'Derrida and Friendship', *Critical Review of International Social and Political Philosophy*, 2(4), pp. 105–130.
Damasio, A. (2003) *Looking for Spinoza*. Harcourt.
Damaska, M. R. (2008) 'What is the Point of International Criminal Justice?', *Chicago Kent Law Review*, 83(1), pp. 329–368.
Davis, M. (1990) *City of Quartz*. Verso.
Deleuze, G. (2001) *Pure Immanence*. Zone Books.
DeLillo, D. (1985) *White Noise*. Viking Press.
Derrida, J. (1987) *The Post Card: From Socrates to Freud and Beyond*. University of Chicago Press.
Derrida, J. (1997) *The Politics of Friendship*, Verso.
Desai, D., Khan, A. and Gevers, C. (2019) 'Sifting through the "Successful Failures" and "Failed Successes" of International Law: Introducing Two Essays on Law and Failure', *London Review of International Law*, 7(2), pp. 143–148.
Dickinson, E. (1998 [1868]) 'Tell All the Truth', from *The Poems of Emily Dickinson*. Harvard University Press.
Dolin, K. (1999) *Fiction and the Law: Legal Discourse in Victorian and Modernist Literature*. Cambridge University Press.
Douglas, L. (2005) *The Memory of Judgement: Making Law and History in the Trials of the Holocaust*. Yale University Press.
Drumbl, M. (2007) *Atrocity, Punishment and International Law*. Cambridge University Press.
Drumbl, M. (2012) *Reimagining Child Soldiers in International Law and Policy*. Oxford University Press.
Dyer, G. (2010) *Working the Room*. Canongate Books.

Eagleton, T. (1999) 'In the Gaudy Supermarket', *London Review of Books*, 21(10), pp. 3–6.
Eagleton, T. (2008) 'Determinacy Kills', *London Review of Books*, 30(12), pp. 1–7.
Emerson, R. W. (1841) *Essays*. Harper Perennial.
Empson, W. (1935) *Some Versions of Pastoral*. Chatto and Windus.
Engle, K., Miller, Z. and Davis, D. (eds.) (2016) *Anti-Impunity and the Human Rights Agenda*. Cambridge University Press.
Fassin, D. (2011) *Humanitarian Reason: A Moral History of the Present Times*. University of California Press.
Fawcett, B. (1986) *Cambodia: A Book for People Who Find Television Too Slow*. Talonbooks.
Felman, S. (2000) 'Theaters of Justice: Arendt in Jerusalem, the Eichmann Trial, and the Redefinition of Legal Meaning in the Wake of the Holocaust', *Theoretical Inquiries in Law*, 27(2), pp. 465–507.
Felman, S. (2002) *The Juridical Unconscious*. Harvard University Press.
Ferguson, F. (1984) 'The Nuclear Sublime', *Diacritics*, 14(2), pp. 4–11.
Ferstman, C. (2002) 'The Reparations Regime of the International Court of Justice', *Leiden Journal of International Law*, 15(3), pp. 667–686.
Firestone, S. (1970) *The Dialectic of Sex*. William Morrow.
Fish, S. (1982) 'Working on the Chain Gang: Interpretation in the Law and in Literary Criticism', *Critical Inquiry*, 9(1), pp. 201–216.
Fish, S. (1987) 'Still Wrong after All These Years', *Law and Philosophy*, 6(3), pp. 401–418.
Fish, S. (1989) *Doing What Comes Naturally: Change, Rhetoric and the Practice of Theory in Literary and Legal Studies*. Duke University Press.
Fisher, M. (2008) *Capitalist Realism: Is there no Alternative?* Zero Books.
Fitzpatrick, P. (1995) '"We Know What It Is When You Do Not Ask Us": Nationalism as Racism', in Fitzpatrick, P. (ed.) *Nationalism, Racism, and the Rule of Law*. Dartmouth, pp 3–26.
Foucault, M. (2003) *Lectures at the College de France 1975–1976, 21 January 1976*. Picador.
Franck, T. (1990) *The Power of Legitimacy among Nations*. Oxford University Press.
Franzen, J. (2012) *Farther Away*. Farrar, Straus and Giroux.
Freud, S. (1905) *The Joke and Its Relationship to the Unconscious*. Penguin.
Freud, S. (1958) 'On Beginning the Treatment (Further Recommendations on the Technique of Psycho-analysis I)', in J. Strachey (ed.), *The Standard Edition of the Complete Psychological Works of Sigmund Freud, Volume XII (1911–1913): The Case of Schreber, Papers on Technique and Other Works*. Hogarth Press and the Institute of Psychoanalysis.
Freud, S. (2003 [1919]) *The Uncanny*. Penguin.
Fussell, P. (1975) *The Great War and Modern Memory*. Clarendon Press.
Gabel, P. (1984) 'A Critique of Rights: The Phenomenology of Rights-Consciousness and the Pact of the Withdrawn Selves', *Texas Law Review*, 62, pp. 1563–1598.

Gabel, P. and Kennedy, D. (1984) 'Roll Over Beethoven', *Stanford Law Review*, 36(1), pp. 1–55.
Gaita, R. (1999) *A Common Humanity: Thinking about Love and Truth and Justice*. Routledge.
Gaita, R. (2011) 'Literature, Genocide, and the Philosophy of International Law', in R. Cruft, M. H. Kramer and M. R. Reiff (eds.), *Crime, Punishment and Responsibility*. Oxford University Press, Chapter 8.
Gaita, R. (2017) *Who's Afraid of International Law?* (ed. with Gerry Simpson). Monash.
Gasset, J. O. y (1925) *The Dehumanization of Art and Other Essays on Art, Culture, and Literature*. Doubleday.
Geuss, R. (2010) *Politics and the Imagination*. Princeton University Press.
Gilligan, C. (1982) *In a Different Voice*. Harvard University Press.
Goodrich, P. (1996) *Law in the Courts of Love: Literature and Other Minor Jurisprudences*. Routledge.
Goodrich, P. (2003) 'Laws of Friendship', *Law and Literature*, 15, pp. 23–52.
Goodrich, P. (2005) '*Lex Laetens*: Three Theses on the Unbearable Lightness of Legal Critique', *Law and Literature*, 17(3), pp. 293–319.
Halley, J. (2006) *Split Decisions*. Princeton University Press.
Hankey, M. (1950) *Politics, Trials and Errors*. Pen-In-Hand.
Harrison, R. P. (2008) *Gardens: An Essay on the Human Condition*. Chicago University Press.
Hartog, F. (2015) *Regimes of Historicity: Presentism and Experiences of Time*, trans. Saskia Brown. Columbia University Press.
Hathaway, O. and Shapiro, S. (2017) *The Internationalists: And Their Plan to Outlaw War*. Allen Lane.
Hatherley, O. (2015) *Landscapes of Communism: A History Through Buildings*. Penguin.
Hazan, P. (2010) *Judging Wars*. Stanford University Press.
Hazzard, S. (1967) *People in Glass Houses*. Picador.
Hazzard, S. (1973) *Defeat of an Ideal: A Study of the Self-Destruction of the United Nations*. Little, Brown.
Hazzard, S. (2003) *The Great Fire*. Virago.
Heidegger, M. (2001) *Zollikon Seminars: Protocols—Conversations—Letters*. Ed. M. Boss; transl. Franz K. Mayr and Richard R. Askay. Northwestern University Press.
Heller, K. J. and Simpson, G. (eds.) (2013) *The Hidden Histories of War Crimes Trials*. Oxford University Press.
Higgins, R. (1994) *Problems and Process: International Law and How We Use It*. Clarendon Press.
Hill, B. (2015) *Peacemongers*. University of Queensland Press.
Hirsch, M. and Lang, A. (eds.) (2018) *Research Handbook on the Sociology of International Law*. Edward Elgar.
Hohmann, J. and Joyce, D. (2018) *International Law's Objects*. Oxford University Press.
Honig, B. (2013) *Antigone Interrupted*. Cambridge University Press.
Hothschild, A. (1998) *King Leopold's Ghost*. Mariner Books.

Howse, R. (2004) *Mozart: A Novel*. Xlibris.
Hume, D. (1817) *A Treatise on Human Nature*. Oxford University Press.
James W. (1884) *What is an Emotion?* Editions Le Mono.
Jameson, F. (2005) *Archaeologies of the Future: The Desire Called Utopia and Other Science Fictions*. Verso.
Jan, C. S. (1991) *Rhetoric and Irony*. Oxford University Press.
Jeffery, R. (2011) 'Reason, Emotion, and the Problem of World Poverty: Moral Sentiment Theory and International Ethics', *International Theory*, 3(1), pp. 143–178.
Jeffery, R. (2014a) 'The Promise and Problems of the Neuroscientific Study of Individual and Collective Emotions', *International Theory*, 6(3), pp. 584–589.
Jeffery, R. (2014b) *Reason and Emotion in International Ethics*. Cambridge University Press.
Johns, F. (2013) *Non-Legality in International Law: Unruly Law*. Cambridge University Press.
Johns, F., Joyce, R. and Pahuja, S. (eds.) (2010) *Events: The Force of International Law*. Routledge.
Kahn, P. (2000) *The Cultural Study of Law*. University of Chicago Press.
Kennedy, David (1985) 'Spring Break', *Texas Law Review*, 63(8), pp. 1377–1424.
Kennedy, David (1995) 'Autumn Weekends: An Essay on Law and Everyday Life', in Sarat, A. and Kearns, T. (eds.) *Law in Everyday Life*. University of Michigan Press, pp. 191–236.
Kennedy, David (2005) *Dark Side of Virtue: Reassessing International Humanitarianism*. Princeton University Press.
Kennedy, David (2006) *Of Law and War*. Princeton University Press.
Kennedy, Duncan (1998) *A Critique of Adjudication*. Harvard University Press.
Kennedy, Duncan (1998) 'Legal Education as Training for Hierarchy', in D. Kairys (ed.) *The Politics of Law: A Progressive Critique*. Basic Books, pp. 54–75.
King, D. (2017) *The Trial of Adolf Hitler: The Beer Hall Putsch and the Rise of Nazi Germany*. W. W. Norton.
Kirchheimer, O. (1961) *Political Justice*. Princeton University Press.
Koselleck, R. (2018) *Sediments of Time: On Possible Histories*. Stanford University Press.
Koskenniemi, M. (2001) *The Gentle Civiliser of Nations*. Cambridge University Press.
Koskenniemi, M. (2005) *From Apology to Utopia*. Cambridge University Press.
Kristeva, J. (1989) *Black Sun: Depression and Melancholia*. Columbia University Press.
Kundera, M. (1996) *The Book of Laughter and Forgetting*. Faber and Faber.
Lacey, N. (2008) *Women, Crime and Character*. Clarendon Press.
Lampedusa, G. T. di (1958) *The Leopard*. Feltrinelli.
Lang, A. and Marks, S. (2013) 'People with Projects: Writing the Lives of International Lawyers', *Temple International and Comparative Law Journal*, 27(2), pp. 437–53.
Lauterpacht, E. (2013) *The Life of Hersch Lauterpacht*. Cambridge University Press.
Lawrence, T. (1895) *The Principles of International Law, Part 2*. D. C. Heath.
Lear, J. (2014) *A Case for Irony*, Harvard University Press.

Linneralli, J., Salomon, Mar. and Muthucumaraswamy, S. (2018) *The Misery of International Law*. Oxford University Press.
Logue, C. (1988) *War Music: An Account of Books 16–19 of Homer's Iliad*. Faber & Faber.
Logue, C. (2001) *Audiologue, A Seven CD Set of Recordings 1958–1998*. Unknown Public.
Lorimer, J. (1883) *Institutes*. Blackwood.
MacGregor, N. (2014) *Germany: Memories of a Nation*. Penguin.
Malcolm, J. (1977) *Psychoanalysis: The Impossible Profession*. Knopf.
Mandel, M. (1994) *The Charter of Rights and the The Legalization of Politics in Canada*. Thompson Educational Publishing.
Manderson, D. (2000) *Songs without Music: Aesthetic Dimensions of Law and Justice*. University of California Press.
Manderson, D. (2011) 'Modernism and the Critique of Law and Literature', *The Australian Feminist Law Journal*, 35(1), pp. 107–125.
McAdams, R. (2015) *The Expressive Powers of Law: Theories and Limits*. Princeton University Press.
McCarthy, T. (2005) *Remainder*. Vintage.
McKay, G. (2011) *Radical Gardening*. Frances Lincoln.
Meerssche, D. van den (2005) 'Calling Themis', *The European Journal of International Law*, 26(1), p. 310.
Mégret, F. (2009) 'Of Shrines, Memorials and Museums: Using the International Criminal Court's Victim Reparation and Assistance Regime to Promote Transitional Justice', *SSRN*, pp. 12–18.
Meron, T. (2000) *Bloody Constraint: War and Chivalry in Shakespeare*. Oxford University Press.
Mieville, C. (2005) *Between Equal Rights: A Marxist Theory of International Law*. Brill.
Minow, M. (1998) *Between Vengeance and Forgiveness: Facing History After Genocide and Mass Violence*. Beacon Press.
Monsacré, H. (2018) *The Tears of Achilles*. Center for Hellenic Studies.
Montaigne, M. (2004 [1580]) *Of Friendship*. Transl. Charles Cotton. Penguin.
Moorhouse, F. (2011) *Grand Days*. Random House Australia.
Moretti, F. (1998) *Atlas of the European Novel, 1800–1900*. Verso.
Morgan, E. (1988) 'Retributory Theater', *Journal of International Law and Policy*, 3(1), pp. 1–64.
Morgan, E. (2007) *The Aesthetics of International Law*. University of Toronto Press.
Motooka, W. (1998) *The Age of Reasons*. Routledge.
Mowbray, J. (2012) *Linguistic Justice: International Law and Language Policy*. Oxford University Press.
Moyn, S. (2018) *Not Enough*. Harvard University Press.
Muldoon, P. (2007) *Oxford Lectures, The End of the Poem*. Farrar & Giroux.
Murdoch, I. (1961) 'Against Dryness', *Encounter*, XVI, pp. 16–20.
Nabokov, V. (1980) *Lectures on Literature*. Weidenfeld & Nicolson.

Nesiah, V. (2002) 'Overcoming Tensions between Family and Judicial Procedures', *International Review of the Red Cross*, 84(848), pp. 823–844.

Nesiah, V. (2019) 'Freedom at Sea', *London Review of International Law*, 7(2), pp. 149–179.

Nietzsche, N. (1969) *Thus Spake Zarathustra*. Penguin.

Nietzsche, F. (2008 [1874]) *The Advantage and Disadvantage of History for Life*. Standard Publications.

Nino, C. (1996) *Radical Evil on Trial*. Yale University Press.

Noonan, J. (1976) *Persons and the Masks of the Law*. Farrar, Straus & Giroux.

Nussbaum, M. (1995) *Poetic Justice: The Literary Imagination and Public Life*. Beacon Press.

Nussbaum, M. (2001) *Upheavals of Thought: The Intelligence of Emotions*. Cambridge University Press.

Orford, A. (2003) *Reading Intervention: Human Rights and the Use of Force in International Law*. Cambridge University Press.

Orwell, G. (1974 [1949]) *1984*. Penguin.

Otto, D. (2016) 'Feminist Approaches to International Law', in A. Orford, M. Clark and F. Hoffman (eds.) *The Oxford Handbook of International Legal Theory*. Oxford University Press, pp. 105–118.

Pahuja, S. (2011) *Decolonising International Law*. Cambridge University Press.

Pamuk, O. (2010) *The Naive and Sentimental Novelist*. Faber & Faber.

Parfitt, R. (2011) 'Empire des Nègres Blancs: The Hybridity of International Personality and the Abyssinia Crisis of 1935–36', *Leiden Journal of International Law*, 24(4), pp. 849–972.

Parker, J. (2015) *Acoustic Jurisprudence: Listening to the Trial of Simon Bikindi*. Oxford University Press.

Peters, J. (2005) 'Law, Literature and the Vanishing Real', *PMLA*, 120(2), pp. 442–453.

Phillips, A. (2000) *Promises, Promises*. Faber & Faber.

Pieterse, M. (2007) 'Eating Socioeconomic Rights', *Human Rights Quarterly*, 29(3), pp. 796–822.

Quirijins, K. (dir.) (2012) *Peace versus Justice*. ITVS Films.

Raine, N. (2017) *Consent*. Faber and Faber.

Rawls, J. (1973) *A Theory of Justice*. Oxford University Press.

Rediker, M. (2004) *Villains of All Nations: Atlantic Pirates in the Golden Age*. Verso.

Richards, I. A. (1929) *Practical Criticism: A Study of Literary Judgement*. Routledge & Kegan.

Robbins, B. (2018) 'Bad Atrocity Writing', *N+1*.

Rodell, F. (1936) 'Goodbye to Law Reviews', *Virginia Law Review*, 23, pp. 38–45.

Rorty, R. (1989) *Contingency, Irony and Solidarity*. Cambridge University Press.

Rose, J. (2003) *On Not Being Able to Sleep*. Princeton University Press.

Roshchin, E. (2017) *Friendship among Nations: History of a Concept* Manchester University Press.

Roth, P. (1995) *Sabbath's Theater*. Houghton Mifflin Harcourt.

Rousseau, J. J. (1938) *The Social Contract and Discourses*. Dent.
Russ, A. (2013) *The Illusion of History*. Catholic University of America Press.
Said, E. (1978) *Orientalism*. Pantheon Books.
Sands, P. (2016) *East West Street*. Vintage Books.
Sartre, J.-P. (1965) *Situations IX*. Gallimard.
Sassoon, D. (2019) *The Anxious World: The History of Global Capitalism*. Allen Lane.
Sassoon, S. (1918) *Counter-Attack and Other Poems*. Heinemann.
Schlag, P. (1998) *The Enchantment of Reason*. Duke University Press.
Schmitt, C. (2006) *The Nomos of the Earth*. Telos.
Schmitt, C. (2007) *Theory of the Partisan*. Telos.
Schwarzenberger, G. (1943) *International Law and Totalitarian Lawlessness*. Cape.
Schwöbel, C. (ed.) (2016) *Critical Approaches to International Criminal Law: An Introduction*. Routledge.
Scott, D. (2004) *Conscripts of Modernity*. Duke University Press
Scott, W. (2008 [1818]) *The Heart of Midlothian*. Oxford World's Classics.
Sebald, W. G. (2002) *The Emigrants*. Vintage.
Sebald, W. G. (2005) *The Rings of Saturn*. Vintage.
Seymour, D. (1997) 'Letter from Shylock', *Law and Critique* 8(2), pp. 215–222.
Shapiro, M. (2011) 'The Micropolitics of Justice: Language, Sense and Space', *Law, Culture and the Humanities*, 8(3), pp. 1–19.
Sharma, J. (2011) *Empire's Garden*. Duke University Press.
Simpson, G. (2002) 'International Law in Diplomatic History', in Crawford, J. and Koskenniemi, M. (eds.) *Cambridge Companion to International Law. Cambridge Companions to Law*. Cambridge University Press, pp. 25–46.
Simpson, G. (2007) *Law, War and Crime*. Polity Press.
Simpson, G. (2011) 'Paris 1793 and 1872', in Johns, F., Pahuja, S. and Joyce, R. (eds.) *Events in International Law*. Routledge, Chapter 7.
Simpson, G. (2014) 'Linear Law: A History of International Criminal Law', in Schwöbel, C. (ed.) *Critical Approaches to International Criminal Law*. Routledge, pp. 159–179.
Simpson, G. (2016) 'Human Rights with a Vengeance: One Hundred Years of Retributive Humanitarianism', *Australian Yearbook of International Law*, 33(1), pp. 1–14.
Simpson, G. (1993) 'Mabo, International Law, Terra Nullius and the Stories of Settlement: An Unresolved Jurisprudence', *Melbourne University Law Review*, 19(1), pp. 195–210.
Skinner, Q. (1978) *Foundations of Modern Political Thought*. Cambridge University Press.
Skinner, Q. (2014) *Forensic Shakespeare*. Oxford University Press.
Slaughter, J. R. (2007) *Human Rights, Inc: The World Novel, Narrative Form and International Law*. Fordham University Press.
Slaughter, J. R. (2019) 'Pathetic Fallacies: Personification and the Unruly Subjects of International Law', *London Review of International Law*, 7(1), pp. 3–54.
Sloterdijk, P. (1988) *Critique of Cynical Reason*. Verso.

Smith, A. (1759) *Theory of the Human Sentiments*. Gutenberg Publishers.
Smith, G. (2011) *Friendship and the Political*. Imprint.
Smith, J. C. (1990) *Psychoanalytic Roots of Patriarchy: The Neurotic Foundations of Social Order*. New York University Press.
Sontag, S. (1979) *On Photography*. Penguin.
Soper, K. (1990) *Troubled Pleasures: Writings on Politics, Gender, and Hedonism*. Verso.
Spence, D. (1982) *Narrative Truth and Historical Truth*. Norton.
Steiner, G. (1981) *The Portage to San Christobal of A. H.* Faber and Faber.
Steiner, G. (2011) *The Poetry of Thought*. New Directions.
Sterne, L. (1981) *The Life and Opinions of Tristram Shandy*. Penguin.
Sterne, L. (2005 [1768]) *A Sentimental Journey through France and Italy by Mr Yorick*. Penguin.
Sutherland, J. (2000) *Henry V, War Criminal?* Oxford University Press.
Tallgren, I. (2002) 'The Sense and Sensibility of International Criminal Law', *European Journal of International Law*, 13(3), pp. 561–595.
Tang, C. (2018) *Imagining World Order: Literature and International Law in Early Modern Europe, 1500–1800*. Cornell University Press.
Taylor, T. (1997) *Nuremberg and Vietnam: An American Tragedy*. Bantam Books.
Teitel, R. (2000) *Transitional Justice*. Oxford University Press.
Tello, V. (2016) *Counter-Memorial Aesthics*. Bloomsbury.
Todd, J. (1986) *Sensibility: An Introduction*. Methuen.
Unger, R. M. (1997) *Politics: The Central Texts*. Ed. Zhiyuan Cui. Verso.
Veale, J. P. (1953) *Advance to Barbarism*. C. C. Nelson.
Venzke, I. (2014) *How Interpretation Makes International Law: On Semantic Change and Normative Twists*. Oxford University Press.
Vinjamuri, L. and Snyder, J. (2003) 'Trials and Errors', *International Security*, 28(3), pp. 5–44.
Voltaire, F. (2005 [1759]) *Candide*. Penguin.
Ward, I. (1995) *Law and Literature: Possibilities and Perspectives*. Cambridge University Press.
Ward, I. (1999) *Shakespeare and the Legal Imagination*. Butterworths.
Warren, C. N. (2015) *Literature and the Law of Nations, 1580–1680*. Oxford University Press.
Weisberg, R. (1984) *The Failure of the Word*. Yale University Press.
Weisberg, R. (1992) *Poethics and Other Strategies of Law and Literature*. Columbia University Press.
West, Rebecca (1984) *A Train of Powder*. Virago.
West, Robin (1988) 'Jurisprudence and Gender', *University of Chicago Law Review*, 55(1), pp. 1–72.
West, Robin (1993) *Narrative, Authority and Law*. University of Michigan Press.
Wheeler, N. (2018) *Trusting Enemies: Interpersonal Relationships in International Conflict*. Oxford University Press.

Wheatley, N. (2020) *Law and the Time of Angels: International Law's Method Wars and the Affective Life of Disciplines*. On file with author.
White, H. (1987) *The Content of the Form: Narrative Discourse and Historical Representation*. Johns Hopkins University Press.
White, H. (2014 [1973]) *Metahistory: The Historical Imagination in Nineteenth-Century Europe*. Johns Hopkins University Press.
White, J. B. (1973) *The Legal Imagination*. Wolters Kluwer.
White, J. B. (1990) *Justice as Translation*. University of Chicago Press.
Wight, M. (1987) 'An Anatomy of International Thought', *Review of International Studies*, 13(3), pp. 221–227.
Williams, B. (2002) *Truth and Truthfulness: An Essay in Genealogy*. Princeton University Press.
Williams, P. (1991) *The Alchemy of Race and Rights*. Harvard University Press.
Williams, R. (1977) *Marxism and Literature*. Oxford University Press.
Willis, J. F. (1982) *Prologue to Nuremberg: The Politics and Diplomacy of Punishing War Criminals of the First World War*. Greenwood Press.
Winter, J. (1995) *Sites of Memory, Sites of Mourning: The Great War in European Cultural History*. Cambridge University Press.
Winter, J. (2006) *Dreams of Peace and Freedom: Utopian Movements in the Twentieth Century*. Yale University Press.
Woods, J. (2004) *The Irresponsible Self: On Laughter and the Novel*. Jonathan Cape.
Woolf, V. (1915) *The Voyage Out*. Duckworth Books.
Woolf, V. (1937) *The Years*. Harcourt, Brace.
Yablonka, H. (2004) *The State of Israel v Adolf Eichmann*. Schocken Books.
Yeats, W. B. (1991) *Selected Poems*. Penguin.
Young, J. E. (2017) '"Memory and Counter-Memory" 9', *Harvard Design Magazine*, pp. 1–18.
Young-Bruehl, E. (1982) *Hannah Arendt: For Love of the World*. Yale University Press.
Žižek, S. (2009) *First as Tragedy, Then as Farce*. Verso.
Žižek, S. (2011) *Living in the End Times*. Verso.

Index

For the benefit of digital users, indexed terms that span two pages (e.g., 52–53) may, on occasion, appear on only one of those pages.

absurdity 52–53, 57–58, 59–60, 70, 79–80
Alexandrowicz, C. H. 124–25
Allott, Philip 18, 196–97, 207
Amritsar Massacre 55–56
Arendt, Hannah 77–78, 94–95, 142–43, 206–7
Aristodemou, Maria 9, 10, 23–24
Aristotle 149–50, 162–63, 165–67, 173, 175

Bandung Conference 181–82
Bell, George 104
Blair, Tony 20, 82–83

capitalism 13, 27, 50–51, 191–93, 195–96
Castro, Fidel 183–84, 208–9
Cavell, Edith 110, 112
Chekhov, Anton 170
China 179–80, 181
Congress of Vienna 98
crimes against humanity 45, 67–68, 73–74, 92, 94–95, 96
Cuba 208–9
Curzon, George 96–97
Cusk, Rachel 203
cynicism 3, 8, 66, 79, 80–82, 83–84

Davis, Mike 203–4
Derrida, Jacques 175–77, 178–79
desire 12, 38–39, 52
Diogenes 8, 78–80, 81–82, 84–85
Dostoevsky, Fyodor 80, 87

Eichmann, Adolf 77–78, 86–87, 94
empire 139, 145–46, 165–67, 204–5
enclave 195–96
excruciation 198

Franck, Tom 56, 82
Freud, Sigmund 11, 59–60, 61, 79–80, 211
Fussell, Paul 58, 65–66

Gabel, Peter 50–51, 88–89, 164
Gaita, Raimond 69–70,
genocide 50, 64, 68–69
Gentili, Alberico 174–75
Germany and Holocaust memorialisation 66, 90, 92, 95–96, 100, 104, 107, 111, 157, 158
George Lloyd, David 46–47, 93, 100–2
Goodrich, Peter 61–62, 164,
Great War 46–47, 65–66, 67–68, 77, 139
Grewe, Wilhelm 128–33
Grotius, Hugo 137–38, 159–60, 167, 190–91

Hankey, Maurice 104, 105–6
Holocaust 51, 90, see also Germany and Holocaust memorialisation

imagination 188–91, 192–98, 204–5
Imperial War Cabinet 93, 96–97, 100–2, 105–6
International Court of Justice 70, 165–67, 174
International Criminal Court 47, 73–74, 96, 106, 141–42, 199
international criminal law 46–47, 50, 88–92, 93, 95–96, 97–98, 99, 101, 106, 107–8–, 112, 126, 139–41, 157–58, 199
International Criminal Tribunal for Rwanda 80–81
international human rights law 89
International Military Tribunal (Nuremberg) 68–69, 94–95, 102, 106

interdisciplinarity 119–20, 121
intimacy 161–62, 174
Iraq War 4–5, 83–84, 187–88
ius ad bellum 153, 170–71, 176–77
ius in bello 156, 176–77

Jameson, Fredric 195–96
Jaspers, Karl 64–65, 90

Koolhaas, Rem 116

Lacan, Jacques 10
landscape 201, 208–10
League of Nations 22–23, 194–95, 204–5
Lear, Jonathan 75–78
literary 7, 15, 19, 22–24, 28, 43–44, 64, 86–87, 92–93, 107–8, 118–19, 143–45, 148
Lorimer, James 159–60
Logue, Christopher 31

Marx, Karl 133, 192–93
Mégret, Frédéric 109–10
Mieville, China 63
Milošević, Slobodan 32–33
Moscow Show Trials 101–3, 141–42

Non-Aligned Movement 149, 181–82, 183
Napoleon 98
Nietzsche, Friedrich 175, 176–77
Nixon, Richard 179–82,
nuclear weapons 64, 65, 70–71
Nuremberg Charter 69–70

Oakeshott, Michael 174
Okawa, Shumei 85–87
Orwell, George 102

Pal, Radhabinod 67–68, 142
Péguy, Charles 112
poetry 16, 20, 30, 36–37, 73–74, 137–38
Prague Show Trial 73–74
Prashad, Vijay 149
psychoanalysis 9, 11–12, see also Sigmund Freud

Rawls, John 161–62, 194–95
Republic of Bolivia v Indemnity Mutual Marine Insurance 159

Rome Statute for the International Criminal Court 44, 106
Rousseau, Jean-Jacques 192–93, 200–1,

Said, Edward 3, 11
Sartre, Jean-Paul 64–65
Schmitt, Carl 123–24, 130–32, 133, 135–36, 158, 169–70
Scott, David 143–44
show trial 101–2, see also Moscow Show Trials and Prague Show Trials
Sloterdijk, Peter 60, 66, 79, 83
Socrates 75–76
Sterne, Laurence 7, 48, 53,
sublime 93–94
Syria 28, 186

teaching 4, 19, 51–52, 195–96
Tojo, Hideki 85
Treaty of Versailles 66–67
Trump, Donald 151, 172–73

United Nations Charter 70, 125–26, 153–54, 167–68
  Article 107: 155
United Nations Declaration on Friendly Relations 167–68
United Nations Security Council 153–54
Universal Declaration of Human Rights 106
US-Iran Treaty of Friendship 174

victims 44–45, 108–10, 206

West, Rebecca 12, 142, 205, 207
West, Robin 33, 35
White, Hayden 57–58, 136–37, 140
White, James Boyd 88–89, 189,
Williams, Patricia 164
Williams, Raymond 203
Woolf, Virginia and Leonard, 205
World Trade Organization 165–67

Yeats, W.B. 149–50

Zedong, Mao 179, 180–81
Žižek, Slavoj 75